To Jim,
All the best!

Paul Tonkin

# Above Us Only Sky

LIVERPOOL FC'S GLOBAL REVOLUTION

PAUL TOMKINS

*"Tomkins' best book yet.*
*Insightful, revealing and entertaining."*

Squarefootball.com

**For Kate, with love and thanks.**

Also for Rebecca Hadley and Susan Edwards.

Special thanks to Chris Hadley, Garreth Cummins, Jimmy Rice, Paul Eaton, Paul Rogers, Tony Barrett, Jonathan Swain, Whitney Louderback, Taskin Ismet, Eric Cordina, Bill Urban, Mel Abshier, Chua Wee Kiat, Dinesh Selvaratnam, Adrian Mervyn, Matt Clare, John Quinn, Ran Stotsky, Alyson Rudd and Akif Butt.

**Above Us Only Sky:**
Liverpool FC's Global Revolution

Published By Anchor Print Group


ISBN 978-0-9556367-0-7

Printed in Great Britain by the Anchor Print Group Ltd.

First edition published 2007

# Contents

# Preface

Hands in pockets, jacket tails pushed back behind him as he strides purposely forward, John Lennon surveys the throng of red-shirted men, women and children from atop his pedestal, as the bleary-eyed hoards gather in the terminal concourse of *his* airport. Peering out from behind his distinctive round glasses, the bronze-cast hero of the city watches the mass exodus of his brethren as they gather in queues at check-in stations *en route* to Athens. It is 4am, 22nd May 2007, and the man who would have us all *Imagine* is forever frozen in that forward-moving stance. Always heading into the future, but never getting there.

Lennon's star first exploded across the firmament in 1963, a year before Liverpool Football Club, led by the equally charismatic and quotable Bill Shankly, reached the pinnacle of the English game and, for almost three decades, stayed there. Nineteen sixty-four saw the start of the Reds' 26-year dynasty that would stretch far and wide across Europe. Indeed, in the last three years of Lennon's life Liverpool FC's name would become a byword for excellence in every continent of the globe, with its first two European Cup successes.

In 2007 the Reds' journey took a new course. Where America would be the final destination for Lennon, for Liverpool Football Club it was a country representing a new beginning.

Liverpool's third season under Rafael Benítez was a tumultuous time both on and off the pitch. In 2007 Liverpool FC finally changed hands, with Americans George Gillett Jr. and Tom Hicks buying the club; work began on a radically redesigned state-of-the-art stadium at Stanley Park; and the team reached a seventh European Cup final. Without doubt a new era has begun.

*Above Us Only Sky* is much more than just the story of one season. As well as reflecting on the recent past, this book looks to the future, to examine how the new regime can make the Reds competitive in all aspects of the game — from silverware, and the pounds (and dollars) that help secure it, through to the players to whom Gillett and Hicks will be looking to achieve success on the pitch, including exciting new signings Fernando Torres and Ryan Babel and a whole raft of promising teenagers. What do the Reds need to do to win a 19th league crown? How the club can move forward with a large and diverse fan-base, both local and global, that has very different needs and desires.

It is about the ongoing struggle towards the day when every Liverpool fan can once again definitively say: *Above us only sky — below us everyone else.*

# Introduction

Have you heard the one about the Englishmen, the Irishman, the Scotsman, the Spaniards, the Brazilians, the Argentines, the Danes, the Welshman, the Moroccan, the Frenchmen, the Chilean, the Italian, the Pole, the Norwegian, the Paraguayan, the Dutchmen, the Ukrainian, the Finn, the Austrian, the Swede, the Australian, the Malian, the Ghanian, the Hungarians and the Bulgarian?

No, not the set-up to the world's most tongue-twisting joke, but the list of nationalities on Liverpool's books, in one form or another, during 2007; senior players, reserves, and those representing the youth team. Add American owners, a coaching staff comprised of Spaniards and a Scot, and fans spread far and wide across the world, and you have a truly global institution.

## New dawn

Dull moments and modern day Liverpool Football Club: rarely do the twain meet. In that sense, Rafael Benítez's third season was not much different from his first two. Highs, lows and cup finals. European Cup finals, at that. While it would be his first season without silverware — and as such he failed to extend his unique Liverpool record of landing trophies in his first two seasons to three — he did maintain his annual ability to make it to a major final.

Between August 2006 and May 2007 there were new levels of drama, with sensations on and off the pitch: a poor start prompting the unthinkable with a long-serving director, Noel White, speaking out against the club's manager; American duo Tom Hicks and George Gillett usurping a Dubai consortium at the last minute to purchase outright the club from a dole-faced David Moores; work finally starting, six years after it was first announced, on a new stadium in Stanley Park — only for the plans to be amended and a new design drawn up, to allow the possibility of expanding to a capacity of almost 80,000; remarkable progress against the odds to another Champions League final, including yet another monumental battle with Chelsea; the final itself, where, as the better team in a second appearance within three seasons, the Reds lost valiantly to AC Milan, the very team they beat while being outplayed two years earlier.

The final, if not overshadowed, was at least marred by Uefa's paltry and offensive allocation to Liverpool, followed by fan protests at the club's redistribution of the few tickets that did come its way. This led to ugly scenes in Athens as some fans with forgeries — or no tickets at all — forced their way into the ground, while fans with genuine tickets were kept out and, for their troubles, tear-gassed and beaten. On top of all this, no one could understand why Peter Crouch — the player no one could understand why Benítez signed in the first place — was not starting in Athens, in the joint-biggest game for the club in two decades. Or, indeed, why Bolo Zenden was.

It was a season of harsh words and extreme actions from start to finish. The tone was set after just a few games. The one thing Rafa Benítez surely never expected when swapping the political machinations of Valencia for the stable-run Liverpool FC was interference from the board. If there are a few things that represent 'The Liverpool Way', be it from the fans or the club, then the boardroom trusting that the manager knows best is at the top of that list. Not so for Noel White, a director and former chairman of the club, who chose to give an anonymous interview to the press criticising the methods of Rafa Benítez in the autumn, when the team was struggling. Even had his criticisms been accurate and full of insight — and they weren't — it would have been the wrong way to go about highlighting them; it was certainly neither the time nor the place. White stated that Benítez didn't appear to know his strongest team by that stage of the season, something the director saw as a must.

In which case, why had the club appointed a manager whose methodology centred around rotation, and who never settled on an exact strongest XI when winning two *La Liga* crowns and the Champions League in 2005? Benítez had his methods that worked in the past, across different competitions, so to expect him to abandon those methods and principles after a few bad results was like expecting a manager to switch from passing with élan to route-one football at the first sign of setbacks. Either you trust a manager and his methods, or you change him; you don't ask him to do a 180° turn on the way he works. It's like asking Xabi Alonso to play like Vinnie Jones. If a manager's methodology needs changing, he will be the man charged with deciding based on his own findings. And of course, rotation really is the most deceptive argument in football, because it simply never gets brought up in the good times, only the bad. And if people are too ignorant to see this basic fact, why are they in football? White eventually stepped forward as the man who made the anonymous comments, and then duly stepped down. Before too long results picked up, despite Benítez — like Alex Ferguson — continuing to rotate.

If that boardroom outburst marred the early months, the season was duly bookended by more tension. In the aftermath of the defeat in Athens there were heated debates in the press and behind closed doors between Benítez, chief executive Rick Parry, and the new American owners about how best to move the club forward, now that there was money to spend. Benítez was frustrated that he was being compared by all and sundry with Ferguson and Mourinho, but without anything like their resources to draw upon. Gillett and Hicks put their manager's outburst down to his understandable frustration following the result in Greece, appreciating that the Spaniard had just spent the night wandering around the city unable to sleep, and replaying the events in his mind like the obsessive character he is. After all, the duo did not want to inherit a manager who shrugged off disappointment and headed out to a nightclub. The discord quickly passed, and cordial relations resumed. But for a while it looked like a baptism of fire for Gillett and Hicks.

All this came from the season, without even mentioning Craig Bellamy's contretemps with John Arne Riise ahead of the Barcelona match that — allegedly — involved the wielding of a golf club. If initial far-fetched reports were to be believed, Riise was lucky to not end up in a wheelchair — or 300 yards down the fairway — as Bellamy swung wildly at him with repeated attacks to the legs, while, at the same time, mild-mannered Jerzy Dudek was apparently busy headbutting various policemen as if he was Arnold Schwarzenegger on a cocktail of cocaine and steroids. Incidents had taken place, and club discipline had been breached, but the severity was always going to be exaggerated by the Sunday tabloids.

Otherwise it was business as usual. No 19th league title; prophecies of doom in the media after a few bad results in the autumn preceding a revival; debates over dodgy goalkeepers as Pepe Reina made a couple of errors, followed by another season as the Premiership's top clean-sheet keeper; and, somewhat deliciously, José Mourinho sour-faced at yet another semi-final defeat to the Reds. Oh, and Harry Kewell, like clockwork, fit in time for a final.

Still, at least Steven Gerrard wasn't thinking over a move to Chelsea. Having said that, in terms of the perpetual rumour-mongering, Benítez was once again linked with a move to Real Madrid — on about six different occasions — and Michael Owen was, as ever, 'reportedly' close to a move back to Anfield (when recovered from his latest injury). On top of all this, Robbie Fowler finally bade his tearful farewells to the Kop, 14 years after it first serenaded him. Rarely a dull moment.

Despite some familiar stories, 2007 undoubtedly marked the start of a new era in the history of Liverpool FC. You can't get much more extreme in terms of changing culture than the club passing from local to Stateside ownership, and, after over 100 years at Anfield, the first bricks being laid in a new stadium a few hundred yards down the road. Perhaps the accents would take a little getting used to, but the new owners certainly said the right things. Just not necessarily in a way we were used to. George Gillett spoke of signing 'Snoogy Doogy', who sounded like a cross between a Gangsta rapper and a snack-loving cartoon dog. Thankfully, he instead sanctioned a move for Fernando Torres.

It wasn't just pan-Atlantic differences that reared their head. Divisions between local fans and the Out of Town Supporters (OOTS) grew increasingly tense, as the 'right' to go to Athens to support the team became a battlefield: with only 16,800 tickets allocated to Liverpool in a stadium that holds 63,000 — presumably because Uefa's fat cats need two or three seats each for their *gros chat derrières* — it was all about fans proving their worthiness. With Americans in possession of the club, some locals feeling ostracised, and Anfield, that most spiritual of homes, about to be abandoned, it seemed like the club's very soul was at stake.

# Frontiersmen and Drunken Sailors

America will always be seen as the last great frontier as far as football is concerned. After all, anywhere that needs to rename a sport isn't exactly welcoming it to its heart. The 1970s saw many of the world's best players — at least those in the twilight of their careers — sign up for the North American Soccer League. Around the very time that Kevin Keegan and then Kenny Dalglish were helping Liverpool secure back-to-back European Cups, Pelé, Johan Cryuff, Franz Beckenbauer, George Best and (erm ... ) Rodney Marsh were playing their trade in the US. But the interest, which only really arose for major games, quickly waned.

Two decades later America staged the 1994 World Cup, but the chances of the country taking the sport to its bosom were about as good as Diana Ross hitting the back of the net from 12 yards. (*Head over the ball*, Diana, *head over the ball.*) Major League Soccer was formed in 1993 as part of the agreement that gave the tournament to a non-footballing nation, but it has led a charmed life, with the country's surprise progress to the quarter-final in Japan in 2002 leading to a vital shot in the arm, at a time when it was on the critical list and fading fast. The latest attempt to gain credibility, or perhaps just publicity, has been LA Galaxy's luring of media-sideshow David Beckham, on wages several hundred times greater than that of his team-mates. Beckham, however, is more famed in the States for his pop-star wife and penchant for wearing sarongs. He is by no stretch of the imagination the definition of an all-American athlete.

And so now, with football still seen by many Americans as a game for young boys and girls to play in front of their screaming 4x4-owning Soccer Moms before they grow up and take part in *real* sports, the Americans have come to England. First Malcolm Glazer oversaw a somewhat hostile takeover of Manchester United, which plunged them into a significant debt (on paper at least — it has hardly stopped them spending fortunes on the team). Then Randy Lerner, with a personal fortune amounting to $1.3 billion, took control of Aston Villa. And next followed George Gillett and Tom Hicks, boasting a combined fortune equivalent to Lerner's, who hitched their wagons to Liverpool.

## Symbiosis

America and Liverpool have long-since shared a peculiarly mixed history. There are parallels, and evidence of a symbiotic existence, as well as extreme cultural differences and no shortage of tragedy.

The Beatles, the world's biggest band at the time, were adored across the pond in the mid-'60s. However, John Lennon was later vilified in the Bible Belt for some misunderstood comments about the band being bigger than Jesus Christ. Lennon, who moved to New York in 1971, was shot and killed in Central Park nine years later. As strange as it may seem to some, Central Park itself has its roots in Merseyside: the architects found their inspiration at Birkenhead Park on a visit in 1850, while gathering ideas for the planned New York parkland.

Then there was the Titanic, at the time the world's biggest, and still its most famous ship. She was registered in Liverpool, but never made it to the United States on her maiden voyage, albeit from Southampton. Dubbed 'unsinkable', she quickly sank. (Rumours that a relation of Graeme Souness was to blame were patently untrue.) This at a time when Liverpool's port was a main source of trade and emigration between the two countries.

Indeed, Liverpool and New York are now siblings, albeit ones separated at birth. In 2001, following the attack on the World Trade Centre, Liverpool granted New York the freedom of the city. This came after New York had approached Liverpool to be its official sister city.

The two ports face each other across the Atlantic, and both were destinations for the hundreds of thousands of Irish souls fleeing the great famine in the 19th Century, who settled and help define the twinned cities.

Hollywood came to Liverpool in 2001, with the film The 51st State, which starred Samuel L Jackson. In a bizarre precursor to Craig Bellamy's alleged antics in the Portuguese training camp, it featured Robert Carlyle as a very angry young man in a Liverpool kit, wielding a golf club. And moving in the opposite direction was Merseysider Daniel Craig, the actor who grew up in Hoylake and who became the surprise sixth James Bond in the remake of Casino Royale, for which his performance was widely applauded. (For those who believe in the perpetuation of tired stereotypes, he stuck to Bond's tuxedo, rather than adopting a dayglo shellsuit.)

And, of course, there was Brad Friedel's brief and unremarkable stint as custodian in the '90s, but it hardly even merits a footnote, such was its relative insignificance. And as bizarre as it seems now, a teenage Souness spent the summer of 1972 playing ten games for Montreal Olympique in the NASL, before making his way from Spurs to Middlesbrough and, in 1978, Liverpool. On the pitch at least, there's been little connection between the countries.

But there is one crucial part of Liverpool FC's history that is as Yankee as the dollar. The club's fabled anthem, *You'll Never Walk Alone*, originated as the closing number in a rather fey American musical. Written by Rodgers and Hammerstein for their 1945 production, *Carousel*, it took the Beatles' Scouse contemporaries Gerry and the Pacemakers to make it a hit on both sides of the Atlantic in 1963, ahead of the Kop adopting it. (How fortunate that Gerry Marsden didn't instead decide to cover *How Do You Solve a Problem Like Maria*.)

## American Resolution

There was never going to be a perfect, please-all solution to the prickly problem of just who invested in Liverpool FC, although it was nice to imagine an old and eccentric Scouse billionaire croaking and leaving his entire fortune to the club in his will, no strings attached — other than that Rick Parry would look after his cat, Mr

Figgles Jr. Or perhaps Jamie Carragher winning the world's biggest lottery and, with Robbie Fowler selling his housing portfolio and Ian Rush auctioning off his medals for their weight in gold, forming a consortium to take control. Of course, even then someone would bemoan three childhood Evertonians owning Liverpool FC.

When Liverpool fans look back at how Malcolm Glazer handled United's takeover — and the contempt he appeared to show them — and even more worryingly, how the fight for control of Arsenal, led by American Stan Kroenke, resulted in turmoil, it's easy to conclude that things could have been much more traumatic. Arsenal, who were just a handful of years ahead of Liverpool in moving to a new stadium, saw David Dein resign, Arsène Wenger take an unusually long time to commit to the club beyond the end of 2007/08, and amidst all this uncertainty Thierry Henry got all huffy and packed his *bagages*. Arguably the three most important people in each area the club — on the pitch, in the dugout and in the boardroom — were destabilised. By contrast, the arrival of George Gillett and Tom Hicks was smooth and peaceful, but not without a few hiccups along the way.

In the Premiership, 2006/07 was the year of the buyout, the year of the takeover. As well as Liverpool's transition into American hands, and Arsenal's troublesome share dealings, the Premiership was awash with new money. Roman Abramovich and Malcolm Glazer were already famously in place when, in 2007, Randy Lerner bought Aston Villa. Across the second city, Hong Kong-based businessman Carson Yeung became Birmingham's major shareholder, with a 29.9% stake. English billionaire Mike Ashley, 25th on the Sunday Times Rich List (23 places behind Abramovich) became the largest shareholder in Newcastle United after buying Sir John Hall's share in the club in May 2007. Franco-Russian businessman Alexandre Gaydamak took control of Portsmouth, and Icelander Eggert Magnússon gained control of West Ham. Yet another American, Daniel Williams, held talks with Blackburn. Most interestingly, former Liverpool suitor Thaksin Shinawatra took control at Manchester City, amidst much controversy. But none of these takeovers was as high-profile or as expensive as the one that took Gillett and Hicks to the co-chairmanship of Liverpool.

Any trip into the unknown can make fans uneasy. Change in life can be unsettling, whatever the context. It's hard to say that two Americans with almost no football knowledge buying the club is *ideal*, but it's a question of who was in the running, and how the deal could be facilitated in the least disruptive manner. The only local interest from a bona fide Red came from building magnate Steve Morgan, but in 2004 he seemed to be drastically undervaluing in the club. The deal quickly collapsed, amidst long-standing acrimony between Morgan and David Moores, the chairman. The major stumbling block was that Morgan wanted to see a greater percentage of the £70m he was putting in (for 60% of the club) invested in the new stadium, rather than going to Moores and the other shareholders. Or, in other words, Morgan would invest in building the stadium if Moores gave him the club on the cheap — valuing Liverpool at just £115m in the process (around half of the figure Hicks and Gillett agreed three years later). For his part, Moores could not be expected to let Liverpool go for much less than it was worth — as some might suggest he should, simply because he loved the club — just as Morgan would never have offered far in excess of what the club was worth, simply because he loved the club. For all their unquestionable affection for the club, these are businessmen, not charities.

At the same time, in the summer of 2004, Thailand's then-Prime Minister Thaksin Shinawatra made a £65m bid, for a 30% interest (therefore valuing the club at just over £200m). However, Shinawatra was deposed of his position in a bloodless coup in September 2006. Undeterred in his aim to buy into the Premiership, in June 2007 Shinawatra sought bought Manchester City. In an act that would send chills down the spines of Liverpool fans, the deal continued despite a committee investigating corruption in the former Thai government ordered that Shinawatra's assets be frozen. However, it didn't stop the appointment of Sven-Göran Eriksson, who instantly spent £40m on a collection of overseas players; shortly before the first of a series of corruption cases was brought against Shinawatra in Bangkok

It was the perfect illustration of how much responsibility David Moores had on his shoulders when it came to selling to the right people at the right price. Morgan may have been the right person in a number of senses, but his price wasn't even close to being acceptable; Shinawatra valued the club at a far more realistic level, but the impending court cases — plus huge concerns at the time about his human rights record — suggest him to be far from the kind of 'fit and proper' person allowed to own an English club (although, at the time of his takeover, Shinawatra had no criminal record, and as such, passed the league's test). While the three years it took to eventually sell the club frustrated many fans, and led to criticisms of indecision and greed on Moores' part, a far worse scenario would have been selling at the first tempting offer to someone who either didn't have the club's best interests at heart, or who wasn't fit to run an institution like Liverpool Football Club.

A number of other investors came and went, including New England Patriots owner Robert Kraft — although in some cases any alleged interest may have been no more than paper talk. The really serious business started to take place in early December 2006, when Dubai International Capital (DIC), after 18 months of talks, agreed in principle a deal to buy Moores' holding at £4,500 per share. DIC, the private-equity investment arm of the Arab state — run by Sheikh Mohammed bin Rashid Al Maktoum — were clearly able to handle a project of this scale: the company owns the Travelodge hotel chain (Europe's fastest-growing) as well as a stake in The Tussauds Group, having owned it outright for two years. Moores would have netted a cool £80m from the sale.

But the deal floundered in acrimony when it was announced Liverpool were also in talks with Gillett and Hicks, two American sports franchise owners. BBC sports editor Mihir Bose told BBC *Radio Five Live*: "Sheikh Mohammed is a very angry man and that is why he has pulled out. He was given assurances by Liverpool that they would go with them but the talk of other offers has unsettled him and he has pulled out." Perhaps key to Moores' procrastination over DIC, and his need to encourage Gillett and Hicks, was summed up by Bose in the following sentence: "DIC saw this as business enterprise but Gillett has told Liverpool that they are a sports franchise and they know how to run sports operations."

Perhaps unsurprisingly in the circumstances, Liverpool FC and DIC disagreed as to why the deal collapsed. The announcements made by the club focused on the time it was taking to tie up the deal, stating that the due diligence — the process of investigation by potential investors — took too long to complete. (It's untrue that they were merely trying to locate Bruno Cheyrou.) There was also the suggestion that David Moores was having sleepless nights, worrying about the suitability of the organisation he was selling to.

Sameer Al Ansari, Executive Chairman and Chief Executive Officer of DIC, went public as soon as the talks broke down. "We won't overpay for assets," he said. "We are very disappointed to be making this announcement," added Al Ansari. "DIC are a serious investor with considerable resources at our disposal. At the same time, we are supporters of the game and of the club. Liverpool's investment requirements have been well publicised and, after a huge amount of work, we proposed a deal that would provide the club with the funds it needs, both on and off the pitch. We were also prepared to offer shareholders a significant premium on the market price of the shares. As businessmen, we move on. As fans, we hope that the new owners would share the same vision as we had for LFC and, of course, in realising the new stadium that is so badly needed to ensure the club can continue to compete at the highest level in the Premiership and Europe."

There were aspects of DIC's bid that didn't ring true with the Liverpool board. DIC was looking to fund the deal by taking loans out against Liverpool, in the way the Glazers did with Manchester United, which in the short and long term would have piled huge debts into the club. It was suggested that they were unwilling to back the club in the transfer market (which seems unlikely), and looking to sell Liverpool within seven years at a profit. These issues were leaked by someone within the DIC team to the UK's big banks and businesses, and ended up printed in national newspapers. David Moores demanded a meeting with Al Maktoum, but the Sheikh sent a DIC employee in his stead. It was clear the Liverpool Chairman was not going to get the reassurances he needed, and suddenly the proposal from across the Atlantic seemed the only viable way forward.

When the club announced it was considering a second bid from Gillett and Hicks, DIC stated that their offer would be withdrawn if they weren't given a quick Yes or No. Liverpool refused to be bullied by this ultimatum, and on January 31st DIC withdrew their offer. The Americans had already carried out due diligence at this stage, so were in a position to move quickly. In stark contrast to DIC, Gillett and Hicks completed the due diligence in just two days. They also offered £500 more per-share than DIC, and just days after it looked certain DIC were going to take control of Liverpool, the club was in the hands of two ebullient Americans. Their £5,000-a-share offer meant that David Moores earned £89.8 million by selling his 51.6 per cent stake, but the Liverpool board was unanimous in declaring that the offer was the right one for the club. In the end, 98.6% of shareholders opted to sell to the new owners.

The deal that saw Gillett and Hicks take control was as follows: an investment of £434 million, which comprised £174.2 million to buy the shareholding, £44.5 million to write off debts and £215.3 million towards the construction of a new stadium in Stanley Park.

The Americans had moved in.

## The Men in Question

Tom Hicks, born in 1946 in Dallas, has a bit of Chevy Chase about him: large doming forehead, bright smile, round cheeks. Like Chase, Hicks stands at an intimidating goalkeeper's height of 6' 3". While not known for his comedic skills, or his appearances in Paul Simon videos, Hicks does possess a performer's charm. Through a producer at his father's Port Arthur radio station he learned the art of public speaking, and eventually became a DJ with his own weekend show. Media relations were never going to be a problem, with charm and ability to woo an audience. In that sense he's very different from Malcolm Glazer, the somewhat gimpish owner of Manchester United, who more closely resembles the *Simpsons'* Mr Burns but with Simon Cowell's taste in high-waisted trousers.

A decade ago Mark Donald wrote in Dallas' '*D*' Magazine that: "Tom Hicks is one of the good guys, or so I'm told — easygoing and unpretentious, straight-shooting and fun-loving, a kinder, gentler corporate raider. Friends and foes alike claim that despite his reputation as one of the hottest leveraged buyout (LBO) specialists in the country, an empire builder who collects corporations the way other people do dust, he still manages to keep his ego in check." Few men that successful in business could expect the same to be said of them. Hicks told McDonald that in 20 years of undertaking leveraged buyouts he had never performed a hostile takeover — insisting only on friendly deals, where the owners want to sell to him. Unlike many others in the field, he did not buy a business to sell off its assets and make its workforce redundant.

Despite his father's relative wealth, Hicks is a self-made man. His company, Hicks & Haas, formed with Robert Haas in 1984, purchased soft drinks makers Dr Pepper and 7 Up. In 1989 Hicks left Haas to co-found Hicks, Muse, Tate & Furst, an investment firm. But investments, as we are told, can go down as well as up, and the early part of the 2000s saw Hicks get his fingers burned. He retired from the financial world in 2004, with the desire to spend more time with his six children and concentrate on his sporting empire.

Hicks had first moved into the world of sports franchises in December 1995, when he bought the National Hockey League's Dallas Stars for $82 million. Two and a half years later he became the Chairman and Owner of the Texas Rangers Baseball Club, purchasing the team for $250 million. He also owns Mesquite Championship Rodeo, which boasts seasonal attendances of 200,000.

One of the major concerns voiced by Liverpool fans was the massive blot on Hicks' copybook: the way he had overspent massively in 2000, when taking baseball's outstanding talent, Alex 'A-Rod' Rodriguez, to the Texas Rangers on a 10-year deal worth $252 million. Seven years later it is still by some way the record contract in sporting history. After three years spent earning an annual $25.2m, for which the Rangers got outstanding performances from the player but in a poor team which continued to struggle, the Rangers agreed to pay $67m of the $179m left on Rodriguez's contract in order for the New York Yankees to take him off their hands. All in all it proved a terribly unsuccessful and expensive move.

However, it showed Hicks was not afraid to pay for top quality performers and make bold decisions. More importantly, it will also have taught him an important lesson: namely that you need to invest in the team as a whole, and not unbalance it with one costly superstar. It's about getting talented players to fit within an overall pattern, and engendering a sense of unity. Balance is a defining trait in all successful teams, from the way the team blends through to the work behind the scenes.

A lot of Liverpool fans won't be overjoyed at Hicks' status as a friend of George W Bush, who, in general, is hardly loved or admired in this country following the war in Iraq and his far-right politics, not to mention that in his public speaking he makes Forest Gump look like Albert Einstein. But it's a fact of life that capitalism was the realm where investors were going to come from; let's face it, neither Oxfam nor the *Socialist Worker* was going to buy out David Moores. In 2003, Hicks ranked 350th on Forbes magazine's list of the 400 richest Americans — with a net worth of $725 million. (He is no longer on the list, but it now requires a billion dollars to make the top 400.)

Then there's George Gillett, the small, avuncular figure with a round face and infectious, toothy smile. At 69 he's almost a decade older than his business partner, and like Hicks it hasn't been all plain sailing for the Wisconsin-born near-billionaire.

He started out in broadcasting, buying up a number of small television stations. But his biggest success came when he acquired Vail and Beaver Creek ski resorts in the mid-80s, with particular focus on customer service when redefining the 'ski experience'. Vail soon became America's premier ski destination, and Gillett would make it a more personal experience by greeting the guests. By 1987 he had also accumulated several more TV stations, with the purchases made using junk bonds. But by 1992 Gillett had declared bankruptcy following a severe interest rates hike that penalised junk bond issuers. He was kept on Vail's payroll at $1.5 million a year, and when the resort went public in 1997 and its stock began trading on Wall Street, Gillett walked away with $32.1 million. Having set up a new company, he then either acquired or built a number of ski resorts across America. By 1997 he had expanded his interests to include big meat corporations, including billion dollar deals with Hicks' company.

By the time he became co-chairman of Liverpool, Gillett had been heavily involved in sports for forty years. First of all he was business manager and minority partner of the Miami Dolphins. Soon after he became owner and CEO of the Harlem Globetrotters, the once-serious African-American basketball team that had by that point already become a touring entertainment phenomenon. Liverpool fans hoping for the same level of jaw-dropping creativity must note that the opposition was often a stooge team. Nor should Reds' fans expect comparable results: between 1962 and 2000, the Globetrotters played 12,596 games, losing only *twice*.

At the start of the new millennium Gillett was part of a consortium that tried, and failed, to purchase the NBA Denver Nuggets and NHL's Colorado Avalanche, as well as the Pepsi Center in which the two teams played. Undeterred, Gillett quickly moved to buy an 80% interest in the NHL's Montreal Canadiens (known officially as *Le Club de Hockey Canadien*) and their home the Bell Center (known then as the Molson Center) for $185 million.

The Canadiens' history bears comparison with Liverpool's. Founded in 1909, the Canadiens are the league's oldest team and a part of the startup group known as the 'Original Six'. They have won more Stanley Cups (the championship trophy of the National Hockey League) than any other NHL team; their tally stands at 24 — or a quarter of the total since its inception — with the Toronto Maple Leafs in second place, nine back on 13. But, in another symmetry with Liverpool, the Canadiens' last success was back in the early '90s. Like Liverpool, their golden era was the late '70s.

Like Hicks at the Texas Rangers, Gillett hasn't brought success to the Canadiens. Gillett is severely hampered by Canada's different tax laws, which makes running the club more expensive than it is for their American counterparts. Despite the top two teams in terms of achievements being Canadian, the last 13 winners have all been American. (Prior to that, eight of the previous ten winners, including the Canadiens on two occasions, were from north of the border.)

Gillett aims to employ ones of his sons to help with his vision of success with the Reds. Foster Gillett was due to take up a role at Liverpool in August 2007 once work permit issues were sorted. "It won't be as CEO and it certainly won't be as manager," his father explained to *The Times'* Oliver Kay over the summer. "Foster will be there to improve communication. This is a very fast-changing sport, where decisions often need to be made very quickly. There was substantial concern on Rick and Rafa's part as to how, with the time differences, we could guarantee quick decisions and quick communication. This is a way of doing that."

## Commercialism

Most English football fans are sceptical about Americans and 'soccer', not to mention a love of razzmatazz in their sports that just seems incredibly *naff* in this country. The two men who now control the club — George Gillett and Tom Hicks — have vast experience of running teams in America and Canada, but that doesn't mean they'll fill Anfield with cheerleaders and hotdog vendors. However, it would be naive to think that they won't be looking to change certain aspects of the way the club is run. Commercially speaking, the need to ramp up operations to be able to compete with Manchester United and Chelsea could not have been stronger. Moving out of the sport's dark ages was essential in terms of being competitive on the field, even if it could potentially mean a further distancing from the 'family' feel of the club. This is one of the trickiest challenges they face, as it's always an uneasy balance to strike.

In July Liverpool announced Ian Ayre as the club's new Commercial Director. Liverpool-born, he is a lifelong Red, and in that sense fans will feel reassured. According the club's statement, he would be charged with "growing sponsorship and merchandising revenues, starting with the selection of sponsors around the club's move to a new stadium in 2010".

His background includes: a spell as Managing Director of Premium TV Ltd, a subsidiary of NTL; a three-year stint as Chairman & Chief Executive Officer of Huddersfield Town FC, which would have provided invaluable experience into the running of a club; and most recently, Chief Operating Officer of Total Sports Asia, which included marketing football in that part of the world.

Within days of this appointment, the club announced that it was finally launching its own TV station, some years after Manchester United and Chelsea had begun to air theirs. It would be a free add-on as part of the Setanta Sports package, so fans were not expected to stump up an additional monthly subscription fee for the channel, in contrast to the other clubs. (But they would still have to pay the additional monthly £9.99 Setanta fee — something many might have done anyway, with the broadcaster essentially taking over the PremPlus pay-per-view games.)

It could be seen as the Reds' first step in a move towards clubs negotiating their own individual television deals once the current Sky/Setanta deal expires; going down the route of Spain and Italy, where the top clubs' revenue has increased massively as a result of cashing in on their individual pulling power (while, of course, weakening the hands of their less-vaunted competitors, and, in time, possibly seriously damaging the league as a whole). Initially, however, the Liverpool FC TV will show delayed coverage of Premiership matches, archive footage, reserve teams games, as well as news and views segments. Even if the club does not wish to instigate a move towards individual TV deals in the future, it needs to be in a position to react if such a move becomes a reality, as well as offering fans a regular diet of niche programming in the interim, for which there is clearly a demand.

Gillett and Hicks arrived in English football at a time of great prosperity. Not only had a total of nine clubs fallen into the hands of wealthy foreign investors, but their first season officially in charge would coincide with the new TV deal, where Setanta and Sky shared live coverage of the Premiership, with Rupert Murdoch's organisation losing out on sole broadcasting rights for the first time since the game was re-launched in 1992. With the new three-year deal, Sky will pay £1.314 billion for 92 games a season and Setanta £392m for 46 games each year. Foreign TV rights will produce £625m in revenue whilst internet and mobile phone revenue will be £400m. To highlight how flush the English game had become, finishing bottom of the Premiership would garner prize money in excess of what Liverpool earned from winning the Champions League: £26.8m, compared with £20.5m. (Liverpool's problem in their two recent trips to the final was that, first of all, in 2005 Chelsea made it to the semi-finals, while in 2007, both Chelsea and Manchester United also reached that stage — meaning they ate into the Reds' share of *English* television money. But in a quirk of the system, and indicative of the differing exposure levels/favouritism on TV, both Manchester United and Chelsea earned more from the 2007 Champions League TV pot than the Reds, despite not doing as well. Liverpool banked £26m, a fraction less than Chelsea. United, meanwhile, earned £28.9m.)

In 2006/07, Liverpool finished 3rd in the league and 3rd amongst English clubs in the prize and TV money stakes from all competitions. United totalled £62.92m, and Chelsea £61.15m. A fair way behind were Liverpool, with £54.71m. Then there was a big jump to Arsenal, with £44.14m, and an even bigger gap between them and their north London rivals, Tottenham, who earned £30.55m. Everton totalled just over £25m.

Winning the Premiership in the next three seasons will result in a £50m windfall, up £20m on recent seasons. It's clearly a good time to become champions. Then again, a lot of clubs will believe it's a great time to finish 17th.

## Fan Hopes

On the whole the reaction from fans to Gillett and Hicks' takeover was more positive than they could have hoped. The dissenting voices were conspicuous by their absence. Perhaps this was partly down to the three years of a mixed bag of suitors arriving, making promises either to the board or to the media, but ultimately either unable to back them up, or unable to convince David Moores and co. that they were the people to whom the club should be entrusted. After some of the apparently shady characters from all corners of the globe, two sports-savvy Americans quickly seemed a better bet than most of those who had tried and failed since 2004.

The promise of a brighter tomorrow is always welcome to a supporter. So in that sense the rich Americans' arrival was always going to whet the fans' appetites. What is true is that the honeymoon period cannot last forever, and whether through any fault of their own or not, they will encounter some tough questions sooner or later. The duo were prepared to dip into their pockets, but to the disappointment of some fans expecting Sugar Daddies, weren't prepared, according to Gillett, to spend like "drunken sailors".

Football fans tend to love the money men when things are going well, but are quick to ask why even more cash isn't forthcoming when the team hits a sticky patch. The fans aren't going to love Hicks and Gillett for their personalities, or their new-found (and apparently genuine) affection for the club, even though these cannot hurt. Owning a football club is a perilous occupation. Getting the fans onside, and keeping them there, is a fine tightrope to tread; even the best can lose their balance. Early statements were well chosen: plans for the new stadium would be reviewed, to see if it could not be expanded further, as well as the utterly crucial promise on recreating the Kop with a definitive stand, so that the more vocal fans could congregate *en masse*. The Kop would live on. But Hicks initially calling the team the 'Liverpool Reds' struck the wrong chord, although it's easy to see how an American would naturally use such a name.

A lot of fans had spent a fair few years expecting modern-day Liverpool to be successful based on a constricting model of the past. No fan over the age of 20 likes the word 'franchise', and marketing is not where we want to focus our attention. A fair percentage of Liverpool fans will continue to rue the plans for a new stadium, even though Arsenal and Manchester United possess far bigger venues than the 44,000 capacity Anfield, giving them the edge in terms of long-term financial strength. Manchester United, with the 76,000-capacity Old Trafford a regular sell-out, take almost double what Liverpool do through the turnstiles. How can Liverpool be expected to overtake them in such circumstances, especially as United had also long-since been 'exploiting' marketing opportunities.

The business side of things is treated as 'dirty' by a lot of fans, but it's an inescapable part of the modern football landscape. Indeed, business has always played a crucial part in the sport. More than 100 years ago fans paid to enter turnstiles and clubs bought players, but the bigger the game has become, the bigger the business decisions involved — expanding way ahead of inflation. In 1904, when Alf Common was transferred between Sheffield United and Sunderland for £520, wealth clearly played a significant factor in the sport; within a year, Sunderland virtually doubled their money in selling Common to Middlesbrough, when another world record fee was set at £1,000. Big money isn't new to football, but the stakes continue to spiral.

So while something like naming Liverpool's new stadium anything other than Anfield seems an unthinkable act of heresy, the money sponsorship could garner would help keep the club's finances strong, long after the initial cash injection has been spent. This is one of the tough decisions that lies in wait. But if Arsenal are recouping £100m from Emirates over a ten year period, for shirt sponsorship and naming rights to Ashburton Grove, it makes it that much harder not to follow suit. Gillett said at the time of the takeover: "If the naming rights are worth one great player a year in transfer spending, we will certainly look at that as a serious option."

Then again, Hicks' recent history might suggest this might not be the case. Hicks sold the Rangers' ballpark naming rights in 2004 to Ameriquest, a loan company, for a reported €75m over a 30 year period. The Ballpark in Arlington became the Ameriquest Field in Arlington. It was still referred to by fans as the Ballpark, or the Temple, its long-held nickname. But on the 19th of March 2007, just one-tenth of the way into the length of the deal, the Texas Rangers severed their relationship with Ameriquest and announced that the stadium would be named Rangers Ballpark in Arlington. Away from a constrictive and exclusive deal, there was wider scope for sponsorship opportunities within the stadium.

The thing with football is that if you don't keep pace with your competitors you can be quickly left behind. And any gaps, be it in terms of league points or bank balances, can take years to claw back. Liverpool were ahead of the game when it came to shirt sponsorship, tying up a deal with electronics giant Hitachi in 1979, before any other British club had gone down that route. Such canny commercial decisions enabled the Reds to maintain their position at the pinnacle of the English game, and indeed, in Europe. It'd take a brave man (or men) to sell the new stadium's name to a sponsor, but Liverpool are in need of some brave decisions in a number of areas in order to fully prosper. It's not about being reckless; but it's not about playing it too safe, either. Whereas other clubs would have struggled financially had they not followed Liverpool's lead with shirt sponsorship, perhaps Liverpool cannot expect to compete without selling the name of the new stadium. Whatever it's called, it won't seem right if it's not Anfield. But that has to be weighed against the chance of further investment in the team.

Liverpool's new wealth has to be sustainable. The influx of cash from Gillett and Hicks is not going to go anywhere near as far, or last as long, as that of Roman Abramovich, with his endlessly deep Russian pockets. The Americans' money has to be invested in a way that will improve annual profits, yielding yearly dividends that the manager can make use of.

All this leads to the dichotomy at the heart of the matter: fans want success on the pitch at almost any cost, while at the same time, perfectly naturally, bemoaning the fallout from *paying* that cost. Every fan wants his or her club to invest heavily in the team, but doesn't want a hike in season ticket prices or more corporate boxes to facilitate it. Every fan wants to attract the very best players to his or her club, and to do the utmost to retain the valued ones already present, but few fans are happy to see players taking home ever-increasing pay packets. The money has to be found from somewhere, and if the team you support doesn't pay them the going rate, other teams will.

A lot of media reports at the time of the takeover mentioned how it's remarkable that Liverpool did not have a dedicated commercial department, and yet a lot of fans have secretly liked that fact; proud that the club did not 'sell out' at the first whiff of money in the 1990s. But it has also become increasingly clear that despite a world-class manager and a nucleus of outstanding players, reaching the next level continues to prove challenging. (That said, the Treble of 2001 and, more significantly, the European Cup of 2005, are up there with the most exciting seasons in the club's history, and in 2007 the club wasn't that far off replicating the great feat of two years earlier. However, most of the focus is on that elusive 19th title.)

Then there has been the 'what would Shanks have made of it all?' viewpoint, used to express dismay. Which is a bit like asking what Henry Ford would have made of a top-of-the-range 2007 Skoda: it might not be the perfect example of an automobile 100 years on, but it's better equipped than an ancient Model T Ford to get you from Liverpool to Athens. In other words, you work within the context of your current day, not the past or the future. BBC Radio Five Live's Nicky Campbell, writing for the Guardian about how he spent the day of the final broadcasting from Syntagma Square, spoke of meeting Shankly's granddaughter, Karen Gill, who lives in Athens and teaches English (not to mention having written an enlightening book on the great man). From that, Campbell move on to how Shankly would have wanted to get his hands on the Americans' money. Shanks saw football as a kind of socialism: "The socialism I believe in is not really politics; it is humanity, a way of living and sharing the rewards." But as Campbell pointed out, Shanks would have gone with the new money "because he wanted the best for the institution he loved and worked so hard to build." And it's easy to see his point. Shanks may now seem old-fashioned in a number of ways — anyone in cloth caps and grainy black and white footage does — but at the time he was forward-thinking. Asking what Shanks would have made of the American owners is a bit like asking what David Ashworth, the Liverpool manager in 1920, would have made of the 4-4-2 formations and constant five-a-sides in training to engender pass-and-move that made Shankly such a success. Frankly, it's not relevant. It's ludicrous to think that if Shankly was in his prime and working today, he wouldn't be looking to innovate within the current framework of the game, rather than rely on the thinking of the 1960s.

Shanks is of course from a different era, and while we can all rue and mourn the loss of certain values and traditions in the sport, we also have to accept that times change, and if you don't change with them you're in danger of becoming an anachronism. The hardest thing is to move with the times and remain competitive, whilst sticking to at least some of your principles.

So what can Liverpool fans expect from the two men in whose hands the future of the club rests? It's fair to say that the pair have had a mixed time in both life and sport. That is not to say failures are necessarily a bad thing (especially if those failures didn't occur at your club). Few people in life get to the top through smooth sailing alone. And it's true: we all learn from our mistakes.

## All Change at the Top

The financial landscape of the English game is changing so fast it's hard to keep up. Millionaires and, more pertinently, *billionaires* are lining up to try their luck with this club and then that, like crazed game show contestants trying to find the gold box into which the special key fits. Many of the same names keep appearing in connection with the latest club under scrutiny: as if it almost doesn't matter what that club's identity is, so long as it includes an invite to the Premiership party. It's almost as if it took a couple of years for clubs to come to terms with the arrival of Roman Abramovich at Stamford Bridge, and most have had little option but to try and follow suit. How else do you compete? It's like Joe Bloggs keeping up with the Joneses next door by working hard at his office job, only for Mr and Mrs Jones to win £10m on the lottery.

If Chelsea's wealth destabilised what was at last becoming a more sensible, stable transfer market, West Ham's has set an even more dangerous precedent: mid-range pros suddenly being paid £70,000 a week, as in the case of Lucas Neill and Scott Parker.

Football is a game of follow the leader. Everyone is out for themselves: the clubs all want to be number one (but only one can), and the players, via their agents, want the best deal they can possibly get — whether or not it's realistic. In desperation a club will make an offer to a player, and the whole wages system spirals. The summer of 2007 saw agents asking for silly money for their clients, because some silly clubs had set the bar. While West Ham will have problems when all their players want £70,000 a week, or their real stars start demanding even more, the problem spreads like a virus to other clubs: a midfielder with one or two England caps looking to join Club X is infected with the same greed, and his agent pitches up looking for what has become the going rate. Club X tells him in no uncertain terms where to go, but Club Y is facing relegation and, in a gamble, decides to break the bank for him. Wage caps are starting to seem more and more essential, but clubs will always find a way around such a measure. It may only lead to more creative accounting.

Separate television deals, as seen in countries like Spain and Germany, could yet be the savour for Liverpool, in terms of breaking free of the closing pack and utilising its core strength: namely, its name, its history. This may seem unfair to other clubs, but it's hard to keep arguing for a fair spreading of wealth between big and small clubs when 'small' clubs are being bought by billionaires. A lot of the meritocracy has gone out of the game, because financial strength is becoming based less on success on the pitch, and bums on seats, and more about which random individual has staked a claim on any particular club. Perhaps it actually makes it fairer, with West Ham and Portsmouth now able to compete on financial terms with more conventionally successful clubs.

If Liverpool could negotiate its own television deal, then as one of the world's top-supported clubs it would thrive in a way teams like West Ham never could. Unlike what's going on at Stamford Bridge, and even at Upton Park, the revenue would be based on business principles — supply and demand — and not simply how rich the owners were from the privatisation of Russian state assets. Liverpool have built up a large worldwide following through success on the pitch in the '60s, '70s and '80s, and while the rich financial rewards were not in place at the time of that unprecedented success, the legacy is that it turned a provincial club into a global phenomenon. The lack of gross financial mismanagement seen at clubs like Leeds United has kept Liverpool at the top — averaging out as 3rd-place finishers over 17 barren league years — and has helped the club stay within touching distance of the leading lights. Hicks and Gillett paid in excess of £40m to cover debts, but was not a figure that was out of the ordinary in the modern game. While not going overboard in terms of spending what it didn't have, the club had still clearly reached its financial limits.

Before the takeover, it would have been easy to throw a lot more money the club didn't have at the problem of toppling Manchester United, Arsenal and, more recently, Chelsea, but borrowing heavily is such a high-risk strategy. While no Liverpool fan enjoys seeing the club away from its perch as the no.1, each can count his or her blessings that the club is still challenging at the top end of the English game and, even more sweetly, has been the joint-best team with AC Milan in European football in the past three seasons — with each club boasting first and second place finishes in the Champions League in that time.

Mentioning Leeds United in relation to financial implosion has almost become a cliché, but it continues to prove the warning example to all clubs whose ambitions outstretch their means. In 2007 Ken Bates, who had taken over control at Elland Road, revealed that the weekly wage of Gary Kelly — to all intents and purposes a fairly average right-back — has been a gobsmacking £46,000 a week since 2001. "Twelve million pounds over five years," said the chairman. "I worked out that all the money that Leeds earned getting to the semi-finals of the Champions League was handed to Kelly with his new contract." Five years later, Leeds find themselves in the third tier of English football, while Kelly retired aged 32, having accumulated not a single trophy. It doesn't seem that much different from West Ham paying a fairly ordinary full-back the kind of money that should only be reserved for the genuine world-class talents. And that's dangerous. It just makes the genuinely talented players expect even more.

The fate of Leeds United seemed bad enough when they were relegated from the Premiership in 2004, just three years after making the Champions League semi-final. It still seemed possible that they would quickly bounce back, as you automatically expect big clubs to do. But by 2007 the club was in freefall. With relegation to the third tier of English football determined before the end of 2006/07, the club instantly went into administration to take the ten point penalty in that season, when it could do no further harm, rather than at the start of the following season (a loophole that has since been closed). With debts of £35m, Ken Bates, as part of a new consortium, then tried to buy back the club with an offer to pay creditors just 1p out of every pound owed. When the Inland Revenue, which was owed £7.7m, refused, Bates upped his offer to 8p in every pound, which was also turned down. This led to the likelihood of Leeds folding, although they started the new season — albeit reeling from a 15-point deduction based on their financial situation. And it all stems back to the Icarian days when, under Peter Ridsdale, the club flew too close to the sun. A time when mediocre full-backs and jobbing midfielders were handed king's ransoms. To say it reached meltdown would be an understatement.

Michael Walker, writing in *The Guardian* in June 2007 on the subject of the massive wage hike seen in recent years, said: "It will be dismissed as anecdotal but within English football, and specifically among agents, the following story is circulating and generating huge excitement. A player from a third-tier club who moved recently to a Championship club — one not so long ago in the Premiership — has seen his basic £1,500-a-week salary increase not five times, nor ten, but 15 times. The player's agent did not demand this sum; it was the club's opening gambit. The belief that wages in football are soaring uncontrollably is understandable. In April a Professional Footballers' Association survey found that the average annual salary of a Premiership player is now £676,000 — £13,000 a week — a rise of 65% on 2000. The accountancy firm Deloitte puts the figure much higher." (This average figure of £13,000 presumably includes all the young players yet to sign major contracts.)

Many fans fail to consider a player's wages when weighing up a particular deal, or the budget they think a club should be spending each summer. Talk of any deal always revolves around the transfer fees alone, never the wages that need to be factored in over a four or five year period. At the end of the 1980s, a top player would cost between two and three million pounds. His wages would be around £5,000 a week, and as such a five-year contract, if fulfilled, would be worth around £1.3m. In other words, less than 50% of his transfer value. Compare that with the current situation, and across the Premiership you will find any number of £5m players who are earning £50,000 a week. That's £13m over five years. Or over two and a half times the transfer value. So these days it's less about the cash to finance the purchase, and more about the cash to actually pay the player. The top players now cost £30m, and their wages over a five year period — almost certainly around the going top-end rate of £120,000 a week — would more than match that figure. Rather than find £30m, the club has to commit to £60m.

A larger stadium capacity is one of the safest ways to guarantee the extra revenue increased wages requires. No team can bank on annual Champions League qualification, nor other performance-based windfalls. But providing the team remains at least competitive towards the top of the Premiership, the sport remains popular, and the ticket prices aren't prohibitive, selling out a stadium should remain possible.

## Stability and Consistency

The most important factor for success at a top club, aside from money, is stability. Even with money at the ready and talent in the team, an unstable environment can lead to disharmony, and without everyone pulling in the same direction a club can be like a badly assembled Rolls Royce: lots of expensive parts, but many working against one another.

Disharmony behind the scenes at Liverpool is rare. All clubs experience difficulties, and disagreements, but by comparison with almost any other English club, Liverpool always remained united in public. In the autumn of 2006 that appeared to be in danger, but once Noel White, who'd spoken out against Benítez, resigned from his position on the board, harmony returned. But then the whole regime changed within a matter of six months, and Benítez was again facing a period of uncertainty. Would the new owners behave impetuously?

Gillett and Hicks inherited a top-class manager in Rafael Benítez. While it's hard to say who is the best club manager around, given the subjective nature of assessing their achievements, it's fair to group the Spaniard with a small collection of other managers at the very top of the game. Three years without a serious tilt at the title, despite success in Europe and domestic cups, could be seen as failure by some, and cause to move on. Perhaps Gillett and Hicks would want a completely fresh start? It couldn't be completely ruled out.

Even had they been in the mood for a firm sweep of their new broom, it's hard to see who could have replaced Benítez and *definitely* do a better job. So that would mean change for change's sake. A replacement manager would mean starting again in so many ways. New managers want new players, and to introduce new tactics and systems. Existing players who are surplus to requirements see their value drop, because a club looking to sell a number of its playing staff always suffers from their need to offload. Unwanted players, however talented, are instantly devalued. Clubs who regularly change managers rarely escape the rollercoaster: no one ever gets the chance to totally remake the club in his own image, and you end up with a mess of half-finished projects and aborted visions.

It was important that, having decided Benítez was as good as they could get, Gillett and Hicks would back him 100%. Benítez had put his identity into the club, in the players he'd purchased and his long-term vision. That needed maintaining — unless there was an amazing fail-safe alternative. Which, of course, there wasn't.

Gillett told Oliver Kay, "For Rafa to say things publicly was a bit of a surprise. But he had had a very disappointing night and was walking the streets of Athens for five hours after the game. We've all been there and said things in a moment of frustration or passion. He's a very interesting, responsible, brilliant man, always trying to do better."

## New Stadium

In May 2007, with Gillett and Hicks finally in full control of the club, work finally commenced on the new Anfield. But no sooner had the first shovel broken earth, news broke of a revision of the plans. Rather than abort the original plans, work on the foundations would continue, with a new planning application presented to the council — one that stuck to the previously agreed 60,000 seat limit, but which would leave room to further expand the stadium in time. If this revision was rejected, the original plan could be stuck to, with work already progressing.

With Manchester United's match-day income far outstripping Liverpool's, and Chelsea's phenomenal wealth enabling them to buy who they want, when they want, the Americans were pinning their hopes of future financial might on having the biggest stadium in Britain. With United having possibly reached the upper limit on how they can expand Old Trafford, and with Chelsea's fan-base, unless it expands exponentially with their new-found success, unlikely to fill anywhere much bigger than Stamford Bridge, it would enable the Reds to become a lot more competitive in the long term; but, of course, the financial outlay required in building a new stadium can leave crippling debts. It's a case of speculating to accumulate, and it can never offer guarantees.

"The city council's planners will receive the final plans on July 25," Hicks told *The Sunday Mirror*. "The initial capacity will be the 60,000 previously approved, but the design will accommodate an eventual capacity in the high seventies."

As with the potential for overseas owners, resistance to moving from Anfield — or rather, to a new 'Anfield' a few hundred metres away — had long-since died away. Not everyone was in favour of it, but the alternatives were thin on the ground. Fan pressure groups, like Anfield4Ever, accepted after meeting with Rick Parry that they could not stand in the way of progress. Tim Kelly, present at the meeting in the early part of the decade, explained in July 2007: "David Moores poured us a lovely cup of coffee as Rick went on to explain the reasons why Anfield was no longer a viable option. The work we put into it (A4E) was recognised by both Rick and David — can't ask for more than that. Six, maybe seven years ago it was that we, and those in support of A4E, finally accepted the inevitable."

The difference in the summer of 2007 was that the two American owners had got hold of the plans, assessed the potential to make an even better, potentially much bigger new stadium, and instructed the architects to come up with a new solution. The plans had to stick to the capacity of 60,000, which had already been agreed, but there was clear scope to increase it by a further third.

Rick Parry explained in a press release: "Our architects HKS have a wealth of experience and have fused a very contemporary and unique vision together with the values that are crucial to Liverpool Football Club. A critical design consideration was to ensure the stadium sat naturally within its park environment, complementing its surroundings and a huge amount of work has been done to ensure this happens. The stadium is a massive investment in North Liverpool and a key driver in the regeneration of the whole area.

"The asymmetric design sets it apart from other new stadia, as it is a clear move away from what is becoming the traditional bowl model. It recognises and makes reference to the fact that English football grounds were historically asymmetric. We make no apologies for that, we've gone out of our way to embrace that culture and it works exceptionally well for both the new ground and its location within Stanley

Park. This new design will be unmistakably Liverpool and instantly recognisable as our stadium."

The point about moving away from bowl designs was particularly apt. It had got to the stage where clubs were using the exact same blueprints: Southampton's St Mary's and Derby's Pride Park are actually identical structures built in different cities. That's okay if you have a limited budget and want an off-the-shelf modern arena, but Liverpool needed to be beyond such actions. Even a uniquely designed bowl would end up close to dozens of others new stadia. While the new design was not to everyone's taste, the club's research and anecdotal evidence from various websites suggested the vast majority were impressed. An impressive 90.5% of Liverpool fans supported the new stadium plans in a poll on the *Liverpool Echo* website.

Depending on your vantage point, the stadium is either curvaceous or sharply angular; from certain positions it is equal amounts of both. Huge steel arcs bend outwards from the ground and up over the roof of one stand, meeting the straight lines that jut from the adjacent one. The club's description of the plans, and how the stadium will fit within Stanley Park, is as follows: "The new ground will also incorporate dedicated facilities for the Anfield Sport and Community Centre and Liverpool Hope University and external facilities will include tennis courts and new multi-use games area. The West side is concave in form effectively embracing the park and providing changing facilities for those young amateur players and their parents who use the existing pitches which will be retained within the park. The North and East facades take a convex form respectively overlooking Priory Road and Utting Avenue across gardens which will be developed in the tradition of Stanley Park. The South facade will be of completely different form, taking on a more formal appearance appropriate to its civic function at the northern edge to the new Anfield Plaza development which will replace the current ground. The stadium will have a stone work base on the North, West and East sides with mainly glass facades above. The South side will be clad in metal and overlook the Plaza. One striking feature will see the South East and South West corners of the stadium visually open, providing views from the park deep into its heart." (Presumably sales in stepladders will rise sharply following this final detail. And as well as 'mind yer car' there'll be scallies selling specs in Stanley Park trees.)

In order to increase the capacity towards the 80,000 mark — a move which could be in place by the time the stadium opens in 2010 — the club would need to make significant adjustments to the local infrastructure. Rick Parry explained: "... we make no secret of the fact that we want a greater capacity [than the initial 60,000] and will consider putting in a second planning application when appropriate. However, we fully recognise for this to happen that all the associated transport requirements need to be in place. To increase the capacity above 60,000 we need a further step change in our approach which is why we, together with Liverpool City Council and Merseytravel, are investigating the possibility of reopening the Bootle Branch railway line for passenger use. That would be a fantastic solution, not just for the club, but for all the people of north Liverpool."

Key to the new stadium will be the Kop: an immense single-tier stand, rather than a seamless, indistinguishable row of seats within a bowl. At a capacity of 18,000-19,500, it will be one-third larger than the current Kop, and three-quarters of the size of the pre-seated Kop at its most populated. At its noisiest the Kop can be worth extra points in a season, or the difference in big cup games, as seen with the two Chelsea semi-finals.

Few stadia seem to be designed with the aim of getting the most out of the crowd's fervour. And yet everyone knows how influential a partisan crowd can be on proceedings. The more intimidating the stadium, the greater the chance of victory; from victory follows the success that everyone at a club craves, from a sporting point of view, and the financial success that is required in order to pay for the stadium in the first place. A soulless arena and you can end up with a monstrous mortgage and a fading team.

The club's willingness to listen to fans in order to help improve the atmosphere at Anfield was highlighted when the '1892' section was announced: a block of almost 2000 seats where the singers could congregate, but also for those most aware of the club's unique customs. The brainchild of fan forum Reclaim The Kop (RTK), the club would reassign seats within the current stand, to group together those who stoke up the atmosphere. The 1892 section will transfer into the new stadium.

"We've also recognised the central importance of the Kop," explained Parry. "It ... will be the heartbeat of the new stadium. The rake of the stand will be steeper and the seats tighter together, with the acoustics of the roof designed to accentuate the atmosphere during games."

It all adds up to what are clearly exciting times for Liverpool fans. Two European Cup Finals in three years, and an increasing core of top-class playing talent that suggests at least the ability to get within touching distance of the league title; the promise of more money to invest in the team courtesy of its new owners; and the opening of a world-class stadium by the beginning of the next decade.

## How Can Liverpool Become Champions?

The number 18 has been on the minds of Liverpool fans for too long, with number 19 thus far having proved elusive. In 1990 Liverpool were like the city's most famous sons: as prolific as the Beatles, with number one hit after number one hit, and respected as innovators in their field. For the 17 years since, however, Liverpool more closely resembled David Hasselhoff: no chart-topping in England, but the occasional über-smash in Turkey and Germany. While all trophies are to be welcomed, especially the Champions League, the success in Istanbul, rather than satiating desire, has only highlighted what is growing into a two-decade failure in the domestic league.

Patience amongst Liverpool fans was tested in 2007 by Manchester United's 16th English league title. Chelsea's triumphs still don't require all the fingers on one hand to count them, but United had moved to within two of Liverpool's record total; decidedly too close for comfort. Solace can be found in the five European crowns to United's two, but the 2007 Champions League final saw the Reds miss a chance to boast a success rate three times higher than that of their rivals down the East Lancs Road.

It was always going to be the case that Liverpool fans' opinions on the success of the 2006/07 season would be dramatically affected by the result in Athens. How fine the line from being crowned Champions of Europe to ending without any silverware to show, and whispers about stagnation. Should all those opinions really ride on one single result? After all, the ability of the team and the manager will not be altered in the face of one game; only perceptions will be.

The Premiership title, because of the wait, is the one that matters most to the majority of Liverpool fans. And, if they are to be believed, to the players and staff, too. But despite this, United's latest success seemed a little devalued; to them it obviously meant a great deal, but there didn't seem to be the usual level of hyperbole in the newspapers.

Perhaps the success of Athens, from a Liverpool point of view, was that the final occupied plenty of column inches — just enough of an achievement to take the shine off the Old Trafford parties. If that sounds a little bitter (and it may well do), it's worth considering Bill Brodhagen's superb catch-all article on America's Onion Sports website, entitled *You Will Suffer Humiliation When The Sports Team From My Area Defeats The Sports Team From Your Area*. The part that seemed apposite in May 2007 was the following passage: "In the past, we have defeated you on any number of occasions. Granted, there were times when your team beat my team, but those were lucky flukes."

The ultimate recourse of any fan is to belittle a rival team's achievements — usually by labelling them as outrageous flukes — while upping the significance of his own team's glories. But there was more to it than that.

Perhaps it was also that there was a sense in the air of both Jose Mourinho, via Roman Abramovich's obsession, and Alex Ferguson, via his own long-standing obsession, wanting to win a European Cup that bit more. The difference between eight and nine league titles was not going to change Ferguson's reputation; but the leap from one to two European crowns would. And while Rafa Benítez remains stuck on one, like Mourinho and Ferguson, he can at least say he got *closer* to a second.

So for the past three seasons no-one has been totally satisfied. Ferguson and Mourinho would gladly swap a Premiership title for Benítez's Champions League alchemy, while the Spaniard would trade another European Cup Final to land a league title.

So what can be done differently in the future to make sure the wait for the league crown does not last as long as Manchester United's 26-year drought, or even longer still? Whether it arrives in 2008 or 2009, or a year or two later, there are a number of issues that remain at the core of a title challenge, not to mention a whole heap of myths.

For the sake of consistency, and given his undoubted talent (and that there is no-one screaming out that they are better), the Reds' board would be advised to have patience with Benítez. Granted, circumstances change, and if things really aren't progressing, particularly domestically, the time for a new direction will inevitably come. No manager can outrun the sack when his time is up. Given that he is the current manager this is written with his stewardship in mind, but much of it would remain applicable to any man in charge. The challenges that face Benítez are those of today, not yesterday.

This chapter assesses the performance of Benítez and his rivals in recent seasons, and what the Spaniard might need to do differently in the future. But before this, a couple of caveats:

Firstly, this assessment does not simply mean suggesting Liverpool buy Player X and Player Y, and sell Player Z. It's easy to bandy names around, and we all know who we think looks good in their respective leagues or Premiership clubs at any given time. Of course, that doesn't mean we're all talking about the same player, or that we'll still feel the same six months later.

Ultimately, no-one outside of the coaching staff can know exactly what type of player the manager and his aides are looking for; nor do we have access to anywhere near as much scouting material, or information on the players' characters and backgrounds, not to mention their willingness to play for the club (and to do so for the right reasons). Mostly we have just a few blurry YouTube videos and some unreliable eye-witness reports to go on. Are we supposed to trust some over-eager teenage internet warrior who may never have kicked a ball in his life over a scout who has spent 30 years in professional football, and who has been to watch the player in the flesh on a number of occasions, as well as studying video footage that is far more extensive than that offered on the web?

Then there's the fact that Benítez and his scouts will be looking for more than an ability to nutmeg or drag-back. The people who will make the decisions about who needs to be bought are the ones who understand the systems these players need to fit into, and the blend that is being sought. They are also the ones who get to look into each player's eyes, and see if the hunger is there.

If it's true that Andrei Shevchenko was bought against Jose Mourinho's wishes, then it could be held up as proof that buying great players who do not fit the game-plan or team ethos can prove counterproductive. You cannot simply expect to sign top players without an idea as to how to integrate them to the team, and if the arrival of a new player means disrupting the balance or negatively affecting someone else's game, it can hinder rather than help.

The first task Benítez faced in the aftermath of Athens — yet another crossroads for the club — was to secure the long-term futures of the key players already on the books. By June 8th the club had announced that Jamie Carragher and Steven Gerrard had signed deals taking them up to 2011, and that Pepe Reina and Xabi Alonso — who was linked with a move to Barcelona, his father's alma mater — had signed new deals tying them to the club until 2012. Steve Finnan and Momo Sissoko soon followed suit.

Any future success surely depends on retaining such prized assets, with the first four players named seen as the quartet Benítez confides in most. Extending the contracts of these players sent a message of unity to the team, its fans and the club's rivals, and kept in place the core of players whose presence will help attract new stars. It would be very hard to envisage Liverpool moving forwards in the hunt for the title without those top-class players who had already gelled within the unit, and whose character and leadership skills were vital to any long-term plans. While it was almost unthinkable to lose any of them, the deals still needed to be struck. To mount a serious challenge for the title, the club almost certainly needs Carragher, Gerrard, Reina and Alonso.

Secondly, this chapter does not attempt to assess the kind of playing style required to be successful, as it's hard to say for sure that a certain style of football wins league titles. You obviously cannot be too cautious and have eleven men behind the ball, or too gung-ho with five forwards, but there are many successful options between those two extremes.

Chelsea's 'cautious', hard-running, physical, target-man 4-3-3 style has been very successful in recent seasons, but so has Manchester United's use of wingers and quick counter-attacking with either a 4-4-2 or 4-5-1 formation. Then there's Arsenal, who intricately passed their way to an unbeaten season in 2004, but who can also pass themselves to death. It's true that 3-5-2 has never proved a championship-winning formation, but Benítez has had some good results on the very few occasions he's opted for it. However, it's hard to see it as more than a third or fourth option.

Liverpool's style under Benítez should not be a problem, as it incorporates elements from each of those three successful side. While small alterations will occur as the team develops, Liverpool show variety in looking to pass short, medium and long; they use the width of the pitch with wingers and full-backs getting wide and forward, and use Peter Crouch's height as a very effective weapon in the way Chelsea look to Drogba. The Reds also have a mix of skill and athleticism, and as of the summer of 2007, an incredibly tall team from front to back. Up front, Crouch is no totem used only for his towering stature, but is as technically gifted as almost any other striker in the Premiership. He's an option, to receive the ball to feet or to win headers, and more than anything, Benítez likes to have options. It stops his sides becoming predictable, with predictability the undoing of his predecessor. Some fans find that he pays too much attention to the opposition, and he may look guilty of this at times. But if an opposition defence is full of small, slow defenders, it's natural to play your taller, quicker strikers.

Under Benítez a lot of clean sheets are kept, and a lot of chances are created — they just weren't converted frequently enough in the league between 2004 and 2007. It's fair to say that the major stumbling block has been finishing, and that's not an issue that relates to the tactics. But it doesn't necessarily follow that possessing a more prolific goalscorer would have solved the problem; it would have needed to be the right kind of striker, whose inclusion kept the rest of the side in balance. Someone like Michael Owen wouldn't have automatically solved the problem, if he hadn't been able to hold the ball up as well as Kuyt or Crouch. The problem with some strikers — particularly diminutive goalscorers — is that they often need another type of striker to help them out; so this can mean changing not just one player but two. Michael Owen could never play as a lone striker; while he has the pace to play on the shoulder of the last defender, he has neither the physical presence nor the skill with his back to goal to perform the role alone. This means a second striker pushed up right alongside him: the bodyguard, as seen with Emile Heskey for a number of years. But if you have two strikers pushed up high, that leaves less scope to play between the lines and create chances in the first place. If you have two strikers who spend all their time in advanced areas then you need both to be prolific, as you cannot afford to commit as many midfielders forward.

## Goals, goals, goals

One of the problem areas identified by both fans and management was the goals-for column. While Manchester United managed 83 goals in the 2006/07 Premiership campaign, Liverpool chalked up only 57.

The obsession with 20/30 goals-a-season man as an absolute necessity is very misleading. A prolific league striker is rarely a bad thing to have ("No, Mr Chairman, take that 60-goal-a-season striker away and bring me Sean Dundee"). However, it is not *definitely* needed, as the last three Premierships have been won with top-scoring strikers who managed just 12, 13 and 14 goals respectively, with one of their own midfielders outscoring them on the way to the title, while the runners-up have possessed the more prolific strikers. Over the last dozen years, the Premiership has been won as often by teams without big-scoring strikers as it has with them.

But if the problem is that your strikers aren't converting enough chances, then that's a different issue. In that case, the key is to add strikers who convert chances at a better rate, but whose inclusion don't lead to fewer chances being created in the first place — from laziness, as an example, or sloppy technique outside the box — as that just leaves you back at square one. It's pointless having the world's best six-yard predator if you can't get the ball to him.

Here's something to ponder. In 2001 Manchester United, champions for the previous three seasons in England, and six times in the previous eight campaigns, finally signed Ruud van Nistelrooy, the ultra-prolific striker who'd made his name at PSV Eindhoven. In five seasons at Old Trafford, the Dutchman scored 150 goals, all inside the 18-yard box, and at a quite remarkable strike rate. But United won only one Premiership crown, and did increasingly worse in the Champions League year on year, despite van Nistelrooy being the competition's most lethal marksman. Van Nistelrooy was then shipped off to Real Madrid and instantly United, without an ultra-reliable finisher, stormed to the league title, and, for the first time in a number of years, made it to the semi-final of the Champions League. Meanwhile in Spain, the man the press dubbed *van Gol* was banging them in at his usual rate. (The nickname *El Caballo Gol* might have been more apt.) Madrid were again eliminated early in Europe, although they did rally late in the domestic season to land the *La Liga* title.

Is the disappointing tally of medals in van Nistelrooy's career — given the goals he's scored and the teams he's played for — all one big coincidence? Surely you throw a man like that into any side — especially a top side — and success follows? The same applies to his time with the Dutch national team, from which he was ultimately expelled. Or does van Nistelrooy represent a certain kind of player, one who plays for himself (and does a damn good job of it) but who ultimately, in some subtle way, disrupts the team?

Let's be clear: any striker who scores goals sees his contribution benefit his team; after all, the goals don't count merely in the top-scorers chart. And van Nistelrooy's time in England did coincide with the best Arsenal team ever seen, who played sublime football, and then Chelsea rampant on the heady mix of Abramovich's cash and Mourinho's bravado. But why did United suddenly get so much better as soon as he left, especially as they only bought one player that summer? While van Nistelrooy's impact at Real Madrid shows how valuable a reliable scorer can be, his time at United showed that it's the best balanced teams who succeed. (Indeed, had Spain used goal difference as a league position determinator rather than the less reliable head-to-head, Madrid would have been runners-up, such was the inferiority of their overall scoring record. Barcelona were the better balanced team, and goal difference, which monitors the whole season rather than just two games, would have been a fairer way to decide the title.)

Arsenal in 2004, and Chelsea in the next two years, won the title with at least one striker barely scoring at all. Dennis Bergkamp's goals had all but dried up at the tail end of his career, while Mateja Kezman and Eidur Gudjohnson barely troubled keepers. (Kezman did trouble a whole host of spectators behind goals up and down the country, plus a few people in the car parks, and on one occasion, someone in a neighbouring county.) But each of these teams had a number of goalscoring midfielders. While Thierry Henry's goals were crucial to Arsenal, the finishing skills of Robert Pirès and Freddie Ljungberg made them difficult to contain. Chelsea, with Drogba managing barely a dozen league goals in each of his first two seasons, was the foil for Frank Lampard, Joe Cole, Damien Duff and Arjen Robben, all of whom could finish when in on goal. In 2007, Wayne Rooney and Luis Saha scored only respectable amounts, while Cristiano Ronaldo led the way, with Ryan Giggs and Paul Scholes also scoring from midfield.

In Steven Gerrard, Liverpool have a midfielder capable of scoring goals from a variety of situations. Getting the captain forward — either to shoot from 25 yards or to get ahead of the strikers into the box — has always been Benítez's priority, and as a result, Gerrard scored 13, 23 and 11 goals between 2004 and 2007. This, having previously only managed a personal best of ten in a single season, and just four, seven and six in the three seasons before Benítez arrived. With other players bought to perform the more defensive side of the game, Gerrard has been freed up to attack. The debate centred around where to play him, with Benítez fond of switching him around, but the manager's aim was always to get him into dangerous areas during games. With additions to the flanks in the summer of 2007, Benítez said Gerrard would be spending more time centrally. But it's an area where the manager's options are vast.

The problems in 2006/07 were easy to spot, but harder to eradicate. Luis García was a gem who, for every minute of football played, had been the most prolific midfielder in the Premiership from open play for a number of seasons. The trouble was accommodating him for something even remotely approaching every minute of every game; something Benítez did not feel was possible. Then, in January 2007, came the injury that ended the little Spaniard's season, and, it would prove, his Liverpool career. Then there was Harry Kewell, who still averages a goal every four games in club football. The Australian's time at Liverpool has been blighted by a succession of injuries, but he remains one of the most natural midfield finishers around, as he showed in his first five months at Liverpool, when he quickly moved towards double figures by Christmas. Having these two players miss so much of the season was detrimental, especially as Mark González, a proven goalscoring winger in Spain and for Chile, failed to adapt to English football.

The trouble was compounded whenever two of Alonso, Mascherano and Sissoko were in the centre of midfield. These three combined will usually manage five goals in a season; all from the Spaniard. (Although Mascherano, usually as prolific as Rob Jones, went crazy at the 2007 *Copa America*, scoring *twice*.) A failure to get enough men forward seems to be a bone of contention for some fans, and the central midfield pairings seem key to this criticism — but it can be misleading. The problem was not necessarily the central midfielders themselves, but getting the balance right around them.

Despite what people think, it is possible to play positive, attacking football with two holding midfielders who don't chip in with many goals. It's a bit like the debate which labels 4-5-1 as negative; it depends on the players concerned as to how attacking it becomes. If Alonso and Mascherano are chosen in tandem it has to be noted that few deep-lying midfielders can be as devastating at starting attacks; so they're not 'negative' players whose presence is merely to destroy. They create, just from deeper positions. Both move the ball quickly and intelligently over short distances, to help moves build momentum, and each can effortlessly find team-mates at longer range (Alonso especially so). They are like fixed central pivots, around which other players can rotate with more freedom. They enable both full-backs to get forward with fewer worries about being caught out, and crucially, allow the winger to stay forward as well, as there is midfield cover to drop in behind.

As an example, in the 4th minute against Arsenal at Anfield in March, Jermaine Pennant and Alvaro Arbeloa exchanged clever passes up by the corner flag. Arbeloa, released by Pennant's back-heel, squared for Crouch to open the scoring. This was possible — in a game eventually won 4-1 — because with two holding midfielders (Mascherano and Alonso), Pennant didn't have to worry about covering for his overlapping right-back, and Arbeloa didn't have to worry about holding back for fear of overloading the attack. Both could hare forward and get at the Arsenal left-back, knowing that if the move broke down, either Mascherano or Alonso — both canny readers of the game with tactical knowledge beyond their years — would shuffle across in time, while the other could stay central to protect the centre-backs.

Meanwhile, on the left that day, Aurelio was getting forward to great effect, with González also having one of his better games. So while the team contained two holding midfielders, there was no lack of forward intent. Far from it, as Arsenal were soundly thrashed. The game proved you can get plenty of players forward in attacks, and keep enough players back — it's simply a more fluid way of doing things; just not as immediately obvious as having a central attacking midfielder catching the eye by sprinting beyond the strikers.

Against Reading a couple of weeks later, Liverpool went in with a central pairing of Mascherano and Sissoko. The Reds had Pennant and Arbeloa again combining down by the opposition corner flag. Soon after, the Spanish right-back had a header at goal from open play, as well as becoming the first Liverpool no.2 in 15 years to score a goal. In the same game, Daniel Agger produced a superb solo run that took him through on goal. So while Benítez had made his team a superb defensive unit, it was not by keeping his defenders back for 90 minutes, or by only sending them forward only for set pieces.

With four central options most clubs would die for — even before the arrival of Lucas Leiva — the option remains to shift Gerrard out to the right. But if Pennant can continue tearing past full-backs, and with the arrival of the tricky and intelligent Yossi Benayoun, maybe the left is a sensible option for the captain? It's certainly the best position for a right-footed player to score goals from, given the way he can open up his body; you only have to look at how often Thierry Henry starts on the left before running infield to score with his right foot. (Even Arbeloa demonstrated this skill at Reading.) At Stamford Bridge earlier in the season Gerrard had two great chances to score, having started the game on the left. If he runs infield and loses his marker, he can be impossible to stop. It was just his finishing that let him down — the story of the Reds' season — but had he put away those two chances in his usual manner, it would have been hailed as a tactical masterstroke. Indeed, the Reds' new Dutch winger, Ryan Babel, specialises in starting on the left and scoring with his right, in contrast to Kewell, who will also go outside his man. So despite Benítez's intentions of playing Gerrard in the centre more often, it's not a cut-and-dried issue.

Of course, fielding two ostensibly holding midfielders does not mean that both have to sit back for 90 minutes. Mascherano's inclusion can help Alonso get further forward. Although the Liverpool no.14 is not a dynamic player who will get ahead of the strikers, in the manner of Frank Lampard and Gerrard, Alonso can advance stealthily towards the edge of the area, where his long-range shooting can trouble teams. (Of course, for Alonso, 18-25 yards is *close* range.) In the 2007 Champions League final he twice had shots from this range, and while he will never be a box-to-box player, the pure holding skills of Mascherano give him a little more freedom to advance with or without the ball. Mascherano's presence will also allow the Spaniard the chance to find a few more killer passes, the kind that are harder to deliver from deep. Sissoko is also extremely good at running forward with the ball; he just needs to work on what he does when he gets there. (Although, perhaps with a hint of things to come, he did finally score his first Liverpool goal in the third league game of 2007/08: a scorching 20-yard drive against Sunderland. It was his 76th game for the club, and was a landmark strike: it was the Reds' 7,000th league goal.)

Those who believe Benítez needs lots of quality options will have been licking their lips at the midfield options open to the Spaniard ahead of 2007/08; those who feel he tinkers too much will have been fretting about how he'll manage to settle upon a consistent team.

The goalscoring problem in 2006/07 was also blighted by the record of Jermaine Pennant, who made the right-wing berth his own towards the end of 2006/07, but scored only one goal in his debut season, and frankly, rarely looked like adding to it. What Pennant did do is create plenty of goals for others. So too did Luis García, albeit with a different style of play, but the Spaniard also scored regularly. Unlike García, whose instincts were always to drift infield, Pennant can give the team good width, and if that helps the side keep an offensive shape, that can open space for others to exploit. But without adding goals to his game, his grip on a place in the side may come under threat. With Steven Gerrard a fairly guaranteed source of both goals and assists from the right, and Yossi Benayoun capable of doing the same, Pennant instantly becomes more of a tactical trump card than a regular winning hand. While he started only just over half of the league games in his debut season, he did make the greatest number of appearances overall. Perhaps most tellingly, he started the first three league games of the new campaign.

Mark González's scoring record in Spain and for Chile suggested he could get towards double figures, but his overall play lacked confidence, and he managed just three goals all season. He started well enough, scoring a crucial goal on his competitive debut on August 9, 2006 against Israeli side Maccabi Haifa, coming off the bench in the 85th minute before coolly slotting the winner three minutes later. In his first league start, against Spurs, he smashed home the rebound after Bellamy had somehow contrived to hit the post from two feet out with the goal gaping. A fine free-kick against Fulham in December was the last of the Chilean's goals.

The one other goalscoring midfielder the Reds possessed was John Arne Riise. Riise is a strange player: limited in a number of ways, and often easy to criticise, but a man who is genuinely versatile and who more often than not delivers the goods. A definite jack of all trades but master of none. Far steadier at left-back than he is given credit for (although in 2006/07 his form dipped), he perhaps only lacks that extra yard or two of pace to be something very special indeed. Given that he has no tricks of any note to use to go past players, that lack of pace hampers his game as a left midfielder. He's not a player like fellow Scandinavian Ljungberg, who gets in behind defenders to score goals, but few players in world football are as dangerous as the Norwegian 30 yards from goal — albeit when a wall isn't waiting to be hit.

Riise's scoring rate is one every ten games, which is good for a full-back but nothing special for a midfielder. One problem is that he rarely scores from left-back. On the other hand, his starts in that position dilute his goalscoring stats when considering his midfield output (so he's probably closer to a very respectable one every five or six games from midfield).

Where Riise can be very effective as a midfielder is in tight away games, where Liverpool will be under pressure; his defensive qualities enable him to double-up on any tricky opposition wingers, and his ability to break with the ball and strike from long distance offers a valuable outlet — as seen in both Barcelona and Eindhoven in the knock-out stages of the Champions League, at home to Spurs in the league, and in the Community Shield against Chelsea.

That last goal was one of the rare Riise strikes scored as a left-back; although in that instance he broke from a Chelsea corner, when formations were out the window. With Finnan (who attacks and crosses well) and Carragher both only weighing in with a goal each under Benítez's reign, goalscoring defenders are thin on the ground. Sami Hyypia was the always the one semi-regular scorer, with 29 goals for the club in 401 games. But the big Finn, whose presence at Anfield for at least another season is to be welcomed, is no longer a first choice defender. His place has been taken by Daniel Agger, who has fortunately maintained, and even improved a little on his Scandinavian elder's strike rate, with four goals in his first 47 games for Liverpool, and an even better rate for his country. For Denmark, Agger's third goal in just 15 caps was unfortunately chalked off when a fan ran onto the pitch to attack the referee, with Sweden awarded a 3-0 win. Agger also scored twice in the Reds' latest pre-season. Elsewhere in the Reds' defence, Fabio Aurelio is a player with a one-in-ten career strike rate, due in part to also playing in midfield, but who has yet to break his duck in England, and who needs to overcome a serious Achilles tendon injury.

With all this in mind, it was perhaps no surprise that, following defeat in Athens, one world-class forward and an array of attacking midfielders were at the top of Benítez's shopping list.

So a title-winning team needs to be able to score a reasonably high number of goals, and from a number of different positions. But three regular scorers from the 'front six', so long as the other three, and a couple of defenders, can chip in the odd goal here and there, is often enough. But of course, how many goals you need to score depends very much on how many you concede. And given that Benítez has pretty much mastered the defensive side of Liverpool's play, it shouldn't require as many as 83 goals to land the title. As long, of course, as the defensive solidity is not compromised in the process of adding more goals to the team. And that's the toughest task. Anyone can find a player who'll at least score a few goals from midfield, but if they don't work for the team it can all so easily fall apart at the other end. Real Madrid, prior to the re-appointment of Fabio Capello, were the perfect example. Before 2006/07, Madrid seemed to eschew every defensive aspect possible, whereas Barcelona played with at least one holding midfielder, and reliable defenders like Carlos Puyol. Capello won Real their first league title since 2003, repeating his feat from a decade earlier of celebrating a one-year spell at the club with the *La Liga* crown. But in true Madrid fashion, Capello was promptly sacked — this, after all, was the club that fired Benítez's mentor, Vincente Del Bosque, after his second Champions League crown. Capello was sacked because the football was not 'sexy' enough, and it makes you wonder why Benítez's name is still perennially linked with his boyhood club. Benítez's teams tend to succeed based on balance rather than outright flair, and, of course, he despises meddling from the top, like any manager worth his salt. And anyway, where had outstanding flair, without balance, got Madrid in the preceding seasons?

Champions do not have to be the league's top scorers, nor have the meanest defence; but one or the other tends to be present, and obviously having both of those distinctions should lead to success. Of course, it's no good going through the season winning 6-0 every other week while also losing each alternate game 1-0. You'd concede only a miserly 19 goals, and score 114, for a record-breaking goal difference, but end up with only 57 points. Consistency is clearly crucial. You don't need a mouth-watering excess of flair if you can win 1-0 game after game. Rather than through mouth-watering displays, Chelsea's two titles came more from grinding out results, and having *enough* skill in the final third to make a difference in tight games. Basically, you don't have to appease the purists, just win games.

(Who are the purists anyway? Are they comprised of Arsène Wenger, Johan Cryuff and Jorge Valdano? Where and when do they meet up? And why do they have such a hold over the aesthetics of the sport? And is there an opposite movement — the impurists, or the ale housers — manned by Neil Warnock and Dave Bassett, who decry the use of the short pass and the failure to leave the boot in?)

One area where the Reds suffered in Benítez's first three years was in finding quick attacking players who suited the system, for that crucial injection of pace. Neither Djibril Cissé nor Mark González managed to exploit their status as the quickest player at the club; neither managed to use his speed in the most devastating fashion. Craig Bellamy was the second-quickest player, after González, but his form was also patchy. On balance, it was not a successful season for the Welshman, although his transfer fee of just £6m, thanks to a release clause in his Blackburn contract, made him a worthwhile gamble; his goal against Barcelona was in itself worth several million to the club, and he left for a £1.5m profit.

But again, can you measure just how much pace is needed to be successful? If someone could field a mythical team of players that included 'prime years' Kenny Dalglish, Eric Cantona, Jan Molby, Graeme Souness, Bobby Moore and Sami Hyypia, it would be hard to back against it winning the league, despite none really troubling a snail over 100 metres. Pace is a great asset, but if you have players who can think quickly, control the ball in an instant and pass it 50 yards to feet — to players on the exact same wavelength — then no sprinter in the world can keep up. Even a slow pass travels far quicker than the fastest player can run. But seeing as it's difficult to create a team with that much natural ability, pace becomes an issue. It's just impossible to say how much of an issue; how long is a piece of string?

Not every great striker has pace, but would Ian Rush have scored as many goals without it? Almost certainly not. He was a lethal finisher, but so many of his chances relied on getting onto the end of a Dalglish master-pass. The best defenders can often get the better of quick strikers with positioning and reading of the situation; but once Thierry Henry is away from the last man there is nothing that defender can physically do to stop him without the aid of a lasso. But if it's a case of all pace and no finesse — an accusation often levelled against Djibril Cissé — then the keeper certainly can. The one-on-one is the preserve of the quick forward, and if he can't take a high-enough percentage of those chances it becomes costly.

However, if a player has skill and pace, as seen with Henry, Cristiano Ronaldo and Didier Drogba, he has the ability to not only go past a man in the first place, but to leave him for dead.

So injecting pace — allied to technical ability — was also high on Benítez's agenda. There was one player who fitted the bill perfectly, given he was also tall and deceptively strong: Fernando Torres.

## Away Day Blues

A manager needs to have more than just a Plan A, unless his Plan A is so faultless it rarely lets him down. His team has to be able to defend a lead, as well as overcome a deficit. Liverpool have a pretty good record in coming from behind to win games under Benítez, particularly in games where the motivation to do so is extra high (such as cup finals), but it's more often the case that the Reds don't concede the first goal, especially at Anfield. Away from home, this was an area where Liverpool needed to improve. It was also where many fans felt the team just weren't attacking enough.

In 2006/07, the away form was not a straightforward issue; it was clouded by a couple of unique conditions. It started with the Reds having to travel to Everton, Chelsea, Bolton, Arsenal and Manchester United — arguably the five toughest away games — in the first six away fixtures. Plus, the campaign started with a tricky away game at Sheffield United, a newly-promoted and passionately-supported club, who were going to treat the game like a cup tie. These six games made gaining confidence on the road that much harder, especially once the media picked up on the fact that the Reds had yet to win away from Anfield.

Liverpool ended up winning just six away games in the league, although there were four defeats — Chelsea, Bolton, Blackburn and Newcastle — where the Reds really should have come away with the points. In terms of tactics and personnel, the right decisions were made; but finishing let the team down, and, at Bolton, a terrible error by the linesman, who incorrectly penalised Pepe Reina for handling outside his area, handed the initiative to the home team with the Reds on top up till then. The away games at Arsenal and Manchester United deservedly ended in defeat, and there's little good to say about them.

The six away victories were all deserved: emphatic wins at Wigan, Charlton and Watford, as well as fairly comfortable victories at Reading, West Ham and Spurs. Had the Reds shown greater coolness in their finishing, and experienced a bit more luck, it could easily have been ten away wins, which would have been much closer to United's 13. It's easy to say 'what if', but in this case it shows that it wasn't really a lack of attacking intent that cost the team on those four occasions, but a failure to be clinical. Add the final two away games, which were lost with Benítez looking to avoid injuries by selecting his reserves rather than going all-out to win, and the results on the road could have been so much better. Better finishing, and a more balanced fixture list, and future away campaigns could be successful if the Reds played the same way. All the same, there was still plenty of room for improvement, particularly in terms of pace going forward.

Craig Bellamy, as the only quick striker on the books, was the ideal weapon for the Reds' travels. But his individual form mirrored Liverpool's away fortunes, and his off-field problems impinged on the campaign to a great extent. At first, he had to adjust to the pressures of being a Liverpool player while a court case for assault was hanging over him. Once he was cleared he instantly found his confidence: on 2nd December he bagged a brace at Wigan in a 4-0 romp — his first Premiership goals of the season, celebrating the team's first away win in the league. His fine form continued in the rest of the winter's away games, but came to a crashing halt following his contretemps with Riise ahead of the Barcelona match. He scored in the game, but was far less effective from then on. Issues off the field had effectively ended his Liverpool career.

## Precedent

As a riposte to the notion that it is Benítez himself who is the problem — the lazy and borderline-xenophobic notion that he doesn't understand English football, as well as criticisms of his tactics — it's worth remembering 2005/06, and Liverpool's domestic record that season. Including the Champions League and FA Cup, Liverpool played a whopping 45 games against Premiership opposition in Benítez's second season, and won 30 of them; a remarkable record which, at 67%, eclipses the best-ever (league only) win percentages racked up by Bill Shankly, Joe Fagan and Kenny Dalglish, and was only ever once bettered by Bob Paisley, in 1978/79, when Liverpool won 71% of their old-Division One matches. As to what Benítez can achieve, it set a precedent.

While including cup games against Premiership sides could be seen as irrelevant, it is designed to show how, in one single season, Benítez managed to get the better of so many top-flight English sides, which, ultimately, is the challenge that faces him in winning the Premiership title. Even more telling is that those cup games included a high proportion of the very best teams, as Chelsea were met an additional three times in cup competitions, and Manchester United one further time. So of the seven games against Premiership sides in the FA Cup and Champions League, four were against the country's top two.

It shows how consistent Liverpool can be over 45 games between August and May. To win the league the task involves just 38 games. Swap the results against United and Chelsea from cup to league, and the title would have been within touching distance. It's easy to say, of course, but that's how close the Reds were, in terms of ability and consistency.

## Big Stick

Then there are other issues that get thrown into the ring when criticising Benítez. Rotation remains his *cause célèbre*, or the giant stick with which he is beaten. In his new role as Setanta Sports' analyst, Steve McManaman wasted no time in stating, with authority, that Benítez needed to rotate less to win the league. The trouble with ex-players going straight into the media is that while they undoubtedly understand the game on a number of levels, it's hard to believe that they actually research and study issues to the level a manager would.

A similar type of discussion took place on Sky's *Goals On Sunday* in 2006, relating to zonal marking. It took Nigel Worthington, the Norwich manager, to point out that statistically speaking, zonal marking is more effective than man-marking at set-pieces. Cue stunned silence from the presenters, including Chris Kamara (who, in fairness, does have some moments of enlightenment in between all the over-excitement). But as a whole, British footballers will get an idea into their heads — perhaps from a few aborted attempts at something like zonal marking, when it was doubtless never given time to bed in (and remember, Liverpool had severe teething problems with it in 2004/05) — and rather than research their facts, they'll trot out a highly subjective viewpoint. Because football is 'all about opinions', too many in the game don't feel the need to look up the facts. They will conclude that something like zonal marking or rotation doesn't work because of limited experience, often at the hands of a manager who was not a visionary and who probably didn't even implement it properly. And of course footballers themselves naturally distrust rotation in particular — especially the better players — as they feel it's their right to play every week. It's an affront to their egos to be rotated. So if you ask the opinion of ex-players rather than experienced managers you'll tend to get just a player's selfish perspective; but managers have to think about the team as a whole. All the debates about Steven Gerrard's best position, for example, tended to focus on where he caught the eye most, not whether or not the team won.

Rotation remains something that is easy to blame because it takes a bit of time to actually research; it's much easier to draw the obvious conclusion, without applying any brain power. Too many ex-players are paid for their opinions based on their playing achievements (or how good they look on TV), but haven't earned their stripes as analysts who actually *analyse* rather than regurgitate received wisdom. They'll be able to explain certain passages of play with great insight, and be able to tell you what it's like to play at Old Trafford or Stamford Bridge, but won't have the ability to provide the necessary bigger picture.

Rotation becomes still more difficult to assess since often you cannot say for sure if players were rested, suspended, injured, or left out for essential tactical purposes. Only the management know why team selections are made, as well as how the players were looking in training. Long gone are the days of settled sides and 14 players featuring all season long.

And of course, rotation is only mentioned after defeats, never after long runs of victories. Benítez was criticised during 2006/07 for having named his 99th consecutive altered line-up, but none of the critics bothered to check that he'd actually won a stunning percentage of those 99 games.

Obviously everyone knows Benítez rotates more than anyone else? (Ergo: *way* too much.) It's a known fact, right? Except, of course, it's not true. Manchester United won last season's league title with Alex Ferguson having made a total of 118 changes to his Premiership line-ups throughout the campaign, at an average of 3.11 changes per game. The season before that, Chelsea won the league with Mourinho also having made 118 changes to his Premiership line-ups throughout the campaign, again (obviously) at an average of 3.11 changes per game. So how many changes did Benítez make in 2006/07? You guessed it, 118 changes to his Premiership line-ups throughout the campaign, at what the eagle-eyed among you will now recognise as an average of 3.11 changes per game. Ah, but in 2005/06, Benítez must of gone crazy with the rotation? Indeed he did, with an outrageous and outlandish *119 changes*, at an average of 3.13 changes per game. This was a very fine year for Liverpool in the league; and yet the rotation, again, was virtually identical to that seen in the country's last two title-winning sides. So why is there this unerring torrent of punditry telling us that Benítez rotates so much more than his rivals? As an example, in the pre-season friendly against Shanghai Shenhua in August, experts Trevor Francis and Gary McAllister (who can be partially excused on account of being a Liverpool demi-legend, and, as far as this author is concerned, for being a fellow member of the bald community) noted that Benítez rotated too often.

Of course, this doesn't take into account rotation that occurs in other competitions, in the games played between Premiership matches. In that sense, it is indeed true that Benítez changes his team fractionally more than Wenger, Mourinho and Ferguson. And, he could argue, with some justification, given the Reds' record in Europe and the FA Cup in that time. But the fact remains that, on average, Benítez has kept his *Premiership* team selections as consistent as Ferguson and Mourinho.

This is indubitable proof that rotation has not been what has cost Liverpool the league title. And, it has to be noted, Benítez made a larger than usual number of changes in the final weeks of the season, when qualification for the 2007/08 Champions League was secured, in order to protect his team's priority interest: the 2006/07 final.

In his 2007/08 preview on Liverpool, *The Guardian*'s Paul Doyle mocked the Spaniard's selections at Sheffield United and Everton in the early weeks of the previous season. The Sheffield United game was just three days before the 2nd crucial qualifying game for the Champions League, with the tie evenly balanced. While the league couldn't be lost in the *very first week* of the season, no matter what the most hypersensitive critics might suggest, qualification for Europe's main competition can falter disastrously at that stage, as Everton found out a year earlier. If drawing in Sheffield wasn't ideal, it wasn't disastrous; losing a tricky qualifier would have been.

Liverpool faced decent, experienced opposition in Maccabi Haifa, and a trip all the way to the Ukraine to play the game. To gamble with playing the same players in three successive games at such an early stage of the season (given a strong team would be needed at home to West Ham), before the players were fully match fit, was unnecessary. As it was in Sheffield, the Reds lost Riise and Carragher to first-half injuries. The team selection at Everton was instantly hampered by injuries, but Benítez, with good reason, opted for ten players who'd previously experienced the Mersey derby, including Robbie Fowler (who clearly understood the significance of the fixture), in what was still a very strong line-up. The only newcomer was Fabio Aurelio, on account of Riise's injury. One problem was that although Jamie Carragher returned from injury that day, he was patently unfit. So Benítez's desire to play a key man, to get close to his strongest side, backfired. Doyle concluded that "Liverpool will still have one big obstacle to overcome: Benítez's seemingly irresistible urge to tamper with his team." A few days later, Paul Wilson of the Observer said "... Being Benítez, sticking to a line-up might prove the problem [with a title challenge]." Alan Hansen, writing for the BBC website, said pretty much the same thing.

The fact that Ferguson named an unchanged team in the league four times last season, something Benítez never did, suggests at the United man's ability to keep a settled side at least on the odd occasion. But in those four games United's results were below their overall season average, and way below the very high average racked up the nine times he made three changes. So for Ferguson, three changes were far better than none. Indeed, it's worth pointing out that Liverpool's best points average came when Benítez made four changes from the previous league match: at an average of 2.5 points in those six games, it shows a rate consistent with a final total of 95 points.

So perhaps Benítez's fault is that he rotates his *key* players more frequently? Or switches his strikers around more than anyone else? As Gary McAllister said on Sky, Ferguson keeps a core of his players in the team at all times, something he felt Benítez never did. Surely this has to be the case? Well, McAllister couldn't be wrong, and nor could every other single pundit who trots out the rotation mantra as fact. The truth is: it's pure fiction.

Whenever Jamie Carragher, Pepe Reina and Steven Gerrard were fit, they were almost always selected, at least up until the pre-Athens 'ease off'. His three indispensable players were never rotated, just rested on occasion or absent through injury. Indeed, Gerrard started 92% of Liverpool's league matches, and was on for a 100% attendance record until Benítez rested him on the 35th game of the season, with Athens looming. Pepe Reina also started 92% of matches. Finnan, Alonso, Riise and Kuyt also started the vast majority of games. Neither Manchester United nor Liverpool had a player with a 100% league appearance rating during last season, but out of United and Liverpool's squads, Gerrard and Reina came closest, with Carragher next in line, with an 89% start rate. United had no-one who started more than 87% of league games.

Overall, both teams had six ultra-key players who started in 76-99% of league games; Chelsea, by contrast, had only four (injuries to Petr Cech and John Terry lowered this from the expected six). Then come the important players who started 50-75% of matches, but were not indispensable.

Again Liverpool had six players in this category, but United only had four (Chelsea had six). So, while Chelsea and Manchester United had only ten players who started the *majority* of league matches, Liverpool had 12. (As an example, centre-backs Agger and Hyypia both started 23 league games, but Carragher was the main man with 34. Agger and Hyypia tended to be rotated, although Agger won priority as the season progressed, and on four occasions all three started.)

This indicates that Ferguson had a slightly smaller core of key players he would always call on; while Benítez had two more 'important' players who featured very heavily. While Benítez used 26 players in total, Ferguson used 25, so there's little difference there. Even looking at those who were little more than bit-part players, the statistics are virtually identical; both had ten players who started less than 25% of Premiership games, many of these in the dead rubbers in late April and early May.

There were ten occasions when Ferguson made only one change or none at all; twice as many as Benítez. So there were five extra times when Ferguson opted to stick with what he presumably considered his best team, or stuck closely to the side that had done well the week before. Benítez's most frequent tinkering was to make two changes, which he did on eleven occasions — meaning a fairly high level of consistency in these instances, with just cosmetic tinkering. Ferguson made two changes just once. This means that there was a staggering 25 league games where Ferguson made three or more changes: three on nine occasions, four on seven occasions, and a fairly hefty eight times in which he made five changes (followed by one seven-change line-up, and one with eight changes). Benítez made five or more changes on seven occasions, three less than his rival. All this means that while Ferguson kept a settled side on a handful more occasions than Benítez, the Scot tended to make a greater number of significant line-up alterations.

Liverpool's best run of league form during the season came in the middle of the campaign, after the difficult away fixtures were out of the way and before the run-in, which had become largely meaningless with the Reds safely clear of 5th place but well adrift of 2nd. In the ten games between Wigan away on December 2nd and West Ham away on 30th January, the Reds won nine times and lost just once. At this point Benítez was making a lower-than-average total of 2.5 changes per game; only going above three changes once, in the home game against Bolton: the four changes that day resulted in an impressive 3-0 win. It has to be noted that, with the exception of Spurs away (three changes) and Chelsea at home (two changes), these fixtures were generally easier on paper. But the run was bookended by disappointing home draws with Portsmouth and Everton, both games in which Benítez made just one change from a league victory four days earlier.

Ferguson rotated almost as much as Benítez in the early weeks of the season, making changes as follows between games one and nine: three, two, three, five, five, one, four and three. United won six of those eight games. But then Ferguson slowed down with his alterations. They won the next four games with a total of just one change, but then dropped two points at home to Chelsea with just one further 'rotation'. Two days before Christmas, at the halfway point of the season, they lost at West Ham in the final time Ferguson kept the same line-up from the previous league game. From that point on the changes came thick and fast until the end of the season: 79 changes, at an average of more than four a game. This meant Ferguson's average from 39 changes in the first half of the season was just two per game. Benítez, for his part, only made 44 changes in the first half of the season, and 74 in the second half: so, again, very similar splits. The most notable difference was in the first four games of the season, where Benítez made 14 changes, to Ferguson's eight; highlighting the difficulty in starting the league campaign whilst having to overcome a win-or-bust Champions League qualifier.

As for strikers, Benítez only really rotated between three — Kuyt, Crouch and Bellamy — until the final three games of the season. Before then, the fourth, Robbie Fowler, started only three times, and only once started a Premiership match between the third and 35th matches; as such he was hardly considered. By contrast, Ferguson rotated between four strikers, with Rooney (like Kuyt at Liverpool) starting the majority of matches, but Saha, Solskjaer and Larsson were switched and swapped regularly, particularly over the winter (Larsson's only time at the club). Alan Smith also started the last six games of the season, to add a fifth name to Ferguson's rotation roster. (Both teams occasionally used midfielders as second strikers.)

It could be argued that Benítez shifts his players around too much within the team — not rotation as such, but still a form of tinkering. This is much harder to measure, as it often involves many in-game changes. But again it's not like he's on his own here: Ryan Giggs played centre-midfield, left-wing and as a striker last season; Wayne Rooney has been deployed on the left of midfield, an act that could be seen as more bizarre than any of Steven Gerrard's many roles; Alan Smith played as both central midfielder and centre-forward. At Chelsea, Michael Essien, their player of the season, played in so many positions it's hard to keep track; suffice it to say he definitely played centre-midfield, right-midfield, right-back and centre-back.

Rotation, like all football philosophies, is not perfect. And, with the aid of hindsight, you can name times when Benítez may have got his team selection wrong. But every manager at a big club gets accused of picking the wrong team, whether he selects the same XI or changes it. Of course, he can pick the right team and still get the wrong result; Liverpool didn't lose at Chelsea because of rotation or poor football, or because Steven Gerrard played on the left, but because Gerrard and Kuyt could only come close from three great chances, while the home team scored with their only real meaningful attempt at goal. In football, the alternative scenario someone puts forward can never be tested, so in their mind it remains the perfect solution. And no one ever says "If the manager had done X and Y, as I suggested, the team might have lost 3-0 instead of winning 2-0".

So perhaps rotating less is not so much the key — given Benítez rotates no more or less than his rivals — as simply having a better squad. On paper that appears to be the case, but time will be the ultimate judge.

Another criticism is that "Benítez prefers early elimination from the English cups/doesn't take them seriously", which has been touted on several occasions, following the fielding of sides comprised of squad players. This, despite reaching the League Cup final in his first season and winning the FA Cup in his second. There's a difference between prioritising the more important competition — which fans surely want — and throwing in the towel. Benítez was criticised for not picking a stronger side against Arsenal in the League Cup in January 2007, in a game that was one of the most bizarre ever seen at Anfield. Both teams had six good chances: Arsenal scored all of theirs, while Liverpool managed only half that amount. Both teams fielded sides comprised largely of reserves/youths, although there was a decent amount of experience in both ranks, and Liverpool's starting XI did feature Steven Gerrard.

But Benítez was seen as the foolish manager, because Arsenal, who had also won at Anfield a few days earlier in the FA Cup, only had PSV to face in the Champions League, whereas Liverpool would be up against the mighty Barcelona. Paul Merson, speaking as a Sky pundit (I use the term 'speaking' advisedly, and the word 'pundit' even more advisedly), openly and disrespectfully mocked Benítez after the game, saying that Liverpool had absolutely no chance of beating the Catalan giants, and as such, had just blown their best chance of silverware. Within a couple of months

Arsenal were out of all competitions and on their way to finishing below Liverpool in the league, while Liverpool were progressing towards the European Cup final in Athens.

## Vagaries

Luck regarding injuries plays a major part in any league title success. No club can have reserves who are as good as their very best players; if they did it would lead to enormous unrest in the ranks. Chelsea have more quality in reserve than any other club, and yet even they couldn't cope with the loss of Petr Cech and John Terry in the winter of '06/07. Manchester United struggled without Paul Scholes the season before, while Arsenal were never going to be as dangerous at any point in recent history while the now-departed Thierry Henry was injured.

There's also luck with refereeing decisions. While every club will suffer bad decisions that favour the opposition, they will also get some fortunate ones in return. But there is no way these can accurately even themselves out over the course of the season. The Reds got a fortunate 87th-minute free-kick 30-yards from goal in the opening game of 2007/08 at Aston Villa, which Steven Gerrard curled home with stunning accuracy to turn a draw into a deserved win. But it was still the kind of decision that rarely results in a goal — not a total 'gimme' like a penalty. A week later, with the Reds 1-0 up and in control against Chelsea in the first big encounter of the season, Rob Styles awarded one of the most bizarre spot kicks ever seen, as Florent Malouda threw himself at Steve Finnan when the ball had already passed. The game was drawn as a result, and Styles later apologised, admitting his error had affected the game. But could it also affect the league title race? He later booked Michael Essien for a second time, but having realised he'd previously booked he seemed to change track, and held the card aloft at John Terry — something he'd already done 30 seconds earlier. It was a shambles. (Of course, when Chelsea said they were going to play with more style this season, perhaps everyone misheard: maybe it was more *Styles?*)

League titles aren't definitely won at home or away, but a notable weakness in either area will undermine any challenge. You don't have to possess the best record in the head-to-heads against all the other top teams; but they're not called six-pointers without reason. Similarly, there's no point beating Chelsea and United only to lose all six games against the three sides who end up relegated. Liverpool certainly need to improve on their away form from 2006/07, where less than a third of games were won. But the previous season's tally of ten wins on the road and only five defeats was more or less in keeping with Chelsea's that season as they stormed to 91 points, and proves Benítez can get it right on the road. So it's more a case of rediscovering that formula, and improving slightly upon it.

Then there's the addition of new players, and how quickly they adapt to the league, to the team's system, and to their team-mates' wavelengths. Last season Manchester United benefited from a settled squad, with just one main addition — Michael Carrick — in need of assimilation. However, in 2004/05 Chelsea brought in a number of new faces, and things clicked quickly into place, possibly because they spent the kind of money that secures more 'proven' players who were not still learning the game, reducing the odds of them being a flop. Not all the signings worked out, although enough did. But they didn't have to gamble on a cheap makeweight like Antonio Núñez.

## Money, Money, Money

All of the things covered above are relevant to varying degrees, but perhaps the most crucial factor is the *wherewithal* a club now needs to win the title.

It can all be boiled down to this: time and money, allied to managerial talent. Either of those first two elements, or the two combined, are what it takes a top manager to win the league in England. Without time, and without money (and by 2007 it's starting to mean seriously *big* money), it appears there's little chance of succeeding.

Every Premiership-winning manager since 1993 had proved beyond doubt in previous jobs that he was a winner. Alex Ferguson did so in Scotland with Aberdeen; Kenny Dalglish at Liverpool; Arsène Wenger in France and Japan; and Jose Mourinho at Porto. We're not talking about plucky seasons at smaller clubs, but delivering titles. And Benítez fits firmly into this category, with his two *La Liga* titles and a Champions League winners' medal. So money alone is not going to land a title.

Good players are a given, but they need not be indubitably the best; nor do they need to be all 'world-class' (whatever your definition of that term is), as the whole can exceed the sum of its parts. Basically, you can't expect to win the title with a great manager and average players, nor with an average manager and great players (examples of which are Claudio Ranieri at Chelsea and, if looking overseas, the succession of Real Madrid managers before Fabio Capello). You need a balance of both: the right man to lead the right players in the right manner.

However, the precise balance between managerial talent and quality footballers is impossible to measure, although there are some things that can be measured and that brings us back to money.

It was never going to be the case that 2007 was a make-or-break summer for Liverpool, but it was certainly an important one, with the new owners determined to make the Reds more competitive across the board, and with Benítez clearly stoked up following defeat in Athens — as if losing had driven him to new levels of determination. There were some frank discussions, and heart-on-sleeve exchanges in the media, but these were was not necessarily bad things. Rather than be piqued, Hicks and Gillett seemed to respond positively to Benítez's outburst the day after the final, straight-talking being a very American trait. It was all aimed at better equipping the team for a tilt at the league title.

Everyone at Liverpool FC acknowledged prior to the final in Athens that, win or lose, and despite so many crucial elements in place, there was still plenty of work that needed to be done. People knew there would be changes; while the squad was considerably better than in 2005, there was still the need for new faces.

Contrary to the 'first is first, second is nowhere' mentality, simply making the final was in itself a significant achievement: proof of an ability to consistently vanquish the top sides in Europe, as the Reds have since Benítez arrived. And not in one-off games, like you see in the domestic cups, but in league stages and two-legged ties, where any luck of the draw is generally evened out with a testing away leg.

But most of all, making it all the way to the final was a significant achievement because Benítez had yet to write any really big cheques along the way.

Expectations at Liverpool remain astronomically high, but phenomenal history and passionate support — while they benefit the team in a number of ways (see the semi-final against Chelsea, perhaps, as proof of both) — only go so far when it comes to signing the very best players, particularly if those players are already under contract at their existing club, and that club will only sell at a premium.

Bargains are always there to be had. But sometimes you unearth a gem, and other times you get what you pay for. This approach can lead to success, but it's a damn sight harder, and takes a lot longer, than the method Chelsea used in 2003 and 2004, when they paid whatever it took to procure a dozen or so big names, and where it didn't really matter if a few expensive signings, like £10m Scott Parker and £14m Seba Veron, failed to deliver, because there were so many others on hand to slot in, and more money to replace them.

If a manager is looking to source the best untapped young talent in the world, and waiting for his top experienced targets to fall out of contract, he can build a great side without spending fortunes; but what he sacrifices is the ability to succeed sooner rather than later. He will have to wait for the youngsters to mature, and bide his time for those experienced players' values to drop.

Of course, Liverpool's history helps attracts top players, as does Anfield and the unrivalled Kop mythology. And top players want to play for Benítez, and play alongside Gerrard, Carragher, Alonso, Mascherano, *en masse*. And while the north-west of England doesn't have as much cosmopolitan appeal as London, or the weather of Barcelona or Milan, the Premiership is where quality players wish to test themselves, and Liverpool remain a big draw.

All senior figures at the club accept that the Reds need to put up a stronger fight in the league, after three seasons under Benítez without ever really challenging (in spite of the impressive win-rate in 2005/06). But it all comes back to money: the thing that can prise that coveted player from the grasp of his owners. As the saying goes, every player has a price. And unlike super-rich clubs like Chelsea and Manchester United, Liverpool weren't able to be persuasive enough on that score prior to the arrival of Gillett and Hicks.

The cheques the club's officials were able to write were not as big as those signed by the chiefs at the only two English clubs to better Benítez's league record between 2004 and 2007. After the first three years of the Spaniard's reign, Liverpool's two biggest signings remained Emile Heskey at £11m and Djibril Cissé at £14.2m, both signed by Gérard Houllier.

Budget is perhaps the only true way to judge managers these days; the 'weighting' used to even out disparate achievements. Everything comes back to spending power. But as an argument it can be abused, as noted by Jonathan Northcroft in the Sunday Times on May 27th. "The idea he [Benítez] has already spent £100m is creative accounting by his critics," he suggested, adding that "Since Rafa Benítez joined Liverpool in June 2004 he has signed 29 players. He has also unloaded 36, thereby cutting his net outlay to around £44m."

Or, one Shevchenko and half a Shaun Wright-Phillips.

While Benítez was saddled with Cissé — a player he could not find the best use for — there was a double-whammy connected with the French forward. Not only had Benítez seen a large chunk (approximately 40%) of what would have been his first summer's transfer budget eaten up by Cissé's arrival, but then, when he was going to recoup around £8m, and therefore reduce his net spending by that same amount, the striker broke his leg representing France. So rather than allocate the money to the deal for Dirk Kuyt, the club had to borrow the money in a personal loan from chairman David Moores. Had Cissé been sold to Lyon in 2006, as was on the cards, Benítez's net spend would have been just £36m after three seasons.

Looking at Benítez's spending on right-backs showed just why it was creative accounting to say he'd spent £100m up to then. There have been a few signed: Josemi, Jan Kromkamp, Antonio Barragán and Alvaro Arbeloa. But Kromkamp arrived as a swap for Josemi, and the Dutchman was then sold to finance the £2.5m deal for Arbeloa, while Barragán was a nominal signing as a teenager who was sold to Deportivo La Coruna for £680,000 (with the option to buy him back for £475,000 in 2008). Add their values together and you could say they cost the best part of £10m, when in true net terms they cost less than a quarter of that.

So why were Liverpool bracketed with the real big spenders in England, given that Chelsea and Manchester United stood alone in terms of outlay? And why are other managers respected for what they achieve on limited budgets, but not Benítez? The reason Steve Coppell was voted Manager of the Year was for what he achieved — namely finishing 8th — on a minuscule budget. Coppell's financial clout was taken into consideration when awarding him the ultimate managerial gong after a fine season.

While Liverpool are clearly a much bigger club than Reading, and have spent much larger amounts by comparison, it's also the case that Benítez hadn't had anywhere near the resources of the top two teams, whom he was expected to usurp. So if Reading did exceptionally well to finish where they did, can it be said that Liverpool had done well to finish 3rd and at the same time reach another European Cup final? After all, only Chelsea and Manchester United domestically, and AC Milan in Europe, finished 'higher' than the Reds, and all three spent significantly more money than Liverpool in the process.

Pound for pound, Benítez achieved more with his outlay than his main rivals. But, of course, no true winner will ever be happy with that. It's not about accepting second best, as no fierce competitor will do that, but being realistic. Just as Reading cannot hope to get even remotely close to competing for the league title, perhaps it's recently become unrealistic to expect a club to win the league without spending a really hefty amount of money on the team.

Money isn't the be-all and end-all, and it never will be, but such has been the spending of the top two in recent years that perhaps, as a rival, you can get only so far without it? Perhaps the limit 'normal' finances place on a club is in the strength of the squad, or in lacking those extra couple of players who can ally real class with consistency over nine months? Not much of a difference, but enough to tell a little in certain games, in order to win a few more points here and there along the way.

Perhaps, with this in mind, cups become the most realistic avenue to silverware, as seen with the Reds reaching four finals in just three seasons, winning two and losing two. Arsenal, whose spending is much closer to Liverpool's than to that of Chelsea and Manchester United, have gone from being a top-two side for eight consecutive seasons between 1997/98 and 2004/05, with three league titles and five finishes as runners-up, to being well off the pace in 4th in 2006 and 2007. And yet in both those seasons they reached cup finals: the Champions League in 2006 and the League Cup in 2007. (It's interesting to note that England's three most recent representatives in the European Cup Final have come in the form of the two less-expensively assembled teams.)

Wenger is obviously an expert in what it takes to succeed in English football, with four FA Cups in addition to those three league titles, and yet his record in domestic football was markedly inferior to Benítez's between 2005 and 2007. Liverpool finished above Arsenal both in '06 and '07, and also won an FA Cup, while Wenger ended up empty-handed.

Benítez proved at Valencia that he could win the league on far lower resources than the opposition; indeed, paltry resources compared with those of Barcelona and Real Madrid. A great achievement, undoubtedly. But when he arrived in this country the difficulty in repeating that feat was that the two rich clubs in England also happened to be more focused and better-managed (from top to bottom) than the two Spanish giants, who seemed to have too much of a self-destruct mentality — certainly when it came to the hiring and firing of coaches, interference from the board, and the existence of a 'superstar' culture amongst their players. While Barcelona and Real Madrid had since come to terms with their excesses of the early part of the millennium, and briefly improved their professionalism and, indeed, shown some sanity, the Premiership landscape remains the same as when Benítez arrived. In 2004, Alex Ferguson had been manager for 18 years at Old Trafford; at the Santiago Bernabéu they were closer to hiring 18 managers a year.

The only real chink in the armour of the top two appeared when Jose Mourinho's relationship with Roman Abramovich became strained in the winter of '06/07; Chelsea's focus and standards slipped, and they experienced a significant drop in the number of Premiership points they'd registered in the previous two seasons. It was a chance to take advantage, but only Manchester United were in a position to do so. And it would still have required Liverpool's highest points tally for 19 years to finish 2nd.

So while Liverpool retain a name as revered and respected as any in football, it's wrong to *unquestionably* expect the club to achieve as much as rivals with far greater resources, based simply on historical success. It's easy to say Liverpool should be challenging for the league title (and I know I thought it was possible after the promise of 2005/06), but the playing field is so uneven.

In terms of managerial talent Benítez is on a par with Wenger, Ferguson and Mourinho, three men who've achieved so much in all areas of the game: each has at least two league titles in one of the world's top three leagues since 2001, and three of the four have won the European Cup. In June 2007 Jamie Carragher described them as the best four managers in the world, and while there are one or two elsewhere whose records suggest they deserve consideration (Fabio Capello's name springs to mind, and, of course, Neil Warnock would naturally include himself), Carragher was not far off.

But how much better than Mourinho and Ferguson would Benítez need to be to overtake them while spending far less? The whole reason David Moores sold the club to Tom Hicks and George Gillett was that the financial demands in competing at the top level had spiralled in recent seasons. And they continue to do so.

A decade ago, Liverpool were able to compete at the very top end in the transfer market, and as recently as 1995 held the British transfer record, with the £8.5m paid to Nottingham Forest for Stan Collymore. This was a time when the Reds were averaging a 3rd-place finish — as they pretty much have done ever since — but when only the League Cup was won following the 1992 FA Cup and before the treble of 2001. Under Benítez, Liverpool have twice finished 3rd, but also twice made the Champions League Final as well as winning an FA Cup.

Four years before Collymore the club broke the transfer record with the £2.3m signing of Dean Saunders, and a further four years before that Liverpool's capture of Peter Beardsley from Newcastle, at £1.9m, had also broken the national record. The only other time the club held the record was in 1977, with what remains arguably the most successful of all record-breaking transfers: £440,000 to Celtic for one Kenneth Mathieson Dalglish.

Working forward, the £11m paid to Leicester for Emile Heskey in 2000 was only £4m short of what had become the British record, set when Alan Shearer moved to Newcastle for £15m in 1996. However, when Liverpool paid what until 2007 remained the club's record fee — £14.2m on Djibril Cissé in 2004 — it was still less than half the fee Manchester United had paid Leeds for Rio Ferdinand in 2002. This gives a clear indication of the widening gap in recent years between Liverpool's finances and those of the club's main rivals. Up to July 2007, Manchester United had spent in excess of that £14.2m on no fewer than *nine* players (including the 2007 signings, Hargreaves, Nani and Anderson). Chelsea had also paid in excess of what had been Liverpool's transfer record on nine occasions before the Benítez finally secured Fernando Torres.

Prior to Roman Abramovich arriving in this country, a 'normal' big club like Arsenal could win the league with its highly prudent approach to buying and selling players, but even they, with their three-times league-winning manager, have been blown out of the water by the new financial explosion. In order to compete they've moved to a new 60,000 seater stadium, for a long-term generation of income. But it's more about keeping pace than setting it. No club can self-generate the kind of money Abramovich has in his bank account, while Manchester United have been expanding both Old Trafford and their money-making ventures since the early '90s.

## Money Talks

We all know money makes a difference when it comes to competing at the highest level. But how much of a difference? In order to get an idea of the correlation between budget and Premiership points, it's worth looking at the average cost of a player in each of the six of the big clubs' squads. The following calculations are limited to each of those clubs' squads main 20 players in 2006/07; the players who, over the course of a season, would feature the most, if everyone was fit. (Beyond a core of 20, it's hard to tell who are the important players at any given club. Making calculations becomes more tricky given varying squad sizes, and the number of youngsters handed squad numbers but who may never go on to play league games for their club.)

Where a transfer fee was undisclosed, such as in the swap deal involving Ashley Cole and William Gallas, the figure used was the one most widely reported by a number of the more reliable media outlets. Also, there are deals dependent on certain targets being met at various stages of the contract, such as appearances and international caps; for these, the full fee has been used, given that all clubs have to be prepared to pay the upper limit. In the case of loan deals, anyone sent away for the whole season was discounted. In loan swaps, such as that involving José Antonio Reyes and Júlio Baptista, the transfer value of the original player was taken. So Baptista is valued at Reyes' original transfer fee, as without the latter player to exchange they'd not have received the former. Therefore the figures can never be 100% accurate, but should still give a very good representation.

Of course, this does not take into account wages, which are an important part of any deal; for example, there wasn't much that was 'free' about Michael Ballack signing for Chelsea for £120,000 a week, or £6.25m per year. But on the whole, discussing wages would involve too much guesswork, given that they tend to not be disclosed, not to mention the variables such as the multitude of bonuses written into some contracts. (It's yet to be confirmed that Ballack got a £1,000 bonus for every time he stood in the centre circle scratching his backside while dreaming of knockwurst, while poor 'Fat' Frank Lampard ran himself into an anorexic husk.)

So, with all this in mind, how did Liverpool compare with their main rivals, both above and below them in the table, when it came to squad cost?

Having cost a total of £86.5m, the average transfer fee of Liverpool's 'top 20' squad for 2006/07 was £4.3m per player. A reasonable amount, and a lot of good players have been bought and sold for less in English football in recent years. But it's not something that in itself suggests that any team should be league champions. After all, if you asked a manager to buy 20 £4m players he'd have his work cut out trying to win the league. Indeed, in 2007 the Deloitte Sports Group published a study showing that £4m had become the *average* Premiership transfer fee.

Compare that with Manchester United's £7.1m per player, and you can see that, on average, United paid approaching twice as much for its main squad, which cost £141.4m in total; this despite having the most youth academy graduates in their ranks. And, of course, this calculation precedes the £50-£80m spending spree of June 2007, at an average of £17-£20m per player, depending on the true fee for Carlos Tévez (who was valued as highly as £30m by some sources, and as a low as just £2m by others).

Of course, if you hadn't already guessed, Chelsea were far and away the biggest spenders, with their 20 main players costing a staggering combined total of £249.5m. There is no better way to put into context the challenge that faced Rafa Benítez than noting the average cost of a player in Chelsea's squad was a phenomenal £12.5m — or in other words, not far short of the fee that had remained Liverpool's *record* outlay. So, basically, Benítez, whose record signing in his first three seasons was Xabi Alonso at £10.5m, had yet to even spend within £2m of the Chelsea *average*.

Perhaps the biggest surprises involve teams who finished below Liverpool; and especially, the spending at Arsenal. The Gunners' youth recruitment policy is perhaps the most deceptively blinding aspect in English football. As with the misconception that Arsenal's team is especially young, the same applies to their transfer values. Because of those young players they procure on nominal fees — they virtually 'stole' Gael Clichy and Cesc Fabregas — it's easy to forget the bigger fees they've paid. The average cost of their main 20 was £4.8m, half a million pounds more than Liverpool's.

Now, of course Arsène Wenger has generated some significant fees from selling players over the years. However, irrespective of how well any manager has balanced the books, and however admirable that is, this is about *current* players as of last season — after all, they were the ones contesting the title — and what a side cost to assemble in relation to how many league points it attained. This is not about the amazing £21.5m profit Arsenal made on Nicolas Anelka all those years ago, just as it doesn't include looking at Alex Ferguson 'wasting' £28m on Juan Sebastian Veron. These were deals done and dusted long before Benítez arrived in England, and as such, were not *directly* relevant to the current landscape. While a manager's net spend is relevant in a number of ways when assessing how he runs a club, and is not being overlooked (and as seen earlier, even now Benítez's remains relatively low), it can distract from the task of evaluating the *actual* squads competing for honours. A club doesn't win the title with players sold to other clubs; it can only win it with the players it has during the season at hand, perhaps due to a canny redistribution of those transfer funds.

By the same token, assessing just the current squad eliminates arguments along the lines of "Liverpool have spent as much as Manchester United over the last decade" — a random statement which may or may to be true — because it will include the spending of managers who failed in their job, and that failure was recognised with their firing. Equally, while it's fair to Benítez to be judged this way, it's also fair to Mourinho: why should he be judged on what Claudio Ranieri spent, if those players were already shipped out? No manager should have to answer for the transfer follies of a previous incumbent. The equality from this is that by 2006/07 both Benítez and Mourinho had more-or-less undertaken what Ferguson had by 1989 and Wenger by 1999: namely ridding from their ranks the inherited detritus and only keeping their predecessors' more astute purchases.

Spending power remains a big issue, and the managers themselves are very aware of how it shapes perceptions and, indeed, creates pressures. It was interesting to hear Jose Mourinho, desperate for more recognition for his achievements and eager to remove the expectation that comes with great riches, almost pleading poverty in the summer of 2007. He told Chelsea magazine: "The spenders will be Liverpool, Manchester United, Tottenham and maybe Arsenal. It won't be Chelsea for sure. I hope that next season the media put pressure on the big spenders because the big spenders, for sure, will not be Chelsea." He followed this up a few weeks later with a similar statement, appearing to single out Benítez for criticism, albeit with a modicum of respect in his words. (It's hard to think of another opposition manager who has spent as much time talking about Liverpool as Mourinho. Indeed, it's difficult to bring to mind a *Liverpool* manager who has spoken about the Reds as much as the Portuguese.)

The point he seemed to miss was that his squad, which he retained, already cost hundreds of millions. To use an analogy, if his neighbours, who were living in more modest accommodation, were adding necessary extensions, Mourinho was already living in the most luxurious mansion imaginable. After all, it's not like he'd sold up and was living in a council flat. Getting in a few free transfers was clearly good business for the Stamford Bridge outfit, as even Chelsea don't want to pay money unnecessarily, but the raft of expensive signings were still in place. Drogba, Essien, Shevchenko, *en masse*, hadn't been given away to charity, and at £13.5m, Florent Malouda was hardly a bargain basement acquisition.

Going into 2007/08, it remains to be seen who will be the main 20 players at each of the top clubs over the course of the season. Some are shoo-ins: Fernando Torres, Carlos Tévez and Owen Hargreaves haven't been bought to spend time in the stands, but players like Lucas Leiva and Nani may have to bide their time. Perhaps less clear is the identity of those players who, as a result of newcomers, will slip down the pecking order, and become peripheral figures.

But a provisional study, albeit based on guesswork as to the identities of those main 20 players, reveals that not a lot has changed. Following the much-heralded investment in the team during Gillett and Hicks' first summer, the average cost of a player in Liverpool's squad of 20 rose from £4.3m to £5.6m, or a little over 25%. (The previous year's average of £4.3m did not include the hitherto record signing, Cissé, who spent the entire season out on loan, so his sale didn't affect the figures.)

Given that Manchester United started the summer with an average of £7.1m per player, with few of Ferguson's previous purchases leaving, Benítez's newly-formed squad was still a fair way behind United's in terms of its overall cost. But the gap grew even wider in the summer, with United's average rising to £9.2m. This is not including Carlos Tévez, but if his fee ends up being as expensive as touted, United's average would be taken over the £10m mark. So rather than the summer bringing a more equal playing field, the disparity between Benítez and Ferguson only increased.

But all the Spaniard could do was concentrate on making Liverpool better; he could do nothing to affect United's strength, although he did table an unprecedented bid for a United player: Gabriel Heinze, the experienced Argentine defender. In response, United's hierarchy stated that they'd never sell a player to Liverpool, Arsenal or Chelsea. Indeed, no player has moved directly between Liverpool and United since Phil Chisnell moved to the Reds in 1962. Heinze left it too late to buy himself out of his contract under a FIFA ruling: the deadline was 15 days after the end of the previous season. Liverpool maintained that there was a release clause in the Argentine's contract, that meant United would have no say in who they'd be able to sell him to, if the price of £6.8m+ was met by a bidder. Nothing was mentioned in the document about a rival like Liverpool being unable to activate the clause, although United claimed that had verbally informed Heinze's agent of the fact. Ferguson went on the offensive, saying there was no way his club would sell to their fiercest rivals, but Benítez claimed he didn't see what choice Ferguson had, and that the lawyers had been called in by Liverpool to resolve the situation. This at a time when United were already in the High Court over the saga surrounding Heinze's international team-mate Carlos Tévez, which had become the most complex transfer in English football history. An arbitration panel eventually ruled that Heinze could not join Liverpool, and the defender was promptly snapped up by Real Madrid, who, in typical fashion, bizarrely offered more than the necessary escape clause fee to land the Argentine.

Chelsea, meanwhile, fractionally lowered their average, following three free signings. Bolton's Tal Ben-Haim, out of contract at the Reebok, replaced £8.5m Dutch defender Khalid Boulahrouz, while Peruvian Claudio Pizarro arrived on a Bosman transfer from Bayern Munich and Reading's Steve Sidwell also moved to west London. (PSV's Brazilian, Alex, finally arrived three years after he became Chelsea property, although no record of a fee has been mentioned.) But Chelsea remained the most expensively-assembled squad, over twice the price of Liverpool's. Still, that was less intimidating than the previous level, which was almost three times higher.

## Ins and Outs

It's fair to say that Liverpool's new American ownership began with really positive action in the transfer market. Targets were identified, and deals were struck before mid-July, in time for the new boys to start their integration in pre-season training. This was in stark contrast to previous summers, where many of the deals seemed to drag on until well into August (at which point a fair few famously broke down). Dirk Kuyt was signed on August 18th 2006, so not only did he miss the entire pre-season programme with the Reds, he also missed the first four meaningful games. Of course, in Benítez's first summer, when Alonso and Luis García also arrived just before the start of September, deals were always going to take longer, given that the manager had only been appointed in mid-June.

The summer transfer window of 2007 saw the first chance for the new owners to flex their financial muscle. By mid-July, Liverpool had signed Atlético Madrid's Fernando Torres for £20m (although reported in some places as as much as £26m), a new Liverpool record, and had also landed their 3rd-most expensive ever, with £11.5m paid to Ajax for rising star Ryan Babel. Yossi Benayoun cost a further £5m from West Ham, with Lucas Leiva moving from Brazilian side Grêmio for £6m. Sebastián Leto, with a £1.85m deal agreed in January, finally moved from Argentine side Club Atlético Lanús. Bayer Leverkusen's Ukrainian international Andrei Voronin, in the side beaten by the Reds on the way to the Champions League success of 2005, arrived as a

Bosman transfer, and a succession of young starlets were procured for fairly nominal fees.

With the sale of a number of players, the net outlay wasn't actually that high. The departure of Bellamy for £7.5m saw the Reds make a profit on the fiery Welshman. Djibril Cissé was sold to Marseilles for £6m, quite a chunk short of the £14.2m paid in 2004; given he had only two years left on his deal, and following two badly broken legs, it wasn't a bad bit of business. Mark González was offloaded to Real Betis for a fee of £3.5m, while Florent Sinama-Pongolle sealed a £2.7m move to Recreativo after a fine season on loan in Spain. Jerzy Dudek, Robbie Fowler and Bolo Zenden were all released at the end of their contracts, easing the wage bill. While approximately £45m was spent, around £24m was recouped. But the transfer fees paid for Torres and Babel were still very symbolic.

Perhaps the most surprising, and disappointing departure was that of Luis García, who chose to return to his former club, Atlético Madrid, in a deal rumoured to be worth around £4m. With only two years left on his deal, and with the player approaching his 30s, the fee was less than his talent alone would have demanded. The transfer was not officially interdependent with Torres', but clearly they were not unrelated either; Atlético had to countenance losing their fans' favourite, and so bringing home another player the supporters were fond of helped smooth the deal.

While practice doesn't always follow seamlessly from theory, the summer of 2007 should — *in theory* — prove the Reds' best in the transfer market for 20 years. It is reminiscent of 1987, when the loss of Ian Rush was offset by the staggered arrival of the mouth-watering attacking quartet of John Barnes, Peter Beardsley, John Aldridge and Ray Houghton. Some pessimists may call to mind another summer of activity: 2002, and Gérard Houllier's ill-fated signings. But the latest crop seem far more talented and more mentally suited to the pressures of a big club expected to push for league titles. Of course, the theory will still need to be put into practice.

After Athens, all Benítez could do, however, was back his judgement and redress the weaknesses in the squad. The signing of so many attacking players was seen in the media as a ridding of the shackles, and the manager himself outlined a desire for his team to score lots of goals.

But even with the impressive rebuilding programme of 2007, success is not just about money. Time clearly plays a key role, too.

## The Gift of Time

One of the reasons Manchester United's squad figure of £7.1m from 2006/07 was relatively low — in spite of a number of big money signings — was because, as well as some younger youth team graduates, their ranks included a number of ageing home-grown players who cost nothing. While the new signings of 2007 have pushed younger youth graduates like Darren Fletcher down the ranks, and seen Keiran Richardson sold, the old guard of Englishmen would remain integral to Ferguson's plans.

In that sense, United remain unique: they are still 'living off' the benefits of youth team graduates introduced by their current manager way back in the early-to-mid 1990s. In other words, players who were promoted into the team at a point when its current manager *had already been in the job for several years*, and after he himself had overhauled the youth system and had time for it to reap dividends.

It's clear that Ferguson didn't have such good fortune back in 1989, when three years into his United tenure; he couldn't call on players like Giggs and Scholes back then. To compare situations, it would be like Benítez benefiting long into the future — in 2020 — from kids at the Academy who are not yet even teenagers. Whereas Ferguson had over half a decade to wait for the fruits of his youth academy, and continues to make use of them, Benítez is expected to be delivering results right now. Is it fair to expect the same level of success with that inequality in mind?

While being in charge for a long time has potential for drawbacks — growing stale, relying on old methods and motivational speaking losing its impact through repetition — it's clearly a benefit to a talented manager, rather than a hindrance. A mediocre manager who's a strong motivator can have a short, sharp shock effect, but the best in the business thrive on time.

If no manager in this impatient day and age can ever receive the time Ferguson was allowed to get things right — and much else has changed in two decades — it's also not fair to expect more recently appointed managers to work miracles. Both Ferguson and Benítez inherited sides that had just finished 4th, with Ferguson doing so in 1986. And yet at this exact stage of his United career, Ferguson saw a banner unveiled by fans at Old Trafford: "Three years of excuses and it's still crap. Ta-ra Fergie." Compare that with the witty and supportive banners seen in Greece this summer and you can get an idea of how supremely better the Spaniard has done in his first 36 months.

In 1989 Alex Ferguson had yet to win even a single trophy at United, and rather than improve the situation he'd actually taken them down to an 11th-place finish; unthinkable for a big club in this day and age. Of course, Ferguson didn't have the luxury of Champions League football back then, in the way that Benítez had a chance to win his first trophy — a European Cup — after Liverpool finished 4th the previous season; it was only open to the champions of each country, and anyway, English teams were banned post-Heysel. But if anything, the ban helped Ferguson weaken Liverpool's dominance, since it affected Liverpool more than anyone, as three-times champions in that era. Everton, twice, and Arsenal, with one title, were also heavily affected, in not being able to compete on the top European stage. (And of course, by the time United were regularly entering the European Cup, in the early '90s once the ban was lifted, the financial rewards were significantly bigger. Liverpool's European successes in the '70s and '80s did not bring the opulent reimbursement that United received for merely competing.)

United would spend big in 1989, splashing the cash on Paul Ince, Neil Webb and breaking the British transfer record for Gary Pallister — but rather than spark a resurgence, it saw them finish way down in 14th in 1990, with Liverpool crowned champions. Of course, Ferguson, as a Scot, would not have been accused of "not understanding British football" in failing miserably in those early years. And yet *eventually* those big signings, like Paul Ince and Gary Pallister, succeeded in helping United land the title in 1993. As with so many other examples, you cannot write off any given player after one single season at a club, especially if from overseas.

In that respect it was surprising to see Benítez offload Mark González so soon, given that the Chilean clearly had some potential, but it's also true that only a manager and his colleagues can judge what it is wanted from a player, and only they can assess him from working together on a daily basis. González had disappointed fans, but you could understand why a manager might give him a second season, given his goalscoring record and his pace. He was disappointing, but never disastrous; he just didn't reach Liverpool standards.

González is yet another example of how a manager, in spite of all the scouting missions and videos, can never know everything about a player until he gets to work with him at close quarters over a period of time; and unless he's worked with the player in a previous job, this must mean that a fee has already been paid. In football there's no 28 day return or exchange policy for the unsatisfied customer. The word from the coaching staff was that González had not proven as gifted as they'd been expecting. They bought the player, but once the packaging was removed, found him to be of insufficient quality. The receipt was of no use. Fortunately they could sell him on, but it didn't help matters in '06/07.

It's also another example of the ruthlessness that this particular manager displays: compare, for example, how long Bruno Cheyrou, a player of a similar age and price tag, was kept by Houllier. Benítez made a small profit on González, which was money to reinvest quickly in the team. The same wasn't true of Cheyrou, whose prolonged presence was a double whammy: his wages needed paying for a second season, while at the same time his value was depreciating markedly. In the end, he had to be released on a free transfer after two further seasons out on loan while his Liverpool contract ran down. While it's good to see players given a second year to prove themselves, no one wants to see a manager flogging a dead horse.

So while large transfer budgets are important, it's a unique advantage to be a manager for such a length of time that you are able to use your judgement to get rid of hundreds of youth team players, and dozens of failed signings (some for megabucks), all the while keeping the great youngsters who pop up only rarely and retaining the rare outright successes in the transfer market.

Of course, you cannot overlook how Benítez benefited from inheriting Gerrard and Carragher, but by the same token he lost Michael Owen as soon as he arrived in England, mainly because Owen hadn't wished to commit to a new contract while the side was stagnating in Houllier's later years. Until things fell away in those later years, Owen had always signed new deals at Liverpool, even when other clubs were interested and could offer more money and a regular presence in the Champions League (to which Liverpool were strangers back in the late '90s). Where would United be if they'd lost either Giggs or Scholes because success on the pitch was not forthcoming? How much harder would it have been for Ferguson, had he taken over more recently, to buy players of that calibre, if the best youth graduates of the '90s had already left for Real Madrid or Inter Milan because his predecessor had lost their respect? And if Benítez didn't want Owen, as has been mooted, he would still have liked the chance to recoup his true transfer value — £20-30m until that summer

— because the England striker was on a four-year contract, rather than approximately half of the fee because he was entering the final year.

So while Ferguson deserves credit for setting in motion the process of finding players like Giggs and Scholes as boys, and for turning them into top stars who even now make a difference in winning league titles, he did much of this work between one and two decades ago. How can Benítez be expected to quickly overtake a man who has spent 21 years shaping his club from the very top to the very bottom, and whose squad cost a lot more per player to assemble? Or quickly overtake Chelsea, whose manager Jose Mourinho, unprecedentedly, won the title in his first and second seasons, but who also had an equally unprecedented mega-budget?

Indeed, the last man to win the Premiership title without either time or money on his side was Arsène Wenger in 1997/98, in his second season. As you can see, that was almost a decade ago now, in the early years of the continental revolution in English football, and it took another four years for him to bag his second title. So much has changed even since that 2002 success, and even more so since the 1998 double.

In 1997/98 only Manchester United were a genuine force to be reckoned with: Liverpool were in decline having fallen away after Roy Evans' bright start; Newcastle had already spectacularly imploded after Kevin Keegan took them close to the title a couple of years earlier; Chelsea, under the raw management of Gianluca Vialli, were only having success in cup competitions; and Leeds had yet to spend excessively in the elaborate gamble that briefly made them a tough proposition (but ultimately 'nearly men') at the turn of the millennium, before a massive fall.

In contrast, Benítez had faced three real forces in his first three years: United, Chelsea and Arsenal, each with a world-class manager. This is not the era of Evans, Gullit, Vialli and O'Leary: each with his own talents, but not in the same class as the managers of the current big four, and none with any prior experience, let alone success under their belts as leaders of a club. These were all total rookies in the art of first-team management, and while three of the men are still in the same age bracket as Benítez and Mourinho, none of the four currently has a significant role in club management. Time has proven them to have been far more limited than the current managers of the 'big four'.

In many ways Benítez arrived at the most challenging time for any Liverpool manager in history. Of course, the club wasn't as low as when Shankly took over, but expectations weren't so high in 1959, and rival clubs weren't immeasurably more wealthy. No other Liverpool manager, bar Gérard Houllier in his ill-fated final season, had faced the mind-boggling riches of a club like Chelsea. Nor had one ever had to better a manager as entrenched at a club, and with as many trophies under his belt, as Alex Ferguson at United. In 2006/07, three of the English big four were in the semi-finals of the Champions League, with the Reds going on to make it to the final. Meanwhile, in 2005/06 Arsenal progressed to the final for the first time in their history — something that had proven well beyond them when reigning English champions.

This indicates how incredibly competitive it has become at the top end of the

Premiership, even if some people don't think that the quality was there below this point.

While a lot of teams are concerned primarily with staying in the top division, given that relegation is a costly affair, the notion that only the top four is strong does not hold up under scrutiny: Spurs looked impressive in the Uefa Cup and, but for some very dodgy refereeing, may have made it to the semi-finals, while in 2006 Middlesbrough, who finished 14th in the Premiership and looked mediocre in that setting, made it to the Uefa Cup final.

It's hard to have seen that happening ten years earlier, when Wimbledon finished in that position. Nor were there world-class players like Mascherano and Tévez at relegation-threatened clubs back then. It could also be argued that teams fight harder for their Premiership lives these days, as they know it's the only place they can afford to be. While some of the smaller teams lack quality, the will to survive at all costs has had to become stronger. In the last two seasons alone, Portsmouth and West Ham have spent fortunes to dig themselves out of trouble.

The obvious worry when Tom Hicks and George Gillett took control of Liverpool was that they'd not show the kind of patience that is required to build towards a title in this sport. Chopping and changing managers at big clubs only leads to uncertainty and a surfeit of unwanted players. However, the backing Benítez has been given is stronger than ever, with new owners in touch with the reality of the task being faced. "I don't know if we are capable of challenging for the title next year," Gillett said at the end of May 2007. "We want to make progress but it is a multiple-year programme. We want to challenge but we won't do it overnight."

Rather than remove Benítez's power, they handed him the keys to the Academy. And while they listened to Rick Parry and David Moores, they seemed to listen to the ideas of the manager even more; not dissimilar to the way Arsène Wenger was given *carte blanche* to overhaul the club from top to bottom at Arsenal in the late '90s, or the way Alex Ferguson restructured United's youth system. It's pointless only backing a manager 90% of the way; it should be all or nothing. And it is the top managers, rather than the chairmen and administrators, who also happen to be the great football visionaries. Bill Shankly didn't just change the playing staff and rouse the troops with his motivating speeches — he altered the whole training ethos, introduced a new diet, and even changed the colour of the kit in order to make Liverpool an intimidating all-red vision.

As of July 2007, there were a lot of parallels with Liverpool and the Arsenal team that started to emerge in the three years before the league and FA Cup double of 2002. Wenger's 1998 success, like Benítez's cup double from Istanbul and Cardiff, was an early fillip, coming less than two years after he took over. But it was five years before Wenger's team really started to make its mark, winning the title in 2002 and, as 'Invincibles', again in 2004. While Arsenal have now fallen away, and are in heavy transition, the Gunners' period between 2001 and 2004 is something Liverpool fans would be only too happy to experience.

Key experienced players like David Seaman, Tony Adams and Dennis Bergkamp — inherited when Wenger took over — were still in place in 2002; for Liverpool, read Jamie Carragher, Steve Finnan and Steven Gerrard. An essential early central-midfield addition from the manager's homeland — Patrick Vieira (Xabi Alonso) — had adapted seamlessly to the English game and become a general in the heart of the action, while a relatively recently-acquired centre-back, Sol Campbell (Daniel Agger), was winning rave reviews, and an old boy, Martin Keown (Sami Hyypia) provided experienced back-up.

Perhaps Wenger's key signings, with hindsight, were Thierry Henry in 1999, and Robert Pirès in 2000; these bear comparison with Benítez's signings in 2007: the addition of that extra bit of attacking flair, and the potential for real match-winning brilliance on a regular basis. It took Arsenal a season of bedding in Pirès, following the arrival of Henry and Freddie Ljungberg shortly before, to become the potent force that made them the best team in England between 2001 and 2004, and, some would argue, the most stylish ever seen in domestic football.

There's also a more recent comparison. Manchester United, league winners in 2003, added Ronaldo months after that title, and Rooney a year later, but it was 2006/07 before these two key, maturing attackers won the club a *major* trophy. There was no shortcut for them.

Building a squad encourages a kind of survival of the fittest. Those who adapt the way the manager hopes get to stay; those who don't are shipped out. The aim must be that, in time, the successes remain in place with years ahead of them to shine, while the 'failures' are let go. If all goes well, with every passing year there will be more key men in place; and so even if only half of the new additions each season are outright successes, their arrival will still mean a significant step forward.

Let's not forget that Arsène Wenger's other 1999/2000/2001 signings — such as £13m Sylvain Wiltord, £8m Francis Jeffers, £6m Richard Wright, as well as a whole host of lower profile flops — can all be overlooked because he got just one or two right each year. Such a list of failures is par for the course in football management.

However, it made it all the more remarkable when an article by James Ducker appeared in *The Times* in July 2007 about how Benítez had pipped Arsenal for Ryan Babel. Ducker suggested that: "As a procurer of young talent, Rafael Benítez's record has been somewhat hit and miss since he took over as Liverpool manager three years ago. Daniel Agger, the accomplished young Denmark defender, may be one of Benítez's better acquisitions, but the failures ring a little louder than the successes. Gabriel Paletta anyone?"

Mark González, 22 upon arrival, was the other notable flop Ducker mentioned. One journalist's misconceptions are not in themselves tantamount to a serious crime, but it shows how people supposedly in the know can think one thing when the facts suggest the exact opposite.

For starters, a player like Paletta, just 20 when signed, and costing only £2m, was at the end of his first season in English football, and a young central defender to boot: that most exposed of positions for a youngster, where there's no hiding from mistakes. While he'd had a torrid time on a couple of occasions, most notably against Arsenal in the League Cup (where the whole 'reserve' team was cut to ribbons), it is too soon to write him off as a player, even if his lack of pace is not going to remedy itself. Perhaps it was this last fact that made Benítez decide to cash in at the end of August 2007, with Paletta sold to newly-crowned South American champions, Boca Juniors, for a fee rumoured to be close to what the Reds paid a year earlier. So if Paletta is to be deemed a flop, it is not a costly one, in terms of money or league points.

And if González, at the age of 22, was also considered a young flop, then what about Xabi Alonso, Momo Sissoko, Pepe Reina and Javier Mascherano, as well as the aforementioned Agger, who were all aged 22 or under when Benítez signed them? Surely, to contradict Ducker, these successes in up-and-coming players far outweigh the failures, both in terms of numbers, and in transfer fees? It's a remarkable omission on the writer's part. Ducker went on to state that Babel had been "coveted by Arsène Wenger, a man whose eye for emerging talent is proven and remains largely unblemished."

Which brings us back to perceptions; or perhaps just misconceptions. How does the £10-17m failure of José Antonio Reyes, 21 when signed, fit in with this picture of Wenger, the master, and Benítez, the failure in the art of procuring young talent? Wenger's judgement is undoubtedly up there with the very best, but would he call his own judgement 'unblemished' when thinking of Pascal Cygan, Igor Stepanovs, Christopher Wreh, Kaba Diawara, Eric Chukwunyelu Obinna, Tomas Danilevicious, Oleg Luzhny, Moritz Volz, Giovani van Bronckhurst, Luis Boa Morte, and the aforementioned Wright, Jeffers and Wiltord? — many of whom were youngsters when they signed for the Gunners, and plenty of whom weren't cheap. And while time is very much still on his side (and like Paletta, shouldn't be judged too soon), Theo Walcott hardly looked a £12m player in his first season in the top flight. But why would you write him off, or use him as an example of Wenger's misfiring aim? You wouldn't, for the sake of fairness.

Why is the perception of Wenger so different from that of Benítez? The latter is building a squad in the way the former did in his early years: some very good buys, a few not-so-good buys, but the strength of the team improving year on year. For instance, Xabi Alonso and Josemi were two early Benítez signings in 2004/05; the former remains a crucial player, while the latter was soon traded in. In 2005 Pepe Reina, Momo Sissoko and Peter Crouch were bought, and remain important figures; by contrast, free transfer Bolo Zenden was released in 2007. Daniel Agger and Robbie Fowler arrived in January 2006; the latter, another free transfer, left after 18 months, having done a decent job, but the former could be at centre-half for the next decade and beyond.

In 2006 Kuyt and Bellamy were signed; the former has the chance to form an exciting partnership with Fernando Torres, while the latter was sold for a profit. In midfield, González struggled after a promising start, but Jermaine Pennant (another Arsenal 'failure', but one with the potential to improve after he left) got better as the season went on, and Javier Mascherano was an inspired addition.

But of course, not all signings can succeed — not only because the law of averages will see some turn out to be duffers, but because there's only room in the team for eleven players, and even with rotation, many of the places in the team are going to be taken by the same players most weeks. Being a squad player will always stifle some talented footballers; it's inevitable. At Arsenal, Pennant, still a teenager, needed games to stand a chance of succeeding, but better players at the time were ahead of him in the pecking order; this in turn led to him losing his motivation, and while he should have remained more professional and fought harder for a place, he needed time to mature, as a player and as a person.

The good thing for Liverpool, as of the summer of 2007, was that out of all Benítez's numerous successes in the transfer market, only Luis García was no longer at the club. Compare that with Arsenal at the same stage: Nicolas Anelka, Marc Overmars and Emmanuel Petit had all wanted moves to Spain, causing another complication in the building process at Highbury. However, their sales did raise nearly £50m for Wenger, and led to the purchases of Henry and Pirès. Perhaps it slowed him down, but it allowed him to eventually build an even better team.

Despite the attempts of Chelsea with Steven Gerrard in 2004 and 2005, and the big Spanish and Italian clubs coming calling for Xabi Alonso and Momo Sissoko in 2007, Liverpool managed to hold onto their much-coveted stars. Even more crucially, as Benítez bought players in their early 20s, he had not had to bid farewell to any due to age. Had he gambled on quick-fire solutions in his first three years — top-class 30-somethings who'd last a season or two at most, or mercenaries interested in getting as many moves in their career as possible — the core of the side could have needed rebuilding. As it was, with youngsters procured and potential big signings grilled over their commitment to the Liverpool cause, the goal is to improve on the notable talent already in place. And keep the disruptive mercenaries at bay.

So despite some (inevitable) failures in the transfer market, and those purchases like Bellamy who didn't exactly fail but didn't set the world alight either, the core of Benítez's side has grown stronger and broader each year. With the possible exception of Steve Finnan (who may yet defy time), and barring serious injury, none of the Reds' key men will be 'over the hill' within the next four years.

In football, the gift of time equates to patience. Rome wasn't built in a day, and good things come to those who wait, yada yada. It's easy to mock the notion, but patience is crucial when it comes to building a team, and also when assessing each individual. Had Juventus shown the patience Arsenal did with Thierry Henry, they wouldn't have so quickly offloaded the player who became the best in the world. Of course, Arsenal, with Arsène Wenger and numerous other Frenchmen, was more conducive to Henry succeeding. But even then, after four months — as it was with Bergkamp and Pirès — Henry was not considered a success.

Which begs the question: so when *do* you judge a player? After one season at Liverpool, Emile Heskey was an unqualified success. After four he wasn't. After one year at Arsenal, Pirès was not a success at all. After four he was a runaway hit. Even the best players in the world have had poor seasons now and again; but two in a row would suggest either an inability to hack it, staleness, serious injury concerns, or an irreversible decline. For most players, the second season is crucial: it's when previously unsuccessful players need to finally prove themselves. It's also when those who did well in their first year have to prove it wasn't down to the element of surprise or being on the crest of a wave and show as well that they can cope with increased expectations and, in some cases, that they will not be guilty of overconfidence. A big problem for young players is that they think they've made it once they've had a good year.

But despite all of the arguments listed above — about the need for money and time — misconceptions remain rife. Including about what Liverpool had already spent.

On the way home from John Lennon Airport after arriving back from the Athens final, I was forced by the driver of our car to listen to a radio phone-in — my idea of hell — and I was reminded of the kind of ill-informed, knee-jerk reactions that the fans of all clubs come out with, whether talking about their own club or, in this instance, when talking about Liverpool.

As well as its callers, its provocative presenter (who made me want to throw myself out of the passenger door at 80mph, and take my chances bouncing around in a busy middle lane) said Liverpool would never win the Premiership under Benítez. The team had barely touched down on English soil having come close to a second European crown in three years when, before any of the anticipated transfer activity had taken place, a man paid to talk about sport was saying the Reds stood no chance of the domestic title while the Spaniard was in charge. What I found remarkable was the assessment that Benítez had spent "big money" during his time at Liverpool; enough to be *expected* to win the Premiership title.

You only have to look at what the teams who finished below Liverpool have spent, and the far lesser expectations they have to measure up to, to see the disparity. The pressure on a Liverpool manager is not related to what he spends as much as what happened between 1964 and 1990. Fans want those high expectations, as it means you're an important team, but they have to be put in the context of the current football climate.

Two teams who finished below Liverpool highlight how true this is. Spurs and Newcastle have pretensions to be 'big' clubs, and in many ways are just that. Both have a lot of supporters (locally, if not globally), and can boast significant achievements in their history, albeit dating back a few years now. And both have spent a fair amount of money over the years. Historically they are important clubs.

So, why aren't they expected to be champions? Or, if that's stretching things a bit, to even get close? Or, hell, even make the Champions League? Is it merely a case of history, where they do not traditionally compare with Liverpool's title-winning credentials? Newcastle consistently spend fairly big, but it's almost universally accepted that their hopes of any silverware will be dashed before August is even finished.

Spurs have got within touching distance of the Champions League in the last two years, finishing 5th both times, but that's the sum of their achievements. No cup finals, let alone trophies. Yes, they impressed in the Uefa Cup, and made the League Cup semi-finals, but that's a million miles from what Liverpool have achieved in the same time period. (And whereas Liverpool were slaughtered in the press when their reserves lost to Arsenal's reserves in the Carling Cup, Spurs' *first team* lost to Arsenal's reserves in the next round.)

Of course, the talented Martin Jol, who arrived in England at the same time as Benítez (albeit taking full control a few months after), has had to take Spurs from a lower position in the league; but Benítez hardly arrived in England when Liverpool were in a position of great strength. Less is expected of Spurs, even though their spending is not far behind Liverpool's. Spurs spent approximately £40m in the summer of 2007, on Darren Bent, Gareth Bale, Kevin-Prince Boateng and Younes Kaboul, without recouping anywhere near as much as Liverpool in return. But despite this, finishing 4th would be seen as a great achievement for Spurs. (Of course, it will now be even more of an achievement, given that they lost three of their first four league games.)

And Newcastle remain the biggest underachievers in English football. Not a lot needs to be said about their failures, as they're all too well known. But suffice it to say that in 2006/07 they finished 13th, with 43 points, just a handful of points above the relegation zone. Their season was obviously hindered by the absence of their record signing, Michael Owen, for all but three games, but even so, they ended up a fraction from being relegated. Sam Allardyce seems to have the personality and methods to transcend the failures of Graeme Souness and Glenn Roeder.

However, Newcastle's signing of Owen in 2005 also shows the high risks in paying excessively on one player: the 'eggs in one basket' syndrome. In 2006/07 Newcastle got precisely zero goals from an already injury-prone Owen in return for their £17m outlay, due to his injury at the 2006 World Cup. For £16m, Liverpool had two strikers — Dirk Kuyt and Peter Crouch — who scored 32 goals between them. Indeed, Liverpool's four strikers cost only £5m more than Newcastle paid for Owen, and while the Reds seemed to lack someone as ruthless as the former no.10 and his best, they ultimately netted a very healthy 48 goals between them.

Owen also provides an interesting comparison in terms of how signings are perceived when they are announced. Twenty-thousand fans turned up at St James' Park for Owen's unveiling in August 2005, whereas the only way 20,000 would have turned up at Anfield to see Peter Crouch was for proof that it was a joke.

Fast forward to the start of December that year, with Owen having scored a number of goals for Newcastle and Crouch almost 20 games into his Liverpool career without having broken his duck. At this point, which of the two players would you stake your mortgage on achieving the following: scoring 31 goals for his club in the next 18 months, while breaking the all-time international scoring record for most goals (11) for England in a calendar year, as well as being the only striker to score for the Three Lions in the World Cup? Six goals in the Champions League could be added, *en route* to the final, but that would perhaps be the only thing to suggest it's not the Newcastle player.

The point of mentioning Spurs and Newcastle, who are not seen as part of the current big four, is that the average cost of a player in their 2006/07 squads was £4m and £3.8m respectively. Or in other words, just a few hundred thousand pounds less than Liverpool's. Now go back and look at the league tables and cup successes from the last three seasons.

So which club, pound for pound, got the most from its spending in 2006/07? This is how many league points each 'big club' got for every million pounds spent on its 20 main players:

| | |
|---|---|
| Liverpool | 0.78 |
| Spurs | 0.75 |
| Arsenal | 0.71 |
| Man United | 0.63 |
| Newcastle | 0.56 |
| Chelsea | 0.33 |

Now of course this is just an indication, but it's still interesting to see Liverpool come out on top, and closest to getting one league point for every million pounds. And this, unlike 2005/06, in a season that did not have the Reds firing on all cylinders in the league. So not only did Liverpool get the greatest value for money in terms of Premiership points per pound spent when compared with the other big club, the Reds also made it to the Champions League final at the same time. (And, as a point of interest, the three clubs Liverpool faced in the final rounds — Barcelona, Chelsea and AC Milan — all cost far more to assemble. Each was outplayed, which says something.)

Liverpool managed more than twice as many league points as Chelsea for every million pounds spent. Of course, that doesn't mean that if Liverpool had doubled their spending they would therefore have ended up with twice as many points (for a start, that's actually impossible, as 114 points is the most available, and doubling 68 leaves you with 136).

The higher up the table you go, the more you have to pay for just a few extra points. And of course, simply spending the money doesn't guarantee anything: you get the impression that Newcastle could have spent £500m in recent years and still not got it right in the way Chelsea did. But all the same, it shows the disparity between the top two and Liverpool and Arsenal. It's also only fair to note that other teams with lower ambitions did even better than Liverpool when it came to points per million pounds. Reading, assembled on a shoestring budget, are the most obvious example. The same can be said of Everton, Portsmouth and Bolton, but all of these clubs' managers got a great deal of credit for their league position.

However, their spending was a lot nearer to Liverpool's than Liverpool's was to Chelsea's. While people expect Liverpool to be challenging Chelsea, no-one expects these clubs to be seriously challenging Liverpool. Then there's the fact that the Reds, for that £4.3m per player, needed to be contesting two major competitions: a 38-game Premiership, and what turned out to be 15 extremely testing and challenging games in the Champions League. For the money Everton, Portsmouth and Reading spent, they only had to focus on the league.

It is probably true that Chelsea and Manchester United are not concerned with value for money when their spending lands league titles. The end justifies the means. And they have also paid a premium for being perceived as cash-rich clubs, having to pay slightly excessive fees as a result. Of course, their ability to pay these fees has still secured the players they craved, while Liverpool could not go the extra mile to sign players like Simão and Daniel Alves. For Chelsea, paying £3m over the odds for a player is like shelling out small change, but for Liverpool prior to the arrival of Hicks and Gillett it was a significant hike. A player's value is determined by what a club is prepared to let him go for, and the amount the buying club are prepared to pay. In the cases of Simão and Alves — the two main targets who eluded Benítez — that middle ground could not be met. It's easy to think that the Reds would have done better in 2006/07 with these two talents on board.

Rick Parry took some criticism for his failure to tie up the deals, but if the asking prices were more than the club could afford, it's hard to see how else he could have manoeuvred. And he's not alone in failing to land targets: all big clubs' deal brokers have lost out to other clubs at the negotiation stage when reaching the upper limits of their finances. Manchester United lost out to Barcelona on Ronaldinho's signature, as just one example. It's usually a case of win some, lose some; but ultimately, money talks, and deeper pockets will increase the chances of better results.

A lot of Benítez's problems stemmed from the final three years of Gérard Houllier's reign. While the Frenchman bequeathed some notable talents to for the Spaniard to make consistent use of, only one of those was signed after 2001. The home-grown talents of Gerrard and Carragher, as well as Riise and Hyypia, were mainstays for much of Benítez's first three years, each playing 100-150 games in that time. But only Steve Finnan, signed in 2003, was a regular bought during the second half of Houllier's tenure. Harry Kewell, another 2003 signing, might have been a further mainstay, but he was rarely fit. While Kewell's signing for £5m remains a great deal in principle, in practice it has yet to yield what was expected.

That left Benítez counting the cost of Houllier's investment in El Hadji Diouf, Bruno Cheyrou, Salif Diao and Djibril Cissé, all of whom were out of the club in one form or another by the end of 2006/07. Having cost approximately £35m, just £4m of it had been recouped (through the sale of Diouf to Bolton) during Benítez's first three years. Include Kewell as a flop (if only on his injury record) and of the last £43.5m Houllier spent, £40m of it was 'wasted'. Of that £40m, the sale of Cissé has since redeemed £6m, but even when added to Diouf's fee that still leaves a big loss on those transfers, with 75% of the money ending up down the drain, along with a large chunk of wages. While Liverpool's board cannot be criticised for trusting their manager with the funds he requested in 2002 — after all, at that point Houllier had earned the right — the legacy was one that, five years later, still affected the club.

## "We will be *Squad*building..."

Penned by die-hard Liverpool fan Elvis Costello in a paean to a shipyard community's hope of a better day during the Falklands war (albeit a brighter day that relied uneasily upon a war), lines from *Shipbuilding* can be applied to the task of rebuilding the Reds on only medium resources. The line about "diving for pearls" sums up the very notion of Rafa Benítez's squad-building: whereas Jose Mourinho and Alex Ferguson can regularly flash the American Express in Hatton Garden for the finest gems, Benítez had to scour the seabed to find his own fresh gemstones.

Benítez has had no choice since Day One at Anfield but to look mostly for youngsters. Unlike Wenger's Arsenal, no-one in the media seemed to appreciate just how young Benítez's side was. That youthfulness, while boding extremely well for the future, comes with a number of drawbacks. The Champions League final was a strong case in point; while the Reds outplayed Milan, the Italians were able to use their greater guile to grind out the result. And had that final been against Manchester United, as appeared likely in the build-up, the Reds' youthfulness could have been cruelly exposed.

As disappointing as it was for Liverpool fans to stomach defeat in Athens, it did not come close to the dejection that would have been felt had Manchester United, beaten by Milan in the semi-final, been the successful team in Greece. And that despair would have been transferred to the players.

Let's make no mistake. A Liverpool vs United final would have been *the biggest game in the history of club football*; akin to Barcelona playing Real Madrid, or a Milan derby — the kind of games yet to be seen on the biggest possible occasion in club football. It would just have been too huge to comprehend, and undoubtedly would have come with a lot of negative aftershocks. It would have been a game that could have easily destabilised everything, and grown way out of proportion, in both victory or defeat. Saying football is more important than life and death, as did Bill Shankly, is now seen as inappropriate, following a number of disasters that clearly show it is not the case. But of course, Shanks was being flippant. Even so, a Liverpool vs Manchester United Champions League final would have felt to fans like being asked to play Russian roulette with three rounds of ammunition and three empty chambers. Win, and the feeling would be a mix of sheer joy and relief, the like of which would never before have been experienced; lose, and, for the time at least, it would feel like the end of the world.

Losing to AC Milan is something that, while disappointing, can be recovered from. Keeping football in perspective is difficult at the best of times, so the hysteria that would have surrounded a bitter north-western derby thankfully never had the chance to surface. Being beaten by United in Athens — and it would have been a 50-50 chance — could have done long-term harm to the progress of what was a fairly youthful Liverpool team. United, with the league in the bag, would have had that notable success as recompense if they were beaten, even though they'd still have had their summer ruined. The Reds would have been less protected by such weighty shock-absorbers. For them it would have been all or nothing. And as it is still a young team Benítez is shaping, such a symbolic setback could have done irreparable damage.

Taking players' ages at the time of the final, Liverpool's average age was far lower than both United and Chelsea's, when comparing each club's perceived strongest XI. It is an example of how Liverpool's team has more potential to mature the longer it stays together, but also an example of its greater tenderness and vulnerability.

So many people in football talk of Arsenal's young team, but the average of the Reds' strongest team in 2006/07 was just 25.6 years — rather surprisingly, a full year younger than Arsenal's best XI, which was 26.6. For all the high-profile youngsters, Arsenal had experienced players like Lehman, Gilberto, Gallas and Henry pushing up their average, plus players like Ljungberg in reserve. While the Arsenal team that plays in the League Cup is always extremely young, these are mostly squad players. Of course, Henry, amongst others, missed quite a lot of football in his final season in England, and Arsenal had to field some of their younger players as a result. But when based on the ages of those players who featured throughout the season, both teams averaged out in the region of 25, with the Reds marginally older than the Gunners.

Still, it's Arsenal and Liverpool, adrift of the top two, who have teams that might be expected to develop most in the next two or three years based on age, and who have the fewest players in need of replacing. How will United, in two years' time, cope without Ryan Giggs, Paul Scholes, Gary Neville and Edwin Van der Sar? If they are to be the long-term replacements for the first two men in that list, then Nani and Anderson, signed in 2007 for a combined fee of £35m, were not a cheap solution. In Ben Foster, United also have a promising English goalkeeper who could replace Van der Sar. But while these new young players all have a lot of potential, they have almost non-existent international experience and limited top-league experience. And while they may prove successful, they will have to be something special to live up to the levels of the men they may ultimately replace.

The only Liverpool player in the Giggs/Scholes age bracket is Sami Hyypia, and Benítez has already found a proven Premiership replacement in Agger, who usurped the great Finn to great effect (even if Hyypia still has much to offer in the short-term). Steve Finnan, recently turned 31, is the only other one who comes close, and Alvaro Arbeloa looks an able young deputy at just 24 years of age, albeit one who still has a lot to prove before being bracketed with Finnan, a master of consistency. However, Arbeloa's versatility is such that it saw him start the new season as first-choice left-back.

The average age of a team is important because almost every successful side around has an average age of somewhere between 27-29, i.e. the ages that are seen as an individual's peak years. It is very hard to find exceptions to this rule. It's that mix of youthful gusto and canny experience that makes teams tick and enables them to stay the course.

A lot was made of United's star younger players, Wayne Rooney and Cristiano Ronaldo, but the average age of their 2007 title-winning team was 28, fractionally higher than Chelsea's (27.2), and a full two and half years older than Liverpool's. One of the main reasons United improved to win the league was because, with the barest of changes to their squad, the group as a whole was one year older. What was interesting was that in the wake of their Champions League semi-final humiliation, Alex Ferguson said his team lacked experience. "We have to keep the team together and grow the team like Milan have done," he noted.

While it's the right principle, how does he expect to keep that team together for much longer, when so many of its key elements are in the twilight of their careers? He may well beat the odds and do so, and obviously Rooney and Ronaldo should be around for a long time, but he clearly can't rely on the older players who form the backbone of the side in the long-term. This is in stark contrast to Liverpool's situation at the end of the season, where all the key players — Gerrard, Carragher, Agger, Reina, Alonso, Mascherano, Kuyt, Crouch — could easily still be in place in five years' time. The same could be said of the new signings that ensued in the coming months, although, like United's new additions, they still have to prove themselves as key men.

At this point in time it's difficult to say with any certainty what Liverpool's strongest XI will be during 2007/08; indeed, it's never been easy during Benítez's reign, given that he believes in a 'horses for courses' approach, and rotates around a core of players. But an educated guess can be taken based on the first few games. Even allowing for the fact that several players had their birthdays over the close season, the average age of what might be considered Liverpool's strongest XI — Reina, Finnan, Carragher, Agger, Arbeloa, Babel, Alonso, Gerrard, Pennant, Kuyt and Torres — was younger at the start of '07/08 than at the end of '06/07: down from 25.6 to 25.2. Based on that fact alone, it looks unlikely that Liverpool will be crowned Champions in Benítez's fourth season, but the exact same eleven will enter the crucial prime-years period during the following season.

While the age of 25.6 was based on what was arguably the Reds' strongest XI during 2006/07, there were still some older members in the rest of the squad. Of those who were 29 or over, only Sami Hyypia now remains, with the Finn 33 at the time of the start of '07/08. The squad members from 2006/07 (therefore not including players out on a year's loan) who were released or sold at the end of the season were Zenden, 30, Fowler, 32, Luis García, 29, González, 23, Bellamy, 28, and Dudek, 34, with an average age of just over 29. These were replaced by new reserve team goakeeper, Charles Itandje, 24, Torres, 23, Babel 20, Lucas 20, Benayoun 25, Voronin 28, and Leto 20, with an average age of under 23. Of these, the first six can expect to feature quite heavily in the match-day squad over the course of 2007/08. And so not only will Benítez be fielding a side that will have a very young average age during 2007/08, but the average age of the rest of the squad will also be extremely low. That said, the aforementioned seven newcomers can boast almost 1100 league appearances between them, so they are not raw.

Of course, it's not as simple as throwing together eleven players with an average age of 27 or 28 and expecting success; they need time to gel as a unit, and it's no good if that happens when five of the players are deep into their 30s. Benítez, hamstrung by the lack of the kind of finances that can procure fully established stars, began in 2004 to build a team significantly younger than that ideal peak; one that can be left to mature while he adds the right ingredients to perfect the blend. With this is mind, it's perhaps no surprise that the league title was out of reach in 2007, even if a better challenge should have arisen.

Benítez also needs to avoid the trap Gérard Houllier fell into of continually lowering the average age. Having said that, it's one thing buying a 22-year-old like Mascherano and another buying a 22-year-old like El Hadji Diouf. The Argentine, like Alonso, Agger, Sissoko and Reina, when they arrived as 21/22-year-olds, or Torres at 23, is mature beyond his years; the Senegalese was like a teenage tearaway.

While Benítez's 2007 haul did indeed further lower the average age of his squad, it was mostly with players who had already proven a lot in world football. And, crucially, these new players were not designed to replace players the manager had previously heavily relied upon. When Gary McAllister, at 37, was released by Houllier in 2002, the manager plumped for Salif Diao, a technically limited central midfielder. Robbie Fowler, scorer of 17 goals in 2000/01 was sold, only for his fee to be spent on Diouf, whose goalscoring record wasn't much to start with, and whose record at Liverpool subsequently proved abysmal. Jari Litmanen and Nicky Barmby departed, and into the squad came Bruno Cheyrou, a technically gifted but psychologically lightweight player, yet to make the international breakthrough, who just couldn't impose himself. So while there are parallels in the way Benítez has replaced some experienced players with players in their early 20s, the contrast is that the signings the Spaniard made in 2007 were proven in many more ways.

It's often ludicrously expensive to buy fully established top-class players; Liverpool have had to look to players like Alonso and Agger, who were rising stars at the time they signed for fees that, while not cheap, were within Liverpool's budget. AC Milan's Kaká, seen as the best player in the world in 2007, only cost in the region of £5m in 2003. Nineteen at the time, he was bought when his class was evident, but when not yet a household name. Another South American, Lionel Messi, is up there with Kaká in terms of talent; perhaps even more gifted. He was snapped up by Barcelona when still a young boy, secure in the knowledge that they had a real gem on their hands. Contrast this with how Chelsea bought Milan's Andrei Shevchenko, aged 30, for £31m. By comparison, £20m for Fernando Torres looks far more sensible; while Torres was still relatively expensive, he was just 23 at the time, and such was his talent that he could be sold back to Spain in four or five years' time, if it suited all parties, for a similar fee.

The age of the AC Milan side that beat Liverpool in Athens averaged out at fractionally above the 30 mark — an incredibly high age — and that did not include Cafu, 36, and Alessandro Costacurta, 41, who was in his retirement year. It did, of course, contain Paulo Maldini, a mere spring chicken by comparison at 38. Their concern would be that perhaps they're *too* old, but their experience was vast. In 2007 they had just enough guile to get them through, although Liverpool were the better team on the night and, unlike in 2005, deserved the win. In the 33-year-old Pippo Inzaghi Milan had they epitome of the canny striker who seems to do nothing but pop up in the right place at the right time. Inzaghi, like many of his colleagues a recent World Cup winner, was just one example of the frightening wealth of experience Milan could call upon. While Liverpool had five players who had featured in 2005's Champions League final, every single Milan player, with the exception of Massimo Oddo, had at least one, if not a whole number of such experiences under their belts.

By contrast, Dirk Kuyt had just a single Dutch Cup success, albeit from two finals, while Daniel Agger and Jermaine Pennant couldn't even boast a domestic final, with the latter not featuring in any of Arsenal's FA Cup triumphs. Javier Mascherano had played in a *Copa Sudamericana* final for River Plate, but this is not as important as the *Copa Libertadores*, which is the equivalent of the Champions League. Even the most experienced player in Liverpool's ranks — Bolo Zenden — had spent a career losing in semi-finals for club and country. Three other outfield players remained from 2005's success, but Luis García's long-term injury was a big blow, and Harry Kewell, while able to enter as a second-half substitute, had missed the entire season and was not fully match fit. Sami Hyypia was only ever likely to enter the action in the case of an injury.

Put all this together and you can see that the potential is there for the side Benítez is forming to really start taking great strides forward. Time needs to turn that potential into Premiership prominence.

## Conclusions

So, in many ways Benítez, after a summer spent rebuilding, entered 2007/08 having had a fair amount of time and a fair amount of money.

But he will know he has not had the most time behind him (Ferguson has 21 years, Wenger 11), nor the most money. After all, there's no way Hicks and Gillett could have doubled, let alone trebled the average cost of a Liverpool player, to bring it into line with Chelsea's.

In finishing above Chelsea, United proved you don't have to possess the most expensive squad to win the league, but they only had to finish above one club who had spent more money. Benítez has to finish above two; and as such, may possibly need both of those clubs to slip up to let Liverpool in. And Ferguson doesn't have to overtake a man with more time and experience in perfecting his job at one club, whereas none of the top clubs have a manager more recently appointed than Benítez.

In other words, out of the four teams expected to challenge for the title, Benítez stands fourth in terms of squad cost, and fourth in terms of time spent at his club (marginally behind Jose Mourinho, who arrived in England two weeks prior to Benítez). That doesn't make getting to first place an easy proposition.

Hope can be taken from the fact that Benítez's record in the transfer market has mostly been excellent — at least when it comes to spending more than a couple of million on stop-gaps or bargain-basement gambles. When Benítez has spent between £5m-£10m on a player he generally finds real winners: no-one can doubt the quality and value for money of Alonso, Agger, Reina, Luis García, Crouch, Sissoko, Kuyt, and on account of his profitable resale, Craig Bellamy. Jermaine Pennant has started to demand that his name be added to the list.

Not all of them have proved perfect (the same can be said of some £30m players), and not all of them will spend the rest of their careers at Liverpool — although each arrived with plenty of time ahead of him in the game, and most had already significantly enhanced their values by 2007. And then there was the impressive income Benítez's signings helped generate with two visits to the Champions League final.

Some, like Momo Sissoko, ended last season out of form, and were therefore easier to criticise when it came to the first 'American' summer, but in the case of someone like Sissoko it's easy to overlook how good he was for the first year and a half, and how young he remains. Like everyone else, however, he will have to compete with some top players for a place in the side, and that includes relative newcomer Javier Mascherano (who was so impressive in a number of games after arriving in the January window, including when snuffing out Kaká in Athens) and the exciting Brazilian prospect, Lucas. If a manager can improve on already impressive players, it needs to be done without sentiment, but it doesn't necessarily mean the end of the road for the man replaced.

The case of Dirk Kuyt, 12 league goals from 27 starts, allied to possibly the most selfless work ethic of any striker in world football, suggests a very promising first season in English football. To put his record it in perspective, he scored one league goal fewer than Spurs' Dimitar Berbatov in three fewer starts, and the Bulgarian, who cost almost £2m more, was hailed as the signing of the season (having scored several more in cup competitions against weaker opposition). Wayne Rooney, fêted for helping United win the league, also scored only two more than Kuyt, in eight more starts. Like Rooney, Kuyt did not play as an out-and-out striker.

The majority of Benítez's main signings offer exceptional quality in one form or another, and most are in their mid-20s or younger. To date, only Fernando Morientes in the £5m-£10m bracket has been a significant disappointment. His compatriot, Luis García, got a lot of criticism from small sections of the Liverpool support, and some would have him in that category too, but 30 goals from 85 starts, from midfield, without any penalties or free-kicks, is a remarkable record, and great value at £6m; especially as it he scored so many crucial big-game goals. The early evidence is that Benítez has spent equally well in the summer of 2007, with Torres, Babel, Voronin and Benayoun all having very impressive games in August, while Lucas looked an old hand in his 30-minute cameo on his debut against Toulouse. But it's too soon to make conclusive judgements.

So Benítez has been battling time and money. And he will continue to do so, albeit to a lessening degree the longer he spends in the job, and as more money is paid out. When signing players he will need to continue to get the most points for every million pounds spent. And if he continues to do precisely that, following the latest round of investment in the team, and in subsequent transfer windows, he stands a great chance of significant success, whether it's this year, or the next.

And, with all this in mind, if he does land the title it will be up there with the biggest achievements imaginable.

Such have been his successes at Valencia and Liverpool with relatively small budgets, it's possible to conclude that, within a couple of years, and with the funds to spend money on the right players, he'll have ended all Liverpudlians' long wait for a 19th title. That doesn't mean the Reds will be able to go on and dominate English football as in the halcyon days, but it would please the fans all the same. Once no.19 is out of the way, then we can worry about what will follow.

# My Way or the Heighway: The Globalisation of Youth

One of the greatest revolutions taking place at Liverpool FC continues to happen largely behind the scenes, and relates to players most fans have yet to see. The Youth Academy at Kirkby has been a cause of controversy since its opening in 1999. Steve Heighway, the old 'Professor' who ran full-backs ragged in the early '70s, oversaw the development of a number of the outstanding Reds who gravitated to the first team in the '90s. But since the expensive complex opened eight years ago, there has been little more than a trickle of talent coming through to the first team. This had led to tensions initially between Heighway and Gérard Houllier, and then, more recently, Heighway and Benítez. In May 2007, having just led the Under-18s to a second successive FA Youth Cup, and only the third in the club's history, Heighway resigned in somewhat sour circumstances.

That success meant Liverpool became only the second club since the mid-'70s to win the Youth Cup in back-to-back seasons. The Reds overcame West Brom, Chelsea, Reading, Sheffield United and Newcastle (thrashed 7-3 on aggregate) *en route* to the two-legged final, which pitted them against Manchester United. The first leg started so well: Craig Lindfield gave the Reds the lead in front of 20,000 fans at Anfield (complete with obligatory high-pitch yelps from the stands). But a second-half penalty from United captain Sam Hewson — who celebrated with the arrogance of Eric Cantona in front of the Kop — and an own goal from defender Robbie Threlfall swung the tie decidedly in the visitors' favour. The return leg at Old Trafford, also played in front of 20,000 spectators, looked an uphill struggle, but the Reds started well, passing the ball confidently, as they had in the first game. As so often happens in football, the scorer of an own goal went on to become the hero, Threlfall smashing home an unstoppable 55th-minute left-foot shot that, without the away goals rule, took the tie into extra time and, ultimately, to a penalty shootout. The juniors mirrored the seniors' ability in this area, and kept their cool, with the poetic sight of Hewson — the penalty hero at Anfield — turning villain with the crucial miss. Heighway went out on a high.

## Success or Failure?

There are a number of reasons for the perceived failure of the Academy, despite a recent upturn in its profile. The FA Youth Cup successes should not disguise the fact that, while it's an important trophy to win, it's not the *purpose* of the Academy. That purpose, of course, is to provide outstanding players who can move up to the senior side. It's not yet clear if that is the case from the recent successful sides; it may be that there is a squad of good players who perform well as a team, rather than the more inconsistent mix of the average and the outstanding that, in the long term, can actually prove more beneficial.

Of the 2006 cup winners, only Adam Hammill, of those who came up through the age groups, looks highly likely to succeed as a Premiership footballer. Craig Lindfield, who featured in both successful campaigns, is another who stands a good chance if he continues to develop, without being anything like the sure-fire thing Michael Owen looked a decade earlier when terrorising defenders who were two years his senior and bagging countless goals. Others will make it elsewhere, in lower divisions: the future Neil Mellors, Jon Otsemobors and John Welshs, who the club can be proud of producing, and who may make it to the top division one day, but who aren't cut out for the very top of the Premiership and sharp end of the Champions League. Some of the recent crop will develop as the years pass, putting on a spurt to force their way to the fringes of the senior squad at the very least.

So, was the Academy solely behind the two cup successes? It has to be noted that four of the key boys from 2006 were actually Benítez acquisitions: Jack Hobbs, Paul Anderson, Godwin Antwi and Miki Roque. And in 2007, another recently-signed player, the gifted Swedish 16-year-old midfield playmaker, Astrit Ajdarevic, was instrumental in the success, as was the Danish goalkeeper, Martin Hansen, also just 16. Considering a lot of boys in the Youth Cup are 18, even 19 by the time the season ends, that two 16-year-olds shone is cause for optimism regarding their potential. It also shows the value in players arriving from overseas.

It could be argued that, without this stepping up of scouting players from further afield, to supplement the local talent, the Academy's reputation would probably still be tarnished. Who, besides Hammill and Lindfield, is a product of the Academy who will go on to flourish? Heighway, upon his departure, said that his captain, Jay Spearing, was ready for the first team. It was said in a way that suggested the player should have been in the senior set-up as things stood. Whether or not it was overdue, Spearing was promoted to Melwood for the start of the 2007/08 season, along with winger Ray Putterill (who did well in the Youth Cup) and goalkeeper Martin Hansen, who would turn 17 by the time the new season started. Fellow FA Youth Cup successes Charlie Barnett, Jimmy Ryan, Michael Burns and goalkeeper Josh Mimms were kept on at the Academy as third years: a kind of halfway house between being promoted to Melwood and being released. It can't be easy to be essentially 'kept back' a year like a failure in the schooling system, but it gives them one more year to impress the senior coaching staff. It's far better than being expelled, or sent to Coventry. Sensing his chances were limited, Barnett was soon having trials at Bolton and Newcastle.

Meanwhile, Spearing was one of five players who signed three-year deals in June 2007, the other four being Craig Lindfield, Ryan Flynn, Stephen Darby and Robbie Threlfall. Benítez told Liverpoolfc.tv: "It is great news these five boys have signed new contracts with the club. They've got a great opportunity now to prove what they can do. They need to keep learning, work hard and show what they are capable of."

To underline his quality, Spearing was named Player of the Tournament in June 2007 at the *Torneo di Renate* in Milan, an annual U20s event. Present at the tournament were Torino, Parma and both AC and Inter Milan, amongst others — so a high-class field. The dilemma surrounding players like Hammill and Spearing is the age-old catch-22 scenario: are top young players seeing their progress to the first team barred by expensive imports, or are they not naturally talented enough to oust them? It can be argued that, without games, the kids won't develop quickly enough. But what manager can afford to throw in kids merely for their education, in the faint hope that they prove good enough? They have to have something to offer the team, even if they're not the finished article.

It's hard to believe that if Benítez saw at the Academy an 18-year-old talent comparable with Michael Owen or Steven Gerrard, or indeed, a Red-hearted Wayne Rooney, he wouldn't have had him at least in the 16 on match-day by now. While Owen and Gerrard gravitated to the first team at a time when there was not much depth to the squad, and when there were weaknesses in the positions in which they played, it was also clear that they were ready. As teenagers, they were good enough — evinced by the fact that both played for England at a very young age: Owen at 18, and Gerrard a day after his 20th birthday.

Perhaps the player who will miss out is the future Jamie Carragher: the honest, committed professional who, at a young age, doesn't appear to have that stamp of class and authority. This is perhaps being harsh on Carragher, who was clearly a very talented young player, but it's also true that, unlike Gerrard and Owen, he needed a lot more time in the team to come of age. But it's down to the staff to spot the talented young players whose skills are not as eye-catching, but whose character will see them attain great things.

However, as Heighway has suggested, it's harder to spot good defenders than it is strikers at a young age, as the skill sets are different. This is perhaps linked to the fact that defending is an art that definitely improves with age, as mistakes are eradicated and positional experience garnered, while a 17-year-old Michael Owen, who missed chances and miscontrolled the ball, as well as running into defenders and down blind alleys, was able to use his phenomenal pace and eye for goal to more than compensate for his rawness. He only had to get one or two things right in a game to win the plaudits (and of course he got those things right with aplomb); a 17-year-old defender would only have to make one or two mistakes to find his career written off by all and sundry.

Perhaps the comparison with Carragher is where Spearing fits in: a versatile player and tenacious character (albeit one who lacks the stature to play at centre-back at a higher level, as he has for the youths) who will have his work cut out getting into the senior side in central midfield, his preferred position. But he has the kind of grit and will to win, allied to enough ability and footballing acumen to be a very fine Premiership player one day. It's just a question of how long that takes, whether it occurs in time for it to be in the red of Liverpool, and whether he can go on and develop even further, to become the kind of international-class player the top teams need to fill their squads with.

There's also the fact that no club is discovering world-class English youngsters on a regular basis. Each team finds a gem now and again; but you can't create them out of thin air. Liverpool cannot summon up a production line of Steven Gerrards, just as Newcastle, situated in another traditional footballing hotbed, have yet to find another Paul Gascoigne, Chris Waddle or Peter Beardsley, 20 years on. What you can do is improve those you do discover. But 'you can only polish a gem, never a turd', as the delightful saying goes. (Quite who spent their time attempting to polish turds in order to prove this fact, heaven only knows.)

In recent years the Liverpool youth team, for so long the preserve of local lads, has become a breeding ground for players from all across the globe. Although he wasn't in the Reds' youth set-up, 17-year-old Argentine Emiliano Insúa would have walked into the side, had he not been moved instantly into the reserves, and then first team squad upon his arrival. He is another example of Benítez looking further afield for talent.

Then there is the issue of playing style. In his desire to be in control of every last aspect of the playing side of the club, Benítez wanted more say in how the youngsters play: tactics and formations that, he felt, should more closely mirror his methods for the senior side. This led to tensions with Heighway, who saw it as an unnecessary infringement into his area.

The problem as Heighway would have seen it is that managers come and go, but the youth development system remains constant. Had the Academy been set up to replicate Gérard Houllier's methods (and not just his broader philosophies), then it would have needed a totally new direction when the Frenchman was sacked. From Benítez's point of view, the chances of youngsters fitting seamlessly into his senior squad would be increased if they understood his particular methods from a young age. His belief is that, while their education will continue apace in the senior set-up, they shouldn't need educating in certain aspects of play, and tactical considerations, upon their promotion. And as a man who started out with youth development, it was always going to be an area close to his heart. Ex-pros from the top level of football tend to enter the level of management higher up the ladder; indeed, until the mid-'90s it was commonplace for stars to instantly become managers or player-managers. But men like Benítez, and indeed Houllier before him, have no such name to trade on. As such they have had to learn to do the job at a lower level and work their way up based on their ability to run a team and improve players; Houllier did so in the lower French divisions (before eventually helping France set up and run its academy of excellence in Clairefontaine), and Benítez initially started out running youth teams, including those of Real Madrid. So it was always going to be the case that each of these managers would want Liverpool's youth academy to be more in his own image, or at least adhere to what they saw as fundamental for the development of players.

It has to be said that so far, few of Benítez's bought-in youngsters have yet to make much progress towards the first team — although it's still far too soon to judge their suitability. Insúa remains an exception, having made his debut at 17 towards the end of 2006/07, albeit in a league game with little at stake. However, it clearly shows the faith the coaching staff have in the Argentine U20 World Cup winner.

But few players in their teens, home-grown or otherwise, are making an impact at the bigger clubs in general; 19, going on 20, seems to be the time when they start breaking through. While it's never been a regular occurrence, there aren't too many players like Arsenal's Cesc Fàbregas, who made his Gunners' debut at 16, and didn't have to wait much longer to secure a place in the team. Beyond Fàbregas, who is now 20, and Wayne Rooney, who is approaching his 22nd birthday, there haven't been many other teenage prodigies at the top end of the English league in recent years. Theo Walcott has thus far been only a bit-part player at Arsenal, and has yet to pull up any trees at the age of 18, in the way Michael Owen already had. Manchester United's Cristiano Ronaldo, and Chelsea's John Obi Mikel are two players who arrived in England for £10m+ fees, and therefore were seen at the time as closer to the finished article; even then, Ronaldo was 19 before he started to look able to handle the Premiership, let alone really shine (he's now 22), and Mikel turned 20 during his first season at Chelsea, and barely featured before that birthday. Teenage talents who are ready for the biggest stage don't come cheap; Wayne Rooney cost almost £30m in 2004. Those who are cheap, however, are the teenagers who are yet to be tied to long professional contracts. Arsenal's snaffling of Fàbregas from Barcelona's youth ranks was as remarkable as any jewel heist in the most far-fetched Hollywood blockbuster. All that was missing was Arsène Wenger in a rubber President Nixon mask.

Tensions between Heighway and Benítez relating to Liverpool's Academy were made public when the former provided *The Times'* Alyson Rudd (a self-confessed Red) with an interview. Heighway said: "Rafa is a terrific manager, tactically astute with qualities I really admire, [but] in my view I'm the best coach of 17- and 18-year-old players in this club. But I no longer get the chance to do that. That's crazy, that's mad; it's to the detriment of the young players at this club."

Inevitably other news sources picked up the word 'crazy', and used it in their headlines. The most revealing part of the Heighway interview was perhaps the following paragraph: "I will admit we [the academy staff] were fairly resistant to the idea of the influx of young foreign players because we were protective of the need for young kids to grow up on Merseyside or the extended area knowing that if they support Liverpool, there is a chance they could play for Liverpool. We've always believed that — from me, through the chairman, through the chief executive. We have always believed there is uniqueness about developing a boy who has come from this area, has come into the club young and then ends up playing for this club. That is an amazingly unique situation. We believe that when you come to the crunch, with two top clubs playing in the Champions League, this club has a bunch of boys who were born half an hour from the stadium whose families just love the club, that when it comes to the final crunch you will see that difference."

While Heighway's viewpoint is understandable, and correct to a degree — you can't beat local talent, if they're up to the task — it also shows a certain narrow-mindedness. Perhaps it's merely the inevitably blinkered approach of a man too close to see the wider picture; too much in love with both the area and the club and perhaps too much in love with an ideal scenario. For all his intelligence and talent, and phenomenal service to the club since 1970, was Heighway ultimately unable to provide the objectivity required? After all, Heighway said that in all his time in the youth management role — 19 years — he only ever knew for certain that two young kids would clearly go on to succeed: Michael Owen and Steven Gerrard. So it's not like he can accuse any Liverpool manager of overlooking a sure-fire world-class talent in the making. And no Academy graduate released by either Houllier or Benítez has yet proven the decision to be a bad one. Meanwhile, neither manager could have put greater faith in Jamie Carragher.

Does Liverpool FC need to act as a community service for Merseyside youngsters, or does it need to protect the interests of the fans, local or otherwise, who pay the money that supports the club? If the difficulty of making the grade deters some local lads from giving their all, then perhaps they lack the necessary gumption. Those who have the strength of character — the Gerrards and Carraghers of the world — will push themselves to the limit; it's an example of survival of the fittest. Liverpool FC should always be open to those Red-mad kids who dream of running out at Anfield, and it still is. But only if they are good enough. It's not like that seminal '70s kids show, *Jim'll Fix It*, where boys and girls were handed the chance to live out their dreams. The right to represent Liverpool should be based on merit. It has to be earned.

Ideally — and not just in Heighway's eyes — all the players at Liverpool would be locals. Even foreign managers would love that to be the case if the talent was there. But that's never happened in the club's history. Even in the halcyon days only a couple of Scousers tended to be present in the ranks, and rarely were they key men; only Jimmy Case, Phil Thompson and Terry McDermott in the 1970s and Steve McMahon in the 1980s stand out, while others, like Sammy Lee and David Fairclough, did well enough but were never indispensable. It's just not possible to find enough top class, or indeed world-class players in one area of the country. Why limit yourself? Especially when rival clubs don't, as they head out to cast their nets far and wide. Since 1998, when Gerrard broke through, has Merseyside produced a top class midfielder to rival Fàbregas at Arsenal? And yet, had Benítez been in charge a few years earlier, there's every chance Fàbregas could have ended up at Liverpool. As it stands, Benítez will have his work cut out finding the next Fàbregas in any country, because the little Spanish international of such a rare talent; but the chances of finding another one in a worldwide search that *includes* Liverpool are indubitably greater than when searching *just* Liverpool.

Where Heighway is undeniably right was in saying "What matters is that the best players in a club get the chance wherever they are from, that's the way it should be." He felt Benítez, like Houllier, was always going to favour overseas players he himself brought to the club — that it was only natural — but by the same token, Heighway would have more affinity with, and a bias towards, boosting the claims of a local lad, even if he wasn't first-rate. These two competing views would always make agreement difficult. You don't nurture talents over a number of years, and develop affections for them as human beings, without wanting to see them succeed at the end of the process. As the manager, Benítez's word had to be final, because ultimately he is the man charged with winning the trophies that matter. His is the head on the block. And it would be a pretty self-destructive manager who showed favouritism that worked against a player who could offer him more; managers need the best players available, to help keep them in a job. For all the accusations that Gérard Houllier also favoured overseas youngsters, he wasted little time in promoting Steven Gerrard from the Academy. Ironically, it was only once an Englishman — Roy Evans — departed the doomed dual-management role that an English lad with the potential to be world-class was instantly taken from Kirkby to Melwood.

While Heighway says that the best players should get the chance, wherever they are from, a manager like Benítez, in supplementing the local talent with imported kids, is merely looking for a broader selection from which to chose those 'best players'. It's especially important to have that depth to choose from given that so many promising 16-year-olds fail to develop as hoped. By broadening the scope, Benítez is trying to increase the odds of top class youngsters playing for Liverpool, irrespective of their passport.

Departing joint Chief Scout Frank McParland, who left to take up a more senior position at Bolton, spoke of the overall ethos at the club: "I'm a great advocate of local talent being given a chance and I'd love to see Liverpool field a team with more local lads in it. To have a team crammed full of Scouse, or just English, lads would be fantastic but as the game becomes more globalised this becomes more and more difficult. And the task facing the Academies at all clubs now is a massive one. The standards here are very high and for that reason it is more difficult for local lads to make the breakthrough. Liverpool is always on the lookout for the top players and if the top player is Brazilian, as opposed to English, you have to sign the Brazilian. Alternatively, if the top player is from Bootle, you must sign him. It's about knowing what's out there and backing your judgement."

This seems a more realistic appraisal than Heighway's.

One of the weirdest things Heighway said to Alyson Rudd was as follows: "There are 26 first-team squad players, most of them are internationals, then there are 18 reserve-squad players and then there is our lot. It's an indictment of English football, but that's the way it is." It makes little sense.

To call it an indictment — defined as 'a thing that serves to illustrate that a system or situation is bad and deserves to be condemned' — makes little sense, from a quality point of view, as well as in terms of competition for places. Rather than an indictment, it could be said that the plethora of internationals shows how good youngsters need to be to gravitate to the first team, and that there is no longer any place for average youngsters. As recently as the '90s there was a litany of youngsters who got first team minutes under their belt before, in the blink of an eye, ending up a long way down the league ladder, or, indeed, out of the professional game completely. Phil Charnock, Leighton Maxwell and Jon Newby, to name just three. These weren't the myriad youngsters released without getting a sniff; these are the ones who got to wear the famous red shirt. Then there's someone like Jamie Cassidy, given a professional contract, but released in 1999 without playing a first-team game. He spent one year at Cambridge United, before quickly ending up in non-league football. Cassidy's story is part and parcel of football.

Heighway put a lot of the bypassing of youth academies down to the advent of the Champions League, claiming that clubs can't throw youngsters into the Premiership campaign because they're competing for Champions League places. This doesn't tally with the past, which Heighway would obviously know so much about; how could Liverpool throw in many young players during the '70s and '80s, given the club was not merely going for top four finishes, with the leeway therein, but instead going for — and demanded to win — league titles? After all, back then only 14 players tended to be used in entire league campaigns, and rarely did they include an untried local lad or a mere teenager. 'Kids' like Ian Rush, Ronnie Whelan and Steve Nicol graduated with honours to the first team, but each of these cost a fee having been scouted when making waves — in the case of Rush and Nicol — at other professional clubs: Chester and Ayr United. Even then they had to patiently bide their time at Liverpool before making their debuts. Rush took six months, Nicol a year, and Whelan two. These weren't products of the Liverpool youth system, and only Rush, from north Wales, was even remotely 'local'.

Heighway then said that managers also can't play kids in the Champions League itself — but if anything, Benítez has been more than generous with the playing time of Academy graduates in Europe, particularly in the qualifiers. Darren Potter played in a number of key Champions League qualifying matches for Liverpool — and not just games where the win was already in the bag — before eventually leaving for Wolves. Danny Guthrie made his debut in the competition in the 'dead rubber' against Galatasary, as did Lee Peltier — who had made the squad for the first time in the crucial qualifier against Maccabi Haifa in August 2006. While the game in Turkey was largely meaningless, Benítez still used it to blood those players. Zak Whitbread (an American who'd grown up on Merseyside, and who was later sold to Millwall) came off the bench for the second game against TNS in 2005 and started the second tie against FBK Kaunas.

Then there's Stephen Warnock. While eventually sold by Benítez to Blackburn for £1.5m, Warnock was clearly given a fair crack of the whip by the Spanish manager: he played over 50 games, when it seemed certain he was heading for the exit under Gérard Houllier. So for Heighway to imply that there was favouritism on Benítez's behalf towards overseas youngsters seems a little wide of the mark.

Take the example of Antonio Barragán, the very highly rated Spanish right-back who Benítez snapped up in 2005. Barragán, feeling homesick, was sold a year later to Deportivo La Coruna, for whom he then made 14 *La Liga* appearances in his debut season. A buy-back clause was inserted into the contract, so that Liverpool could recall him in 2008 or 2009 at a discount price. However, in his first season at Liverpool, Barragán played only a handful of minutes, as a substitute in the third qualifying round against CSKA Sofia. So Barragán — of whom Benítez thought a lot — received less playing time than some English youngsters who were arguably less gifted.

Heighway concluded that the League Cup has become the only place where kids can be thrown in — and yet, as recently as 10-15 years ago, it was a competition teams took seriously enough to not try out a string of rookies. So if anything, the League Cup has become a bonus — the Premiership's breeding ground for new talent — where young players can face the first-teams of lower division clubs, as seen when

Arsenal made it to the 2007 final with a fledgling side. Benítez has followed the lead of Arsène Wenger and Alex Ferguson by throwing in boys for their debuts in a competition that to all intents and purposes has become a high-profile and live-televised competition for reserve and youth team players, rather than the neglected, low-profile senior team one it had become by the mid-'90s.

It's not just young players eligible for the youth team that the Reds have been so busily scouting in recent years. A high percentage of the key signings of the Benítez era have been in their very early twenties: none of Momo Sissoko, Pepe Reina, Xabi Alonso, Javier Mascherano and Daniel Agger were older than 22 when signed. Of that list, it was the impact of the last name that pleased departing scout Frank McParland the most since taking the role in 2004, as he explained the process involved. "There's been a lot of signings that have pleased me since becoming joint Chief Scout but I think the one that stands out is Daniel Agger. Dan's come on really well and has great potential to get better and better. He's a fantastic professional. We initially spotted him a while ago and myself and Paco Herrera did a lot of work before completing the deal. That's not to say it was just down to us, however. Far from it. All of our scouts watched him and liked him. That's the way scouting works. It's not just about one opinion. We all have an input then, at the end of the day, it's down to the boss to make the final decision."

Agger had a superb first full season, coming of age at the heart of the Liverpool defence and doing the unthinkable: usurping Sami Hyypia, not only from the Premiership but from European games too, where the Finn had recently set a new club record for consecutive appearances. Agger's all-round game, from solid, aggressive defending to skill on the ball, passing, and scoring goals, saw him voted the club's Young Player of the Year, as well as scooping the Reds' Goal of the Season, with his 30-yard swerving rasper in opening home game against West Ham. He also notched arguably the most important goal of the season, stroking home with aplomb the set-piece routine that led to Chelsea being overcome in the Champions League semi-final. Not bad for a player for some reason labelled a 'flop' by *FourFourTwo* magazine after his first four months in England, when, as a 21-year-old fresh from Denmark, he was both bedding in and, at the time, merely a back-up option to the in-form pairing of Carragher and Hyypia. That Agger had done very well in his four appearances made the label all the more bizarre, but if you are not a close follower of a club you can easily fall into the trap of thinking: £5.8m + only played four games = failure. Agger was always an investment for the future, to learn from Sami Hyypia; it just so happened that the apprentice turned master quicker than expected.

Agger's story also highlights the difficulties in either buying young English players or developing them yourself. Carragher aside, Merseyside has not produced a central defender of Agger's quality and potential in decades; the last top-quality centre-back to hail from the area was Phil Thompson. (Unless anyone could seriously count Alan Stubbs?) And to buy an established English centre-back of Agger's quality would at least cost three times what the Reds paid, as seen with the fees of Rio Ferdinand and Jonathan Woodgate. Again, it does nothing but prove how right Benítez was in looking overseas.

McParland's exit was a blow to Liverpool, with the Scouser having established himself as a key member of the backroom staff, having also been involved in youth development. With his departure came warm words for the man who had become his mentor. "I can't speak highly enough of Rafa or thank him enough for everything he's done for me," he said. "One of the reasons I feel confident enough to take on a role like this at Bolton is because of what I've learned working close to Rafa. I've learned more from him in three seasons than the rest of my career in football."

His words — as a local who had cut his teeth at Liverpool at the Academy — were a firm testament to the Spaniard's abilities. "For as long as Rafa's at Liverpool," he added, "the club is in safe hands. I'd also like to thank Rick Parry because it was he who gave me my start at the club. He interviewed me for a job at the Academy ten years ago and I've been able to move through the ranks from there. I'll always be grateful for that."

## Frustration

Rafa Benítez's message on the eve of the 2007 Youth Cup Final highlighted his frustrations at the lack of genuine top class talent coming through the ranks. "It's important to see the players progressing in the youth team and we all hope they will win, but the most important thing is to see them develop into good first team players," said the manager. "There are some good players but they will need to work really hard if they are going to play in the first team in future."

Benítez then underlined his credentials in the field, that mark him out as so much more than a manager. "I have a lot of experience of working with academies from my time in Spain and the key is always not to win trophies at that age, but to produce players. If you can do both, it is perfect. In *La Liga* there are currently 43 players who started in the youth team at Real Madrid. That's what you can say is a success. As a manager, I would be really happy if we could find one player to come from the Academy into the first team every season."

As well as failing to provide the senior team with enough top class talents, there have hardly been any 'handy' squad players, who might give a few years' commendable service, playing more than a handful of games in the process, before moving on when the time is right, for a decent fee, to be a bigger fish in a smaller pond within the Premiership. Dominic Matteo came through in 1993, David Thompson in 1996 and Stephen Warnock in 2004. But while Benítez suggested 43 Real Madrid alumni were plying their trade in *La Liga* (not to mention those like Alvaro Arbeloa graduating to other top leagues), at the end of 2006/07 it was possible to count only six Liverpool FC youth graduates who were in Premiership first-team set-ups. These were Steven Gerrard, Jamie Carragher, Michael Owen, Robbie Fowler and David Thompson, although Danny Guthrie would return to the Premiership from a loan spell in the Championship. And even then, Fowler and Thompson were released by Liverpool and Bolton, and are unlikely to be seen in the Premiership again. (Former no.2 keeper Tony Warner was a Fulham player but spent the season out on loan at Leeds and Norwich in the Championship, although he started Fulham's first Premiership match of '07/08, but had such a bad game Fulham moved for a new keeper, and there also was Kevin Nolan at Bolton, who was released by the Reds at a very young age.) So while Liverpool FC produced some sensational talents in Heighway's time, going back to Steve McManaman, the well had clearly run too dry.

Benítez continued: "If you can have one Carragher every season, and one diamond like Gerrard every five seasons, it would be perfect. If after five years I had five more like Carra and two like Gerrard, I know I would have a team that didn't concede goals but scored and created a lot of them." Perhaps it's unrealistic to even expect players of this ilk to emerge that frequently, but the truth is that since 1998 no Academy player has even come remotely close.

Perhaps Steve Heighway's legacy will be the emergence of two or three top class individuals from the group that won those back-to-back FA Youth Cups. But by his own admission, if Heighway was 100% sure only of Owen and Gerrard when they were kids, then that suggests he is not 100% sure of any of the current crop. So rather than a budding Gerrard being present, it leaves only the hope of a Carragher. (Although presumably, given he wasn't listed, another Fowler, too?)

Heighway ended his association with the club in mixed circumstances: success with trophies (won with the aid of some bought-in players), but a question mark hanging over a system that, in recent years at least, failed to provide Liverpool managers with the one or two gems they could have made great use of. With that in mind, it was perhaps best for all concerned that a change occur.

## The Loan System

Such an important part of the development of a young player at a club like Liverpool is sending him out on loan: it's a bit like throwing him in the river to see if he sinks or swims (without the risk of having to fish him out of your own river). If he swims, how well does he swim? Just enough to get by, or with real skill and strength? And even if he nearly drowns, can he benefit from the experience?

This is standard practice at most big clubs, as it's the only way for these players to gain experience by playing under the pressure of must-win situations, and in front of demanding crowds. In Liverpool's case, under Benítez players not been sent on loan straightaway, but after a period of acclimatisation at the club, where they can first be fully monitored and assessed.

And unlike a lot of the deals under Gérard Houllier, the outward-bound loans of young prospects who are thought to have a future at the club have been exclusively within British football; in contrast to the way Djimi Traoré, Alou Diarra, Anthony Le Tallec and Florent Sinama-Pongolle were loaned out to French teams when part of the manager's long-term plans. Upon signing for Liverpool, the latter three instantly went back to their homeland, and as such, did not become used to English football, while Traoré spent a season at Lens in 2001/02, after a couple of years at Liverpool. Perhaps it was better for their development as footballers to be in the French top division rather than getting *le merde* kicked out of them at a lower English level. But it did not help them quickly come to terms with the idiosyncrasies of this country's play.

The one exception was young defender Miki Roque's move to Xerez CD of the

Spanish *Segunda División* in July 2007. Roque played four games for Oldham at the end of the previous season, but Xerez would offer him a good place to develop as a player after two years at Anfield.

This is different to the way, in the summer of 2006, Le Tallec was loaned to Sochaux, Djibril Cissé to Marseilles, and Sinama-Pongolle to Recreativo Huelva. All three were surplus to Benítez's requirements, and in need of both first team football and a shop window to help facilitate permanent moves away from the club.

Sinama-Pongolle's loan was a particularly notable success, as he notched 12 league goals, helping the newly promoted Spanish club to record a highly respectable 8th-place finish. In May, Recreativo took up their option to make the move permanent, sealing a £2.7m deal; although, with hindsight, the pre-agreed fee ended up seeming cheap, even if it did break Recreativo's spending record. There was never any doubting Sinama-Pongolle's technical ability, nor his pace and his willing attitude, but he found it hard to find a place in Benítez's system, and failed to score regularly enough when given a starting berth. He will of course be remembered for crucial substitute 'turnaround' goals against Olympiakos and Luton Town, which saved Liverpool from early exits on the way to winning the Champions League and FA Cup. As with other 'flops' such as Fredi Kanoute and Diego Forlan, he found *La Liga* an easier environment in which to demonstrate his talent, settling quickly and getting into double figures for league goals. It vindicates Houller's faith in Sinama-Pongolle's ability, even if the player never reached the heights expected of him in England. Liverpool recouped the fee paid out in 2001, and, with those absolutely crucial goals in 2005 and 2006, received a priceless repayment from the player himself.

Le Tallec, another one of the bright teenage prospects who didn't live up to the overbearing hype, failed to do as well at Sochaux in terms of individual impact, although the French team did finish seventh in the league, as well as winning the French Cup. Indeed, Le Tallec scored the equalising goal in a 2-2 draw in the final against Cissé's Marseille, for whom the former Liverpool no.9 bagged a brace, with the game settled by a penalty shootout.

Cissé's loan was the most crucial for Liverpool, given that the striker, who would have been sold in the summer of 2006, badly broke his leg just days before the World Cup; the second time in two years he'd suffered such a serious injury. He needed to prove he could come back a second time, and, from Liverpool's point of view, rebuild his reputation and, with it, his hefty price tag. He started well at Marseilles, the club he'd supported as a boy, bagging a hat-trick soon after his return to football in December 2006. But as often happens with players returning from a long layoff, his form dipped after a few games — when the adrenaline rush of being back had worn off — although once he established his proper match fitness towards the end of the season he was regularly back amongst the goals, ending the campaign with 15 from just 27 games. (And thus in keeping with his usual 30-goal haul in French football.) Marseilles eventually paid £6m to make the deal permanent.

As for the players loaned out for their own progress, with the intention of being brought back to Liverpool, goalkeeper David Martin and 19-year-old centre-back Godwin Antwi spent some time at Accrington Stanley towards the end of 2006/07.

Both did well, with Antwi becoming a firm fans' favourite at the Division Two side, who compared him with Sol Campbell. It's obviously a far weaker level, but the basement of English football is not an easy place for a teenage centre-back to ply his trade. He will certainly have learned a lot about the aggression required, as well as how to extract a centre-forward's elbow from the side of his head and six studs from his upper thigh. A year later he had moved up a level in the league, with a season-long loan agreed with Hartlepool United. Manager Danny Wilson hailed the loan signing as a major coup. "He's come in from a terrific football club who think a lot of him," Wilson told his club's official website. "He has good experience, great potential and has played in a lower division and he had a lot to do for Accrington Stanley during his time there. That will put him in good stead for us. He has great pace and will be a big acquisition for us."

Besian Idrizaj, the tall 19-year-old Austrian forward who said "I would even have swum across the channel" to join the Reds, was sent to Luton Town in March, where he failed to make an impact but did score in the final league game of the season. He caused a bit of a sensation in pre-season back at Liverpool by scoring a fine 19-minute hat-trick against Wrexham in the Reds' first game ahead of the forthcoming campaign. It was a handy reminder to Benítez of his talents, but it was never going to earn him an instant rise to the first team once the senior players returned to the fold after their extended summer breaks. All the same, it did earn him an extended stay at the club, and new year-long loan to Crystal Palace.

Scott Carson's loan to Charlton was the highest profile move by any of the Liverpool youngsters. Aged 20 when he moved south for the year, he proved himself to be one of the league's outstanding goalkeepers; all the more impressive given his tender years for such a responsible position. Voted the London club's Player of the Year, despite Charlton being relegated, it was proof that Liverpool invested shrewdly when signing him from Leeds for just £750,000 in 2005. He went to the 2006 World Cup, just a year after winning a Champions League medal as the unused substitute keeper (but having played *en route* to the final). Not a bad start to his top-level career, just four months after joining the Reds.

Despite Carson's fine season at Charlton, the situation regarding his Liverpool future has simply become more cloudy. Dislodging Pepe Reina was not going to be an easy task, especially as the Spaniard is also in the early stages of his career — albeit with an incredible 300 senior appearances to his name at the age of 24. Carson has proved he was good enough for the Premiership, and in so doing, made it less likely he could be happy as a mere second-choice — which, as a goalkeeper, can mean a year spent sat on the bench twiddling oversized thumbs.

It's also worth noting the different challenges a keeper faces at opposing ends of the table. At Charlton, where there were fewer expectations of him keeping clean sheets, Carson ended up so busy he could pull off a number of top-class saves and build his confidence, even if a couple of shots slipped past him. This was in stark contrast to Pepe Reina's season at Liverpool, where the Spaniard spent long stretches of games as a spectator, but remained alert enough to make that one high-pressure, game-defining save when needed. With Carson at Charlton, Reina started the season in indifferent form, letting in a vicious, mis-hit cross against West Ham (a partial error) and a real howler against Everton in the last minute, when the game was already well and truly lost. (In his defence, the mistake also showed his general positivity: he was trying to keep the ball in play, rather than concede a corner as he normally would, to help start an attack to get the Reds back into the game with time almost up, but ended up handing Everton a third goal.) From this, Reina was lambasted in the press, although he quickly recovered and put the mistakes behind him. Unlike at a club like Charlton, any error a goalkeeper makes at Liverpool is instantly blown out of all proportion. At times the criticism descends into mass hysteria, as David James experienced.

Then there is the issue of footballing ability. Liverpool's high defensive line calls for a 'sweeper keeper', something Reina does to near-perfection with his quick thinking. But it's more than this: a goalkeeper has needed to be a good passer ever since handling a backpass was outlawed. In less ambitious teams, the role of the keeper can be to simply hit a backpass long and hard to clear his lines; at Liverpool, the aim is to keep possession. No keeper in English football passes as well as Reina, and as well as keeping the most Premiership clean sheets for the second year running, and winning a Sky.com vote for the season's best custodian, Reina's value as a *footballing* goalkeeper makes him almost undroppable. At times he is the eleventh outfield player, and frequently had a hand in creating goals through his quick and canny distribution.

This leaves Carson caught between two stools: too good for a long-term future on the Liverpool bench, but, injury to Reina aside, only likely to remain a deputy. Under contract until 2011, Liverpool retain the option to cash in by selling the Cumbrian for a hefty profit; some sources put the price tag at £13m. But Benítez wants two top-class players for every position, and Carson clearly fits the bill. At the end of June 2007, Benítez said, "I was speaking to Scott recently and I told him he will be part of our first-team squad next season. He must fight with Pepe Reina now for a starting place. We knew when we fought off Chelsea to sign him he was a talented goalkeeper. He got some good experience last season and now he is coming back to us."

With Jerzy Dudek finally departing the club, the second-choice spot had come up for grabs, and the time looked right for Carson; the time was right for him to see off Dudek, even had the Pole managed to hang around for another year. The 21-year-old Italian youth international Daniele Padelli arrived in January on loan from Sampdoria as another option; the new keeper had a poor debut in the final league game of the season — ironically against Carson's Charlton, but loan rulings meant the English keeper was unable to play against the club that owned him. Padelli's loan was not made permanent, and he returned to Italy when the season ended.

Just as it looked like Carson was set for a season on the Liverpool bench, he secured a late loan move to Aston Villa. With the European Championships in 2008, Carson has his international career to think of; staying at Liverpool would not only limit his first team football at club level, it would freeze him out of the England set-up. The loan will also provide Carson with experience of a club with expectations in between those of Charlton and Liverpool, as he steps up his education. But it seems increasingly clear that he will never again be the Reds' no.2. With the signing of Charles Itandje, the 24-year-old RC Lens keeper, Benítez has someone more ideally suited to the role of understudy: talented and with plenty of first-team experience, but not necessarily destined for the very top. With Reina seemingly in for the long-haul, it could be that a new back-up keeper arrives every year, unless Itandje is prepared to hang around.

Also heading out on loan in '06/07 were Darren Potter, whose move to Wolves was made permanent in January 2007, and Danny Guthrie, who moved to Southampton two months later, and just three months after his first start for the Reds, which came in the Champions League game at Galatasary. Both players appeared in the Championship play-offs, each on the losing side in their respective semi-final matches. Guthrie then secured a season-long loan for 2007/08 to Bolton, where Sammy Lee had taken charge, assisted by his new General Manager, Frank McParland.

Adam Hammill's spell at Scottish Premier League side Dunfermline was the highest profile and most successful of the deals involving Academy graduates. The tricky Scouse winger, by his own admission always a bit of a show-pony in the Reds' youth and reserve teams, came to terms with the demands placed on him in senior football, and grew up a lot in the process. To use the earlier analogy, rather than sink he swam. And with some style.

Although the East End Park outfit were relegated, 19-year-old Hammill was described by their fans as 'the jewel amongst a collection journeymen'. Hammill arrived north of the border in January when the Pars were well adrift at the basement, and although they failed to escape, they managed to close the gap enough to take their survival down to the final week of the season. In a weird symmetry that stretched from Liverpool's first team, through their youth team, and onto the two forwards loaned to Sochaux and Marseilles, Hammill ended up contesting a cup final. Liverpool's ability to reach cup finals in recent years had grown highly contagious. (Remarkably, the list continued to grow over the summer months, with Javier Mascherano in the beaten Argentina side in the *Copa America*, new-boy Ryan Babel starring for Holland in their U21 European Championship Final, fellow new signing Lucas unexpectedly reaching the prestigious *Copa Libertadores* Final with Grêmio, and Emiliano Insúa winning the U20 World Cup with Argentina.)

Dunfermline's progress to face Celtic in the Scottish FA Cup Final was totally unexpected, and the Pars held out valiantly until the 85th minute, only to lose to a late goal. Given that the Scottish FA Cup starts in January, it highlights how much better the second half of the season was for Dunfermline after Hammill's arrival.

He summed up the changes to his attitude, and to his game, in an interview with the *Scottish Sunday Times*. "When you're in the reserves at Liverpool you're wanting to impress and I think I overdid it by trying to be too individual at times," said Hammill. "You try to do that bit extra to make people watch you and say, 'Wow, look at that!', but here I've learned there's no place for that. Extravagant little flights don't really work in your own half, you've got to be workmanlike and solid. It's not all about you, as long as we win I don't really care. Since I've come here I've matured and become a team player." Such a statement will be pleasantly noted by Benítez.

Hammill is now at the same age Cristiano Ronaldo was when started to impress for Manchester United, and while Hammill lacks the Portuguese's blistering pace, he can certainly match his trickery. He just needs to prove he can match the Portuguese's commitment. "I think Liverpool will see a big difference in my attitude and commitment because it wasn't always there with the reserves," Hammill admitted. "It wasn't that I couldn't be bothered, I just became a bit lackadaisical. It's been an eye-opener coming to Dunfermiline and a real taste of what football's about. Joe Cole's the perfect example for me. If I got a tape of him playing at West Ham I think it would be similar to how I was before coming to Dunfermiline. Looking at him at Chelsea now, he tracks back and defends, which I never used to do when I was younger. Here it's the least expected of you."

It's not that Hammill has eschewed his flair to become like Salif Diao; he simply knows there's a time and a place where tricks can hurt the opposition, rather than put his own team in jeopardy.

The winger paid tribute to Steve Heighway, the man who converted him to that position at the age of 15 from his previous role of second striker. "I've done a lot of training with him behind the scenes. I never played left midfield until I was 15, Steve basically converted me from playing in the hole because he saw my potential." When it comes to tuition in the finer points of left-wing play, there he could not have had a better tutor. Given that Hammill is a very passionate Liverpool fan whose burning desire remains to represent the club at senior level, he will be well served by the education he received north of the border. There's still some way to go for him, but the penny has dropped that talent, without application, will not get you to the very top. He returned to Melwood a different prospect to the one who left, even if there remains a big leap between Scottish and English football. His next struggle will be to remain focused, as he cannot expect to walk straight into Benítez's squad. Especially as several other promising youngsters arrived during the time he spent in Scotland, and more were procured over the summer months in 2007. While Hammill has potential at the age of 20, Ryan Babel, at the same age, was already delivering for a top international nation.

Indeed, following those arrivals, Hammill was loaned to Southampton for the upcoming season, in what should prove another valuable education. While the Championship does not contain teams as good as Celtic or Rangers, it appears to have a more consistent level of quality spread across the division, with many of the teams superior to those in the Scottish Premiership, particularly those fighting for promotion and those recently relegated from the Premiership, such as Southampton themselves. As the Premiership has filled with superstars, players who were of Premiership standard a decade ago now find themselves in the second tier of English football. With the Saints one of the favourites for promotion, Hammill should enjoy a lot more of the ball, which will be more like what he can expect at Liverpool than was his time north of the border; having said that, he had yet to make a start by the end of August, having to content himself with a place on the bench. In the division he may also be pitting himself against Robbie Fowler, one of Liverpool's greatest ever youth team graduates, who opted for Cardiff City after his release by Benítez in May 2007.

Of all the new arrivals, closest to Hammill in playing style is Moroccan U20 international, Nabil El Zhar, who joined from Saint Étienne in the autumn of 2006. El Zhar, 20, was born in France and represented *Les Bleus* at U18 level, but eventually opted to play for his parents' homeland. Abundantly skilful, he was one of the stars of the 2005 FIFA World Youth Championship, but was not tied down to a professional deal by his French club, for whom he'd yet to play a senior game when Benítez stepped in.

His first two games for Liverpool both came in brief substitute appearances against Portsmouth in the Premiership, a combined 26 minutes at home in November 2006 and away in May 2007. He then doubled his playing time at Craven Cottage a week later, playing another 26 minutes in what, as with the preceding game, was a weakened Liverpool team on account of the impending Champions League Final. It's fair to say that he didn't really impress in those brief cameos, but they weren't just his opening games with Liverpool but his first professional run-outs; like all overseas newcomers he also had to deal with the culture shock of English football. That he was thrown in by Benítez suggests the manager has seen enough to believe that he warrants a future at the club, but his game needs to continue to develop to make a real breakthrough. It remains to be seen whether he or Hammill will progress quicker, and whether either has a long-term future at the club. With Hammill packed off to Southampton for the year, El Zhar took the opportunity to shine in pre-season against Auxerre, opposition from the country of his birth. It was the first time Liverpool fans got to see just what he was all about, with skill on the wing and several attempts at goal.

## Influx

The list of newcomers goes on. Defender Ronald Huth, 17, arrived from Tacuary FC in Paraguay. Spanish youth international midfielder Francisco Manuel Duran, 19, joined from Malaga, for whom he had made four appearances. Arsenal also offered Duran a deal, but he opted for the greater Spanish connection at Anfield. And tall 19-year-old Dutch striker Jordy Brouwer was snaffled from Ajax, where he'd been top scorer in the youth side. Stockport County's 18-year-old winger Ryan Crowther joined the Reds in August 2007.

There was the signing, in May 2007, of two teenagers from Hungary: Krisztian Nemeth and Andras Simon from MTK Hungaria — runners-up in the country's top division. Nemeth, 18, and Simon, 17, starred for Hungary in 2006's Uefa Under-17 Championships. The duo are both strikers, although Nemeth — with a hugely impressive 14 league goals in his first 36 senior games (many of which were when he was just 17), and seven in six Hungary U21 matches — also plays in midfield.

The deals were the start of a partnership between the two clubs, with Liverpool beating a number of European giants seeking to arrange a similar mutually beneficial arrangement. Sky Sports reported that as part of the agreement, Liverpool will financially support MTK's Karoly Sandor academy and the schooling of its attendees, meaning the Reds could cherry-pick the best talents from MTK's youth system. In return, Liverpool can send their own youth players and reserves to play in Hungary if they fail to make the grade at Anfield. MTK general director Laszlo Domonyai told Sky Sports, "This is a milestone not only for MTK but for the whole of Hungarian football because Hungarian talents will get such an opportunity from this agreement that they could only dream about before." In August, goalkeeper Peter Gulacsi became the third player to arrive from MTK, joining Liverpool on a 12-month loan.

Perhaps the most audacious capture was that of Barcelona's 16-year-old Daniel Pacheco who, like Cesc Fàbregas and Fran Merida (Arsenal), and Gerard Piqué (Manchester United, and loaned to Real Zaragoza), has left the Spanish giants at 16 to try his fortune in the Premiership. Yet another of Barça's future stars has decided that his future lies elsewhere.

Losing the striker — whose style and stature leaves him resembling Michael Owen — was a big blow to the Catalan outfit. García Pimienta, his manager for the U-16 A-team, said he was a big loss for the club "because we're talking about a striker with lots of quality and a goalscorer. He's been our top goalscorer, reaching almost 30 goals and he's already played with the U-18 A-team, so I don't think this is a sporting issue, because he is highly valued at the club". The coach considers that "he is one of the U-16 players with best prospects that we have, but there is nothing we can do now. It all happened very fast".

Bulgarian Nikolay Mihaylov, 19-year-old son of the former wig-wearing Reading keeper, packed his gloves and, like his father, has come to try his luck as a keeper in England. Mihaylov Jnr left Bulgaria after 64 games for Levski Sofia by the age of just 19; these games include Champions League experience, and he has also been capped by his country. Benítez has signed yet another promising young keeper, but with his immediate chances limited, Mihaylov was loaned to Dutch team FC Twente for the year. The same week, 18-year-old Athletic Bilbao defender Mikel San Jose was signed for for a reported fee of £270,000. "For us it is bad news, but Mikel has decided on the choice of Liverpool and it was impossible for us to fight against a European giant," Athletic Bilbao said in an official statement. San Jose said: "It was a surprise for me but I have decided to accept the chance at Liverpool. I am very excited but now I know that I have to work more each day to get in the first team."

Liverpool then swooped on transfer deadline day for Lyon's French youngster, Damien Plessi. The 19-year-old holding midfield player will be added to the reserve ranks at Melwood. "He is a good player, big and strong, and we're sure he'll do well for us," said Benítez . "He's only a young boy with plenty of time to work on his game but it depends on his progress how quickly he can force his way into the first team."

How many of these players will we still be talking about in five years' time? Or even just two or three years' time, for that matter? After all, not all of the young players can make the grade at the club, otherwise there would be a squad of 200 players. Many will come, do little, and leave, like the Welsh U21 striker Ramon Calliste. Calliste is the perfect example of a 'punt' worth taking — released by Manchester United in 2005, having been very highly rated in his early teens, Liverpool took a year, at no real expense, to look at him up close, to see if that untapped potential was still present.

He didn't do enough to impress, and ended up at Scunthorpe in 2006 (where he broke his ankle, and never played a game, only to be released in 2007.) But if just a handful these myriad promising young players from dozens of different backgrounds make the grade, it could save the club millions in the long term, not to mention helping achieve the ultimate aim: serious success on the pitch.

What Liverpool have started to do under Benítez is increase the turnover of players; having them long enough to get a good look at them, but also making a decision within a fairly short timeframe and not procrastinating if the talent isn't evident. The same applies to the senior squad, where any failures are quickly shown the door. It is not until a manager or coach gets to work with a player, and to see him day in and day out, that he can really understand just how good (or bad) he is, and how he can fit in to the systems in place. Top established players cannot be taken on trials ("Hola, Señor Presidente, can we have that Torres fellow of yours for a week before we make a decision on buying him?"), but youngsters can. Even then, a week or fortnight isn't a foolproof indicator of a player's potential, but it's enough to decide on the option of taking a lad for a year, for a better look, or deciding he's not up to scratch.

Ross County's Gary Mackay Steven is one such example, having impressed on a trial in early 2007. The 17-year-old never got a senior game for the Victoria Park outfit, but had enough potential to catch Liverpool's eye. A statement from Ross County explained what the Reds saw: "As an individual Gary has always been willing to put in the hard work and training to go alongside his exceptional natural skill, and we all look forward to seeing him light up the Premiership in the coming years."

Only time will tell if that's the case. But Liverpool have little to lose in waiting to find out. Making a move once the player was established could have cost the Reds ten times as much.

## New Future Takes Shape

The overseas revolution at Liverpool gathered pace during the summer of 2007, with the appointment of a Dutchman as spearhead for the Academy. On June 27th Liverpool confirmed former Ajax player Piet Hamberg as the new Academy Technical Director. Hamberg, who played in both the Dutch and Swiss leagues, joined from Grasshoppers of Zurich, where he had overseen the youth set-up. Prior to this he successfully coached youth development in Africa and the Middle East. When talking about technique, you can't get much better than an Ajax connection, with the club still considered the best breeding ground for a footballer in the last 40 years. It's the watchword of good practise, but Hamberg has influences from elsewhere, too.

Hamberg is part of a new-look Academy management structure introduced by the club in the wake of Heighway's departure. John Owens, England U15s coach a decade earlier, moved from his position as Reds' Under-18 Coach to become Academy Manager, while Malcolm Elias, who joined from Southampton's successful youth set-up in the summer of 2006, has been charged with overseeing all Academy recruitment.

Elias has an impressive record in spotting and developing young talent. He was approached by Chelsea at the start of 2004/05 to oversee their academy. "I know people will think I'm mad to turn Chelsea down," he told Southampton's website at the time, "but, among other factors, I genuinely believe at Southampton the boys have a real chance of getting in the first team." They did, but only to be sold following Southampton's relegation in 2005. In the end his left the Saints after seven years — during which time Theo Walcott and Gareth Bale came to the fore — to join the Reds. Those two players alone will bring Southampton transfer fees of over £22m, based on subsequent appearances for Arsenal and Spurs respectively.

Rick Parry explained the new arrangement: "Following the departure of Steve Heighway, we took the opportunity to review the Academy structure and decided to separate the very distinct roles. Piet will come in with the specific brief to head up the coaching and development side, while Malcolm will be in charge of all recruitment. But continuity is also very important, which is why we are taking full advantage of John's many years of experience within the youth system by promoting him to Academy Manager."

It remains to be seen whether the players will receive the kind of personal touch Heighway brought to the role, for which his charges remain eternally grateful. But John Owens is a sensible choice, and another man the players look up to as an English 'father figure' type. A greater emphasis on technique with the arrival of Hamberg can only benefit the club in the long-term, providing the idea of producing players with a good attitude is not sacrificed along the way; there's no reason it should be. With Owens and Hamberg the club can get the best of both worlds.

Owens explained more about how he saw the system working, following the arrival of two new overseas 16-year-olds: German striker Marvin Pourie, from Borussia Dortmund, and Swedish winger, Alex Kacaniklic, from Helsinborgs. These two, along with five local lads from the U16 side, were handed full-time scholarships. Owens said: "We have lads coming in from Dave Shannon's under-16s' team to start full-time as scholars. They are Steve Irwin, Sean Highdale, Nathan Ecclestone, Joe Kennedy and the goalkeeper Chris Oldfield. That is five who have come through the schoolboy ranks. As well as those second years still with us. Then we have a couple of signings.

"Signings from overseas are not quite the same as from here. Sometimes players are attached to clubs, but when they get to this age (16), they are free to look at offers from clubs around the world. We have been looking at that. Here [in England] we would have to put in a bid and go through the compensation process, but that is not the case [in Europe]. But that is something we will continue to do and try and blend that with boys from this country."

Owens took time to reflect on how, as well as getting things right, the Academy also had its shortcomings. He explained: "It gives me a chance to look at the past, obviously at the tremendous job Steve Heighway has done and to carry that on. I will have this overview of the whole Academy in the same way that Steve did. Anytime you work as assistant to someone, like with Steve, there is a lot we agreed on and things that we had different ideas on. Now it gives me a chance to look at the situation, how it has gone over the past few years and put my stamp on it. See how the players and staff react to those decisions."

Rick Parry believed that Liverpool's decision to split former Academy Director Steve Heighway's role in two was the only way of ensuring Liverpool get the very best out of their youth set-up; the job had become too big for one man to handle. "People should not assume that because we have a foreign coach we will suddenly be bringing in a raft of Dutch or German players, for example." Parry said. "Their views are very similar and they are looking forward to working together."

So a new era has begun at Liverpool, and at its state of the art Academy at Kirkby. If, in five years' time, none of the young players mentioned in this chapter are established Liverpool stars, something will have gone very wrong. And unless major trophies have been procured regardless, questions will be asked.

## The New Recruits

In keeping with every previous summer during Rafa Benítez's reign, the close season of 2007 proved rather eventful. As before, players came and went in great numbers. But something was different. This was a definable new era. If Benítez wasn't exactly starting again — after all, so many good players had already been brought to the club and a few gems remained from before his arrival, while his methods were firmly established — then he was finally getting a budget to stretch for the players he really coveted. The net spend wasn't enormous, but the fee paid for Fernando Torres was of the kind only topped in England by Chelsea and Manchester United. Torres was just the icing on the cake.

### Israeli Golden Boy

Yossi Benayoun's arrival at Liverpool could be seen as something of a good omen. A £5m signing from West Ham, he became the third Israeli to join the Reds, following Avi Cohen and Ronny Rosenthal, both of whom won the league title in their time at the club. Indeed, Rosenthal had an incredible impact after arriving in late March 1990, scoring seven goals in eight league games in helping the Reds finish strongly to see off Aston Villa for the championship.

Benayoun impressed Benítez in *La Liga* when at Racing Santander — a somewhat unfashionable Spanish club. Arriving in England 12 months after the Liverpool manager, the attacking midfielder enjoyed a superb first season in English football. It ended with the Israeli as one of the stars of the FA Cup Final, overshadowed only by Steven Gerrard, whose two goals, sumptuous assist and penalty success stole the headlines and cup from the Hammers and Benayoun.

Upon his signing, some Liverpool fans suggested Benayoun was not as good as Luis García, the man he effectively replaced in the squad, but the Israeli's record in the top Spanish division, in a weaker team, was arguably more impressive than the departing no.10's. Also, Benayoun was only 21/22 at that time, and fresh from Israel. And before West Ham's myriad troubles in 2006/07, which could be seen as extenuating circumstances, he had proved he could more than cut it in the more physical English game, winning rave reviews and being courted by Arsène Wenger at Arsenal. Of course, Luis García himself split the fans, between those who loved his game-winning ability and those who lamented what they saw as his sloppiness in possession.

Benayoun had begun making waves in Israeli football circles by the age of 11, and become a national celebrity by 13. At 15 he was snapped up by Ajax, recent European Champions, where he became the star player and top scorer in the youth team. As a result, he was offered a four-year professional contract. But Benayoun failed to settle in Holland, and within a year had returned to his homeland, where he would remain until his national service was complete at 21.

It's fair to say that Benayoun is a 'footballer's footballer'. He's not overly flashy, and has a low SOR (Step-Over Ratio). He hasn't played for fashionable clubs or a major nation, and as such will never be a worldwide superstar. But he really understands how to do those classic Liverpool-like things: find space, pass and move, and play with intelligence. He's a team player, who should prove comfortable taking part in the fast, passing football that helps to unlock defences. Closer to a Ray Houghton than a John Barnes, he has a lot to offer, as seen against Toulouse, when he put in a fine performance topped with a canny through-ball to Kuyt for the fourth goal. His problem will be getting a regular game on the right-hand side of midfield, where Jermaine Pennant began to really impress in the second half of the 2006/07, and where Steven Gerrard and Ryan Babel can also be utilised. Benayoun will need to show a lot of character to keep his form when in and out of the side, as it will take exceptional performances to come as close to cementing a place as anyone can get under Benítez. But the Israeli is also a player who can cut infield from the left, or play as the second striker, so he's not hamstrung by a lack of versatility.

## No Such Thing as a Free Transfer

It's clear that Ukrainian forward Andrei Voronin, who turned 28 soon after joining Liverpool, was not a 'glamour' signing to appease the fans; indeed, his signing was met largely with shoulder shrugs, and little expectation. As a free transfer the pressure was off, but at the same time Voronin didn't have bags of goodwill wishing him to succeed, a situation exacerbated by fans' hopes of signing players like Barcelona's Samuel Eto'o; hopes raised unrealistically following the new investment. But the Ukrainian striker, with his distinctive '80s porn-star ponytail, was the revelation of the Reds' pre-season, and went some way to winning over the sceptics. (Then again, Bruno Cheyrou had a promising pre-season in 2002.)

Upon the no.10's unveiling, Benítez said it was hard to list Voronin's strengths, as he had so many. His new capture was a player with pace, strength and good technique, who could chip in with goals from deeper positions as well as creating them for others and, if necessary, use his pace to get in behind teams. He had a good attitude, would work hard for the cause, and possessed good game intelligence. So while none of his strengths would see him labelled as world-class, he had a bit of everything in order to be a very effective footballer at the top level.

At Bayer Leverkusen Voronin scored 32 league goals in 92 games, at a rate mathematicians will spot as approximately one every three games. He faced the Reds in the Champions League games in 2005, as an early substitute in Germany and from the start at Anfield, but so outclassed were the Germans in both games that he hardly had a chance to shine. Voronin had previously represented Cologne, for just one season, and Mainz, the German club who later went on to shock Liverpool in the 2006 pre-season with a 5-0 win. Voronin had been just 16 when he first moved to Germany, to begin his professional career with another club etched into Liverpool's history: Borussia Mönchengladbach. With just a handful of appearances and a single goal to his name at Mönchengladbach he moved to Mainz, who were in the German second division. Voronin began to win rave reviews and score goals: 29 in 75 games.

More of an all-rounder with good a football brain than an out-and-out goal threat, he is another player capable of meeting Benítez's desire to have four interchangeable strikers scoring approximately 15 goals each. He also likes to play 'between the lines' — which Benítez usually requires from one of his two strikers.

Voronin couldn't have started his Liverpool career much better: scoring on his full debut with a rasping 25-yard drive in Toulouse to win the opening tie of the Champions League qualifier 1-0. The game was played in near 40° heat at 3.30 in the afternoon, and the French, while not a side to be feared, provided stiff opposition at that stage, given that they'd finished third in what remains one of the stronger European leagues. It was certainly more of a challenging tie than the teams Liverpool faced at the same stage in 2001, 2004 and 2005. He followed it with the second goal at Sunderland on his first league start, having assisted Momo Sissoko's opening strike, and the fifth goal against Derby, having only just come on as a sub.

## Ryan Babel, Dutch Master* (*Cliché alert)

The loss of Luis García could have left Liverpool even shorter in an area — scoring goals from midfield — which was already an Achilles heel. But it was the area to which Benítez added the most numbers over the summer of 2007. In came Benayoun, Lucas Leiva, Sebastián Leto and, with his ability to play in deeper positions, Voronin. None of these were of any great surprise: Voronin announced his impending move to Liverpool in February, at a time when Leto had also announced to the Argentine media that he was Anfield-bound. Lucas announced he would be signing soon after the Champions League final, and Benayoun had been on Benítez's radar for several years, with the deal mooted in the press many weeks before. As expected, it came to fruition.

But one player whose name was not linked to the Reds at any point before his surprise move was that of Ryan Babel, the player who spent the first few weeks of the summer terrorising defences in the European U-21 Championships with Holland; Babel was named Man of the Match in the 4-1 final win over Serbia. He seemed destined for Arsenal, who had been tracking him for a number of seasons. He was seen as a typical Arsenal signing.

Having made his Ajax debut at 17 and his full national debut at 18, he began learning the game in public, and arrived in England still not the finished article. With searing pace, and intimidating bulk and height, Babel offers a different dynamic to García. From the neck down he resembles John Barnes at his physical peak, before the waistline became Molbyesque. Like Barnes, he appears too muscle-bound to be quick and nimble, but then he exhibits adroit close control and a surprising quickness off the mark.

Babel's goals record for a young winger, who also plays behind the main striker, is fairly impressive. Most wingers become increasingly prolific after a few years of steady development in their early 20s (see Barnes, Harry Kewell and Cristiano Ronaldo). The early seasons are all about adjustment. Scoring goals as a winger is an art that takes a bit of learning: knowing when to get into the box and when to stay out wide. Unlike young strikers, wingers aren't guaranteed lots of chances, so have to learn how to beat top-class keepers with fewer opportunities, not to mention when to go for goal or look for a striker who may well be better placed. As an example, a young Michael Owen missed lots of chances, but given that he could play centrally, on the shoulder of the last defender, he knew he would get in on goal a few times in each game. A winger may get in on goal just once in a match.

Inevitably too much too soon will be expected of Babel. At 19/20/21 Ronaldo (like Wayne Rooney) wasn't a player who could make enough impact, either creatively or in terms of goals, to push United towards a title. But at 22/23, he was. Even though Ronaldo clearly had promise, the jury was still out; 73 step-overs are all well and good, but where was the end product? By 2006/07 he had matured sufficiently. Had he been that good in 2003, either he'd have cost United three times as much, or someone like Real Madrid or AC Milan would have outbid them. It's often about buying players on the cusp of greatness, as AC Milan did with £5m Kaka, because those already fully established as great just don't change hands very often, and if they do, it's for megabucks. Babel wasn't exactly cheap, but it seems almost certain that in years to come he'll be worth far in excess of the £11.5m paid.

Babel claims his favourite position is up front, but it will be up to him to prove what is his most effective position for Liverpool — not where he wins rave reviews as an individual, or enjoys it the most, but where he can help the team win games. It could well be the case that in a few years' time he establishes himself as a striker, but it seems that Benítez's initial use for him is on the right flank, or as a left winger cutting in on his favoured right foot.

Babel's first goal for the club — the Reds' second against Derby County at Anfield at the start of September — was a real gem. Receiving a squared pass on the edge of the area, it looked 100% certain from his body shape that he was going to blast in a drive. That made his quick change of feet all the more remarkable; two defenders were instantly taken out of the game as they threw themselves to block a shot that never came. Somehow Babel readjusted and slammed home a superb side-footed shot. It was a finish made all the sweeter for sending the keeper the wrong way.

At just 20, Babel already had four international goals in 14 games for a major footballing nation upon his arrival in England, as well as being so far ahead of most other players of the same age he starred as the Dutch won the U21 European Championship. He may not have been as developed as Chelsea's Florent Malouda, who Liverpool initially bid for, but at eight years the junior of the French wide-man, he has the potential to be much better and last much longer.

Indeed, Marco van Basten, the Holland manager and without doubt one of the game's greatest centre-forwards, said Ryan Babel could become as good as the game's current star striker. His public assessment was delivered on the eve of the 2006 World Cup. "He has all the potential to become the next Thierry Henry," Van Basten said. "The pace, movement, finishing, feel for the game — it's all there. If he keeps developing and improving there is no saying what he might achieve in the game."

Van Basten should know. He organised one-on-one training sessions with Babel when the youngster was at the Ajax Academy; Ronald Koeman, manager at the Ajax ArenA at the time, offered his erstwhile colleague a chance to work with the young player, following the legendary striker's completion of his coaching badges. Before long Babel made his full Ajax debut, at the age of 17, and just a year later found himself called up to the senior Holland team by Van Basten, who by then was the national manager. Babel didn't disappoint, becoming his country's youngest goalscorer for 68 years when, having come on as a sub, he rounded off a 2-0 win in Romania.

Comparisons with Thierry Henry won't help keep expectations down to a realistic level for a player just 20 years of age. Interestingly, Fernando Torres is also somewhat reminiscent of the ex-Arsenal star: tall, extremely quick, skilful. But that doesn't mean either will be the 'new' Henry; after all, English football waited 140 years for a player like Henry in the first place. Being reminiscent of a world-class player does not mean being an identikit, or a cast-iron certainty to reproduce his achievements. But it's better than resembling Robbie Savage.

Foretelling which players will succeed is almost impossible. Djibril Cissé looked a good bet to be a massive hit following his scoring exploits in France, but while he had the physical attributes needed to succeed in England he lacked the necessary control, both of the ball and, at times, of himself. He also had to play under a manager who didn't seem to fully trust him, having been signed by his predecessor, and he also suffered two terrible broken legs that were never going to help him fully succeed. How could that be foreseen? Fernando Morientes had the control and was a decent size, but lacked the pace, and didn't have the best of luck with niggling injuries that further inhibited his ability to cope.

The players Benítez bought in 2007 appeared to have no such shortcomings, be it mentally, physically or in terms of technique. All the same, it's important to give them time to adjust to the Premiership and grow into their roles in the team. Rather than go for grossly overpriced or merely average Premiership players who may need less time adjusting, Benítez took the necessary long-term view.

It has to be remembered that no player is a robot; you can't transpose him from one environment to another and expect him to put in the exact same performances. Like those warnings on financial advertisements, 'your investment can go up or down'. A new club, new city/country, new manager, new team-mates, new training regime, new tactics — all these things affect a player, either positively or negatively. It's a big upheaval off the pitch, and that can affect a player on it.

A bigger club with better players and a really top-class manager can lift a player to new heights. Competition for places can propel him to new levels of consistency. A bigger stadium, more passionate support, and higher-profile games can inspire him. Rotation can keep him hungry and fresh. Alternatively, he can struggle to get onto the wavelength of his new team-mates or manager. Competition for places can make him insecure, perhaps leading to him trying too hard or going the other way and losing heart. The pressure of a big club can see him wilt. Rotation can disrupt his flow, break his rhythm. These are universal truths, but they aren't always considered when judgements are hastily made.

## Torres – Enter *El Niño*

There's no getting away from who was the star attraction in the summer of 2007. Fernando Torres, golden boy of Spanish football for the previous half-decade, was finally prised from Atlético Madrid's clutches. The boy had become a man.

Some young footballers are blessed with greatness, touched by the hand of God (or whichever deity they believe in, and who has a bent on touching people). There is something about them that marks them out from an early age as having everything necessary to be up there with the very best. They seem to emerge from the womb with uncanny balance, and while others are still finding their feet these toddlers are juggling rolled-up nappies and nutmegging their fathers with a teething ring following a reverse-dragback. By their late teens they are world stars.

Inevitably, such players are later doubted in many quarters; 'yes, he's great, but is he *that* great?' Couldn't he have been so much more? Think George Best, Paul Gascoigne. But these were tortured geniuses whose mentality saw them self-destruct (albeit after leaving an indelible mark on the game). There was also a trio of Liverpool legends: Kenny Dalglish, John Barnes and Alan Hansen, who should somehow be above all criticism following amazing exploits at club level, but who, the critics said, 'never did enough at international level'. There is Thierry Henry, who, it is said, goes missing on the very biggest occasions. Or Ronaldinho, who could be even better if he just put in a little more effort, or Ronaldo, whose weight stopped him getting away from defenders in the manner he once had. Or Zinedine Zidane, whose two headed goals in the 1998 World Cup final were arguably overshadowed by his headed *butt* in the 2006 final: the pearler that connected with Marco Materazzi's ribcage. Or Wayne Rooney, who scored in the Premiership at the age of 16, and was a world star by 2004, but who then went two years without a Champions League or competitive goal for England, but who now has a league winner's medal. Then there's Michael Owen who, no matter how many goals he scores, will 'never be the player he once was'; something that was being said regularly at the age of 19 and 20, before he became the 2001

European Footballer of the Year and scored 28 goals for the Reds in 2001/02.

Fernando Torres is one such player. Not temperamentally flawed or injury prone like some of the above, or yet as proven as world masters like Zidane or Dalglish, he has been marked out for greatness from a tender age, and any example of him being merely mortal — a bad game, a missed chance — is inevitably met with 'oh, he's overrated'. It's virtually impossible to live up to such hype, but once that hype is stripped away you're left with one very special player; just not the superhuman hybrid of reincarnated legends Pelé and Puskás.

Torres had the nickname 'El Niño' ('The Kid') bestowed upon him when he was literally just that. Making his Atlético Madrid debut at 16, he was a boy playing in a man's game. He did well considering his tender years, scoring seven goals in his first 40 games, all played in the *Segunda División*, into which the club had recently been relegated. This was one of Spain's biggest outfits, a club that had made the European Cup Final in 1974 (when a certain Miguel Reina, father of Pepe, was in the defeated Spanish team), and which had won the ninth of their Spanish Championships as recently as 1996.

By the time Atlético were promoted back to the top flight in 2002, The Kid was fast becoming a man. And to prove it, his club would soon set his release value at a prohibitive €90million. The goals duly flowed: 75 in 172 *La Liga* games over the next five years, at a rate of a goal every 2.2 games. This, despite spending some time on the wing and playing in a side that, for all Torres' goals and effort, could not even make the Uefa Cup in that time. They made Newcastle United look like extraordinary overachievers.

As time passed, Torres became increasingly worried about growing stale, something he stated in several interviews. As much as he adored his hometown club, he was naturally concerned that any ceaseless loyalty would be to the detriment of his career. As honourable as it is to be loyal — and Torres had been just that, spurning numerous advances over the years despite his club's perennial failure — a player also recognises that as soon as he is no longer useful to the club, through injury or loss of form, the club won't show any extended loyalty in reply. A club won't let its heart rule the ruthlessness of its head. Football clubs cannot afford to be sentimental. That's how the game works; if it wasn't, Kenny Dalglish would still be playing up front for the Reds aged 56. You only have to look at how Liverpool's very own 'God', Robbie Fowler, was sold against his wishes by Gérard Houllier in 2001. Whatever the rights and wrongs of the sale, both seen at the time and with the 20-20 of hindsight, it was not exactly the reward Fowler had in mind for his stunning early seasons and his desire to see out his days in a red shirt. Liverpool made a business decision, and he had to move on. Having allowed a number of years for Atlético to finally awake from their semi-slumber, the time was right for Torres — Atlético's Fowler, circa 1996 — to take his talent to the next level.

In June 2007, Atlético Madrid found themselves in a quandary: sell the fans' idol and risk their wrath (street protests even took place at the first suggestion of a possible move to Liverpool), or try and hold on to a player who clearly needed a new challenge, and whose effectiveness might diminish as a result. By cashing in they could build a team, rather than try to rely on one clearly over-burdened young man. They moved for Villarreal's reborn Diego Forlan, a player who was linked with Liverpool (well, he did only ever score goals at Anfield), as well as Liverpool's very own Luis García, a man who'd had his best season in Spain for the Madrid club in 2002/03, and who wanted to return to *Atléti* when the time was right to head home. These appeased the fans' frustrations, but only so much; Torres was irreplaceable in their hearts, even if the team could grow in his absence. Once the deal went through, though, rather than see Torres as a 'Judas' he was given a hero's send-off. Of course, this wouldn't have been the case if he'd left to join Real Madrid, but that was never in the player's thinking.

Torres is not a player whose reputation has been founded on hard, cold figures; he was not a prolific goalscorer in Spain to the degree that his stats were uttered in hushed tones, as proof of some outrageous talent. He is a footballer who needs to be seen, a footballer who elevates a team with his presence and all-round ability. Rather than a great goalscorer, he had been a scorer of great goals. Not for the sake of artistic merit, but because he can score the kind of goals only special players can, from situations where 99% of other players would have to pass instead.

While he may never be ultra-prolific in the way a 'fox in the box' might be, he has that special gift of scoring goals out of nothing: a curling shot from distance, an outrageous lob from an unlikely angle, a spectacular flying volley, a thumping header. There are those strikers who score a lot of goals, but need all the chances to be created on their behalf; Torres is someone who, like Thierry Henry, can create his own. And that's a priceless commodity. Anyone who can score goals out of nothing is a valuable asset, especially if there's someone else in the box, such as Kuyt or Crouch, who can score the scrappy goals.

It's fair to say that Torres is also someone who misses a fair few chances. On his debut against Aston Villa this was in evidence. But such was his movement and skill on the ball, he created each of the three opportunities himself — one following a sublime nutmeg that earned him a half-chance. The opening goal of the Reds' campaign was another case in point. Having turned a Villa defender in the box, and shown remarkable balance in springing back to his feet when appearing certain to fall flat-faced to the ground, he composed himself in a fraction of a second and calmly stroked a shot towards the bottom corner. Stuart Taylor made a great save low to his left, but it was a shot that gave him a chance; perhaps Torres could have opted for more power. Dirk Kuyt kept the ball alive by trying to find Torres with a fired-in cross, and the ball was swept home for an own goal by Martin Laursen. So while it highlighted that Torres was not necessarily a clinical finisher, his performance also showed how teams cannot handle his movement, pace and skill, and that goals and victories can follow as a result.

A week later Torres got off the mark against Chelsea at Anfield, and it was a goal highly reminiscent of Thierry Henry. The Spaniard picked the ball up 30 yards from goal, following a sublime Gerrard pass into the inside-left channel. Tal Ben-Haim, who blocked the striker's path to goal, knew Torres preferred it on his right foot, so he showed the Liverpool no.9 onto his left. Undeterred, Torres took the invitation and whipped the ball past him in the blink of an eye. Although he only ever used his right foot in the process, Torres went to the *left* of the defender. Like Henry so often did, he guided a right-instep shot across the keeper into the far corner. Had the ball then been more to Torres' left it would have meant a left-foot shot or nothing. But he was so skilful in his bypassing of Ben-Haim it allowed him to use his right foot. Special players have a way of fooling defenders to work the chance onto their favoured foot. And with the goal Torres put a seed of doubt into every Premiership defender's mind, saying: I may prefer my right, but I will happily go past you on either side. His second and third goals came against Derby County, the first of which saw him twice go past defenders onto his left side, only this time he stroked home a left-foot shot.

While Kuyt and Crouch shared an impressive 32 goals last season, 30 came from within the penalty area — with just the goal apiece they notched at West Ham coming from beyond the 18-yard line. In Kuyt's case, hardly any of his goals came from further out than 12 yards, and the majority were six-yard poaches. But it's not just that the pair finished these chances in the box — without fail, they either received the ball inside the box or right on the very edge. That requires accurate supply. What Torres provides is the ability to take the ball into the box himself (as he did against Chelsea and Derby), perhaps from as far back as his own half; or to score from outside the box with his powerful shooting.

Chelsea were sniffing around Torres in 2006, following his outstanding World Cup, and Inter Milan were hopeful of his signature at the same time. But Torres stayed in Spain, loyal to *Atléti*. While Liverpool holds an attraction to any overseas star — given its history and regular appearances in the Champions League (not to mention two recent finals) — it was always going to be the Spanish connection that had the greatest pull on the young striker. He was not motivated by money, but by being successful in an environment in which he felt valued; indeed, like Benayoun he even took a wage cut to join the Reds. Torres would be joining international team-mates Pepe Reina and Xabi Alonso, as well as a dozen more Spanish speaking players, many of whom came from *La Liga*. And more than anything, there was the lure of Benítez, the best Spanish manager around.

Guillem Balague, Spanish football writer and a Liverpool fan from his time in the city in the 1990s, interviewed Torres once his compatriot had sealed his move to Anfield. Torres explained how he was walking his two dogs near his house in Madrid in late May when his mobile rang with an unfamiliar number on the screen. Seeing it was a UK code, he broke the habit of a lifetime to answer a call from someone whose number he did not recognise, assuming it was either Pepe Reina or one of Arsenal's two Spaniards.

"I cannot remember if he said, 'Hi, it's Rafa' or, 'Hi, this is Benítez ... I was surprised but did not realise the dimension of what I was hearing till I hung up," Torres said. "Then I thought, 'Wow, this club that can get anybody in the world has rung me, they want me." And so began the move that would take him from Spain to England. It allowed Torres to escape the unbearable pressure he had been under at Aléti.

One of the biggest problems a new Liverpool player has to deal with is the pressure of representing a club with such high expectations. If the transfer fee also happens to be big, that just doubles the pressure. But if anyone has shoulders broad enough to carry these expectations then it's Torres. He explained to Balague that he felt like a weight had been lifted from his shoulders.

Balague described it thus: "... at 19, he became captain and the only person responsible for everything that was good and bad at the club. He was mobbed, criticised, scrutinised. He couldn't breathe." The most encouraging point was how he noticed that: "... In the press conference at Anfield, the weight had gone. It was another Fernando Torres and the smile he wore that day has not abandoned him since."

At Liverpool Torres will be important, but as another one of the main men, in a nucleus of great players, rather than out on his own.

## New Beginning

Homesickness and culture shock are two of the greatest problems facing anyone moving to a new country, but for Torres, Liverpool was more like 'Little Spain'. The football might be different, but adapting to it would be made easier by familiar faces and a common language in an Iberian enclave. And the weather was not going to be a problem: Torres stated that his girlfriend was from Galicia, where, he said, it always rains.

Just as Arsène Wenger made had made Arsenal formidable by signing the best of his compatriots to form the core of Arsenal's side for years to come — Thierry Henry, Robert Pirès, Patrick Vieira, Nicolas Anelka and Emmanuel Petit initially — Benítez mined Spain in similar fashion. The first knee-jerk assumptions, back in 2004, were that he was not doing what Wenger had done so successfully, but what Houllier had done so catastrophically: signing too many average examples of his fellow countrymen (or anyone playing in his homeland) in a policy doomed to failure. The big difference was the quality of Houllier's purchases from France — unproven, often mentally suspect, and nowhere near the quality of either Wenger's Frenchmen or, subsequently, Benítez's Spaniards.

Torres should prove difficult for Premiership defences to play against: tall enough, at 6ft 1in, so that teams won't want to defend too deep, but so quick they won't want to defend too high up the pitch either, and leave gaping holes in behind. His presence could give Dirk Kuyt the chance to push up higher, alongside him.

From a tactical point of view Torres ticks all the boxes. Whereas in 2006/07 Liverpool's only genuine pace up front was from Bellamy, the Reds now had a striker who could play centrally as either a lone striker or the more advanced of two. This latter role never suits smaller strikers, who can't offer the physical presence, and usually require a 'bodyguard', and it instantly limits things if you have to include a player just to get the best out of another. Both Kuyt and Crouch are capable of holding the ball up — especially the latter — but neither can choose, having taken hold of a pass, to turn the last defender and make for goal. Defenders know that. What those strikers can do, however, is follow behind someone like Torres — who *can* turn and head for goal — looking for a squared pass if the keeper holds up Torres or any rebounds from a shot. (This is precisely what happened on the opening day: Kuyt, as the link-man, created the chance for Torres with a dummy, but was able to get to the loose ball after 'following in'.)

For all the many positive things Peter Crouch offers, his lack of pace means teams can often keep him where they want him: as far away from their area as possible, because any header won in and around the box spells trouble. Indeed, Crouch doesn't even have to win the header: his mere presence caused Chelsea's backline to panic at Anfield for the first goal in the January 2007 league game, leaving Kuyt free to score. Kuyt's lack of that extra yard of pace also means teams can afford to defend a higher line against him, so someone who can help push them back towards their own goal should prove a big help.

## Complete

One thing Rafa Benítez was not able to utilise during his first three years was a 'complete' centre-forward: the quick, strong and tall striker who could be relied upon to score goals as well as link play intelligently, create chances for others, and hold the ball up. Until Torres' arrival, he was always relying on combinations of players to offer the full gamut of attacking skills.

Think about someone along the lines of Blackburn-era Alan Shearer, when at his quickest, or Nicolas Anelka, when he burst onto the scene. Or more recently, Didier Drogba and Thierry Henry. Ruud van Nistelrooy was another; even though he was only ever a goal threat in the box for United — never scoring a single time from outside the area — he was big, strong, quick, and good on the ball, and as seen against Arsenal a few seasons back, he could go on powerful runs (unless, of course, a particularly vicious gust of wind happened to sweep him over). It's notable that the aforementioned players all led the line in league title triumphs. And in Drogba's case, he did so twice without scoring that many goals.

First Benítez had Milan Baros, an instinctive striker and forceful dribbler, but very hit-and-miss in front of goal, and someone whose head-down approach had its limitations; certainly he was certainly no target man. Then there was Fernando Morientes, who had the technique, intelligence and stature, but lacked the pace to be a real threat in behind defences, and even failed to offer his famed aerial brilliance as his confidence evaporated. There was Djibril Cissé, who had the pace, but not the composure, nor the temperament; in many ways still a natural goalscorer — he was much happier scoring rather than creating, and his instincts were to get into the right areas — he did not fit with Benítez's team-first ethos, and his hold-up play was lacking. Peter Crouch — perhaps the most criticised of all Benítez's signings at the time of purchase — enhanced his improving reputation, with great ability on the floor and an 'unplayability' in the air, as well as increasing his goals-per-game ratio in his second season; but his lack of pace will always limit how much he can offer in certain situations. With pace, Crouch would without doubt be regarded as world-class, and while, as an intelligent footballer, he will get better with age and experience, he will not get any quicker. Robbie Fowler arrived — the most natural goalscorer of the lot, and, along with Crouch, the most surprising of all Benítez's deals — but the manager pondered how perfect it would be if only he had Bellamy's pace. And Fowler, like Bellamy himself and Florent Sinama-Pongolle, lacked the physical presence to play as the lone striker, which limited his deployment. Then came Dirk Kuyt, second only to Fowler in terms of ability to sniff out a chance. But the Dutchman was rarely deployed as an out-and-out striker in his inaugural season, in order to help balance the team and make use of his phenomenal stamina and will to win. However, Kuyt, while strong as an ox and able to take up clever positions in the box, is not the tallest, nor the quickest.

Every one of these players possess certain attributes that makes him special in his own way. In particular, Kuyt and Crouch remain hugely effective players and, in their mid-20s, are still improving. No-one in England offers more sweat for the cause than Kuyt, and no-one in the Premiership can pose the same kind of problems Crouch does. These are assets to be celebrated. But every one of the players mentioned has a shortcoming of one kind or another that affects the tactical master plan. However, as well as being ideal for the lone-striker role he played so well in Spain, Torres' pace and movement also make him the ideal foil for the more static Crouch, while Kuyt can also benefit from the Spaniard's style.

There are very few players in the world in any position who are so perfectly rounded they can tick all the boxes. At Liverpool, Steven Gerrard is one such player. He can fit into the team anywhere, and the team does not need to be adjusted to accommodate his weaknesses: bar the odd minor flaw, they don't exist. But there are few other such players in the game. In the aftermath of Athens, Benítez pondered that "Some players, even playing isolated up front, can change the game. They can receive the ball, dribble, pass, and they can change the game." It's the one thing Benítez's teams had lacked.

Torres, however, fits this criteria.

Tall, strong, highly motivated, level-headed, and with the twin assets of blistering acceleration and great feet — not to mention excellent game intelligence to make the best use of them — Torres has everything needed to be the perfect centre-forward. The plaudits picked up before his arrival in England sum up the regard in which he is held.

Take the words of Raúl, talisman of Atlético's rivals, Real, as well as the Spanish national side, when talking about Torres in 2004: "He's got a lot of character. There are plenty of talented players who don't have the desire that Torres has. Since I saw him make his debut, I've always said: this guy's the real thing. He's going to be the player of his generation for club and country. He can take advantage of his pace, youth and desire. He's a great football player and in a few years time he'll be even better. He's got it all, it's frightening, his speed is overwhelming. He's big and strong and his head's in the right place too."

Raúl's co-striker at Real Madrid at the time, the legendary Ronaldo, said: "Torres is one of the greatest players in the world, he's young and he's going to learn a lot, although he's already an eye-catching player." As players at Atlético's fiercest rivals, they were hardly saying these things for the mere sake of it.

Carlos García Cantarero, coach of Atlético Madrid in 2001, spoke of the youngster who had started making waves at the club: "Fundamentally, Fernando is a very mature player in all aspects of the word. I particularly notice that he always chooses the best available option in any situation — that's where his goalscoring prowess comes from. Off the ball he plays the game very well, he has a remarkable change of pace and innate skill. These three factors are what make a player great. All that, added to excellent technical ability are what make Torres a special player."

The words of Pedro Calvo, the Spanish youth coach who oversaw the development of Torres at the end of the '90s, are interesting, as they highlight the natural ability and character of the player as a youngster: "I got to see the best of Fernando in the youth teams. It was the period of the Nike Cup and the European Championship Fernando won with the under-16s, when he was named Best Young Player in Europe. Even as a lad he had the mean streak he's got now. I'm talking about on the pitch — something vital in people, the same as Fernando's other qualities like courage, ambition and the will to win. He was captain, which wasn't easy at that time because of the differences between the lads who'd just arrived from outside Madrid and those who had been in the organization for a while. Nevertheless he knew how to handle the responsibility, young as he was, and to top it all he had to put up with the odd undeserved telling off without letting his team-mates get in trouble. That kind of responsibility, acquired so young, together with his footballing prowess, has propelled Fernando into the elite. In as much as the game is concerned he's always been a technically superior player, he especially stood out from the rest in that he was always in the right place in the tough situations, thanks to which, without wanting to put the other lads down, we managed to win the Nike Cup. The day Fernando was missing we had problems, and that was something all his team-mates were aware of. He was and is a footballer who makes the difference."

Two more familiar names paid testament to Torres' ability. First, David Beckham (media-shy ex-Real Madrid midfielder) said: "For me Fernando Torres is one of the best players I've come up against in Spain, and he's one of the best forwards in Europe. The problem is that, as he is a forward, people only look at his misses but he's a great player". Meanwhile Frank Rikjaard, successful manager of Barcelona, enthused: "Fernando Torres is a forward's forward, and he gives a team depth. He's fast, direct and dangerous in the box. He's still very young but he's doing really well. He accepts responsibility and he has a great future."

Taking these comments together, from people within the game who worked closely with the player or who were pitted against him, paints a clear picture of an all-round forward with no real chinks in his armour. If you didn't know the identity of the player about whom all those comments were made, it would be easy to think they referred to Thierry Henry, the man who left for Spain as Torres made the trip in the opposite direction. One difference between the two is that Torres is not as liable to sulk or pout.

Perhaps most encouraging of all is the characteristic that runs through all these plaudits: Torres' determination, his character, his will to win, and his ability to remain grounded. These are things that will not show up on YouTube compilations or in cold, hard stats, but which suggest an ability to keep improving, and a desire to integrate himself into the team, for the greater good. He is that best of breeds: the individual talent who can go it alone with a ball, but who will get his head up and pass to someone better placed, and who will work for the team when the going gets tough. What more can you ask for?

While Torres' goals record is not yet remarkable, there are precedents that suggest he could yet turn into a real goal-machine. There are no guarantees, of course, and there will always be so much more to his game than goals, but two of modern football's greatest goal-getters were actually far less prolific at the same stage of their careers.

Torres arrived in England a fraction older than Henry was when he started his Highbury love-in. Before his move to London, Henry had scored just 23 league goals in 126 games for Monaco and Juventus. While also utilised as a winger, Henry was not noted for his clinical finishing when playing as a striker. After a difficult first five months in the Premiership, his potential gave way to the realisation of a great talent. In a better team, and under a compatriot and mentor who understood him, Henry came of age at Arsenal. His overall career strike rate went from a goal every five games to one every two; and his Arsenal ratio, without the earlier failure to distort it, was better than a goal every 1.5 games.

So if that's the example of the overseas star who came good at 22/23, there is another example closer to home. Along with Thierry Henry, Alan Shearer is the most successful striker in the Premiership's history. (Andy Cole scored fractionally more than Henry, but in seven extra years.) While this ignores the feats of bygone greats like Ian Rush and Jimmy Greaves, the Premiership is still the modern currency most people use to compare and contrast. And Alan Shearer showed little sign of what was to come when, aged 22, he moved from Southampton to Blackburn in 1992, when the league's name was changed. While he'd just enjoyed a fine season at the Dell, he left the south coast with very similar figures to pre-Arsenal Thierry Henry: 23 league goals in 118 games. In four seasons at the Lancashire club he notched a phenomenal 112 Premiership goals in just 138 games, followed by 148 in 303 league games for Newcastle.

The arrival of Torres will also take the pressure off Kuyt, who spent his first season as the expensive striker expected to score bags of goals. Kuyt should also have a better season in 2007/08, injury permitting; benefiting not only from the arrival of Torres but from having had a first year to acclimatise. After just one season, a lot of fans seemed to have written him off as not fitting the bill for the 20-goal striker they felt the club needed (which, in itself is a contentious issue). He's a goal poacher, but also such a tremendous team player, and spent much of his debut season in deeper areas, helping the team to victories in places like the Nou Camp and in games like the Anfield semi-final against Chelsea, rather than spending 90 minutes helping himself to the glory. The Dutchman is not one of those strikers who stands hands-on-hips in the area while a team-mate beats seven men on a breathtaking run, and then, when the ball is squared, taps home the cross from six inches — only to wheel away in the opposite direction to his supplier, celebrating the goal as if it was all his own work, and suggesting that he's the main man.

It cannot be said that Liverpool got the Champions League Final in spite of Kuyt. There is no way that the team 'carried him' with him not scoring *en route* to Athens. He started in virtually every game, and played a crucial role in wearing teams down, creating space for others and leading by example when it came to giving every last ounce of energy.

Even so, last season he was close, in some regards, to being that 20-goal striker. He got a very respectable 14, and 12 in the league (one fewer than Spurs' much-heralded Berbatov). But the Dutchman also hit the woodwork no less than six times. All of the 14 goals were from open play. Had he taken the Reds' penalties, certainly in the manner in which he took his Champions League semi-final shootout spot kick, then he could have had those 20 goals and no-one would have questioned his scoring rate. And all this despite often being the second striker.

Strikers often need time to acclimatise. In his debut season, Didier Drogba also scored 12 league goals for Chelsea as they first won the Premiership. He scored 13 the season after, as they retained it. Last season, when they finished 2nd, he exploded into life, getting 20 league goals, and 33 overall.

As previously stated, Kuyt had a tough time breaking his Champions League duck, eventually doing so in the very last minute of the competition. But for a linesman's unusual accuracy of vision and bravery in allowing a goal in a hostile environment, Kuyt would have got that longed-for goal in Barcelona; the decision to give it to Bellamy was correct, but Kuyt, for all his mileage that night, was on hand, in true poaching fashion, to make sure from close range.

But, lest the number of Champions League goals be used as an indicator of lack of ability at the highest level, it should be remembered that in 2005/06 some fans were doubting Crouch's ability, and using the fact that he didn't score in the Champions League as proof of his deficiencies. Then in his second season he was second-top scorer in the whole competition, netting six times (plus once more in the qualifiers), despite not starting in five of the final seven matches. Indeed, it took Kuyt just one start in the 2007/08 campaign to surpass his previous season's tally, when he netted twice at home to Toulouse in the qualifying round.

If there's one thing that hints that Kuyt can be the poacher people crave it was the close-range headers he bagged against Arsenal, Reading and AC Milan. Rather than power headers, they were like Robbie Fowler's first goal upon his second-coming against Fulham. They were about positioning, finding half a yard of space, being alert, and then reacting quickly.

So, in theory at least, the Reds now have far more options going forward. It is up to the players to put it into practice.

# Samba and Tango: Latin America

Buenos Aires, Argentina. A port of passion on the South Atlantic with an immense harbour, at which point the *Río de la Plata* — the River Plate — spills out to sea. A strong sense of European culture pervades the city: it is often referred to as the "Paris of South America", and boasts a large immigrant Italian population. It's nearly 200 years since the city broke free of Spain's clutches, with the Spanish Viceroy ousted on 25th May, 1810 — the date now celebrated as a national holiday: *La Revolución de Mayo*. It is of course also a date close to the hearts of Liverpool fans: half of Merseyside would also like to declare it a public holiday, following events in Istanbul 195 years later. (In 2005 the situation was reversed somewhat: the Spaniards of Benítez, Alonso, Luis García and co. gaining victory over Argentina's Hernán Crespo.)

The British introduced football to Argentina back in 1867, coinciding with the formation of Buenos Aires Football Club. Club names like Newell's Old Boys and Quilmes Rovers Club (which became Quilmes Atlético Club) clearly reveal the sport's British origins. When looking at the nature and style of Argentine football today, something is readily apparent: technically it bears little resemblance to the English game. In the early part of the 20th Century Italians usurped Brits in the country's teams, and it shows.

Tim Vickery, South American football correspondent for the BBC and Sports Illustrated, is clearly a man to trust when it comes to assessing the merits of that continent's football. In his column on the BBC website he recently spoke of a belief in Lucas Leiva's ability to succeed at Liverpool, as well as accurately predicting in the summer of 2006 that Gabriel Paletta was making a mistake in leaving for the European stage before he had experienced enough senior foootball in his homeland.

In July 2007 I ask Vickery for his thoughts on Liverpool's recent move into a part of the world that had been previously untapped by the club. Why was Rafa Benítez focusing so much on South America, where he set up an extensive scouting network, when it's not been a continent whose players have transferred well to the English game in general?

"He's looking for a differential," Vickery tells me. "The pool of talent is now global. Arsène Wenger and Jose Mourinho have mined Africa, so Benítez is turning to a region where a) he has a cultural affinity, and b) where other English clubs have been slow to go. If South American players can tip the balance in the German league [where a lot of Brazilians have succeeded], then surely they can adapt to England. A big problem so far is that — mainly because of work permit restrictions — there haven't been enough of them."

This latter point has led to all sorts of controversies in recent years, such as when Edu was found to be in possession of a fake Portuguese passport when signing for Arsenal, only for the problem to be solved upon discovery of Italian lineage on his father's side. (Many South Americans have Italian passports: Lucas Leiva and Javier Mascherano also possess them.) For the world's second-strongest footballing continent in terms of league strength (after Europe), which also contains the game's most legendary nation in Brazil and gave the world its two most lauded players (Pelé and Maradona), South America is represented in the Premiership by a very small percentage of players.

While all fans think about a player's ability to adapt to English football, Vickery doesn't feel that English clubs are necessarily prepared to welcome them in a manner to which they are accustomed, and which would smooth over their difficult transition. "South Americans are baffled by our concept of personal independence — clubs have bought players and then left them completely to their own devices after training. Hernán Crespo in his first spell at Chelsea spoke about the problems he had getting his car fixed or having the guy from the phone company come round. Juan Pablo Ángel at Aston Villa — his wife was ill and the club gave him no support. In Germany, for example, this would be less of a problem because there are plenty of other South Americans around to form a welcoming committee and help the newcomer ease in."

The way things are going, the same could be said of Liverpool, where there are now five South Americans (Mascherano, Leto, Aurelio, Lucas and Insúa) and a further fourteen Spanish-speaking staff members. These are comprised of six on the coaching/fitness staff and eight players, including youngsters Godwin Antwi and Miki Roque (loaned out for the season), and also including Momo Sissoko and Yossi Benayoun, who both spent a few years in *La Liga*. (Benayoun acted as translator for Mascherano and Tévez at West Ham.) Brazilian Fabio Aurelio obviously learned to speak good Spanish during his six years at Valencia, and that will help Lucas, as the one player who speaks only Portuguese. Even with the best will in the world, the most comprehensive teacher and extensive do-it-yourself CDs, it can take a while to learn English. And while English is the language used at Melwood, Spanish will of course be used at times for new players needing instructions (better to give them directions they understand than to leave them clueless). Settling into life in a new country is that much easier if you have friends who share your native tongue.

So what is English football's reputation on that continent? Has it moved away from the physical, toiling, long-ball fare of the dark ages? Vickery tells me that its profile "has risen unbelievably in South America over the last ten years — and is hugely popular in Argentina, where the game shares a lot of the collective working class roots of industrial society, and they can relate to the atmosphere in the English stadiums. Argentina's sports paper held a survey last year to find the best league in the world — patriotic vote meant that their own came first, but England came second. In Brazil the Premiership would still be seen behind Spain and Italy in terms of profile, but it's much more popular than it was."

So how does this support manifest itself?

"In Argentina there are lots of United shirts in the streets [and this before Tévez signed], and Arsenal as well. I'm also starting to see a few Chelsea. You don't see too many Liverpool, but I'm sure it's just a question of time."

This last point, whilst purely anecdotal, is interesting: suggesting that success in the Champions League doesn't have as much impact in attracting these new fans as their domestic form, given that the trio mentioned represent the last three champions of England, going back to 2003/04. If English football has become far more popular in the last decade, then it makes sense that the successful teams in that time would draw most support, but Liverpool's 2005 victory over Milan would have been expected to garner a lot of affection. The weekly exposure of the Premiership seems to have more impact.

It's almost certain that the Chelsea fans Vickery mentions have been seduced since 2004, so that's an interesting comparison: in the same timeframe Liverpool have reached two Champions League Finals. If this support was based on a long-standing admiration tied in with historical success, then Liverpool would obviously be up there with United in Argentina's affection. While Chelsea have boasted Hernán Crespo, and United have had Gabriel Heinze and Juan Sebastian Veron (who also popped up briefly at Stamford Bridge), Arsenal's popularity debunks the idea that they are merely following the exploits of their countrymen: Arsenal have had no notable Argentines in their history. (In contrast, their neighbours, Spurs, had England's most notable Argentine imports: Osvaldo Ardiles and Ricardo Villa, who arrived in 1978 as newly-crowned World Cup winners, into a league with few overseas players, and were still registered with Spurs when the Falklands War broke out in 1982.)

You would expect that with so many Argentines at the club, and in particular a high profile one like Javier Mascherano, Liverpool's appeal will increase in that country — although Mascherano is not a 'fantasy' type player who will capture the imagination of young fans, unlike his compatriot Carlos Tévez. The success of Mascherano, and in particular Tévez, in the English league should however help encourage other players to follow suit.

The success of South Americans being transferred into English football has been very mixed, although of course the success of *English* footballers transferred within English football has been similarly so — and this includes highly-rated ones who disappeared off the radar following an unsuitable transfer. Not everyone makes the grade following a move, be it from overseas or within the domestic framework. However, if you list all the South Americans bought by Premiership clubs in the last decade — even ignoring those imported before the cultural revolution seen in English football in the mid-'90s, such as Newcastle's Mirandhina, who arrived before the league was conducive to them succeeding — then it still doesn't make the best reading.

Of the outright successes, you'd list Tévez and Mascherano, but at the time of writing based purely on the second half of 2006/07 and the first month of 2007/08. Newcastle's Nolberto Solano is a Tyneside hero, and someone Benítez tried to sign in 2005, so the Peruvian is an unqualified success. Going back to the point when overseas players started flooding into the English game, Brazilians Juninho and Emerson were very successful at Middlesbrough, especially the former during his first spell at the club; he fared less well on his two returns to the north east. Arsenal had some success with Brazilians Edu and Silvinho, although neither was totally outstanding. Juan Pablo Ángel's record at Aston Villa was impressive under John Gregory and David O'Leary, but the Columbian was not trusted by Graham Taylor or Martin O'Neill, and never quite lived up to his £10m price tag. Like Ángel, Hernán Crespo was another relative success, and would have been seen as a great buy at £5-£10m, but a £16.8m price tag (and his previously held record as the world's most expensive player at £35.5m in 2000) raised expectations to the point where even an impressive 20 league goals in 49 games for Chelsea (over half of which contributed to the victorious league campaign in 2005/06) was seen as some kind of failure. Beyond these players it's hard to see any other South Americans who succeeded, although Manchester City's Brazilian Elano, after a promising start at the Eastlands, could well join the list of successes, having become an established Brazilian international in 2006.

The flops — or at least disappointments in one form or another — read as follows: to start with there's Diego Forlan and Júlio Baptista, whose only good games seemed to come at Anfield. There then follows Mark González (who could have done with a few more good games at Anfield), Kleberson, Faustino Asprilla (despite some good moments), Juan Sebastian Veron, Antonio Valencia (who as yet has done okay at Wigan, but no more), Mauricio Pellegrino, Ulises de la Cruz, Agustín Delgado, Christian Bassedas, Daniel Cordone and Clarence Acuna. (The list may have some omissions, simply because the players were so forgettable.) It's worth remembering that this was a mixed bunch of players to start with — not everyone in it was expected to be a world-beater.

## Jewels

South America remains a place to find players blessed with outstanding technical ability. Since Brazil eschewed pure fantasy football for a more balanced approach, allying skill to physique, they've become more like Argentina, whose gifted players always possessed a more ruthless, physical streak. In many ways the continent now breeds players for export, ready-made for the European leagues.

The way Kaká ended up in Italy is an example of the route that Liverpool are following. Winner of the Brazilian Footballer of the Year when playing for São Paulo aged 20, Kaká left for Milan a year later in 2003, going on to become one of the world's top players within a couple of years. In what will hopefully prove a fitting parallel, Liverpool moved in May 2007 to capture Lucas Leiva, the most recent winner of that prestigious award, and also just 20 years of age. Indeed, being three months younger than Kaká was when he won the award, Lucas became the youngest-ever winner of *Placar Magazine*'s esteemed accolade.

Lucas is a very different kind of player to his illustrious predecessor, but has the potential to make a similar impact. Prior to Lucas' honour, the three previous winners of the best player in the Brazilian league were Alex, now at Chelsea after excelling on loan at PSV Eindhoven, Robinho, the Real Madrid winger, and Carlos Tévez, the Argentine striker who earned the title playing for Corinthians. So it's a pretty good indicator of an ability to succeed in Europe's major leagues.

Indeed, Lucas is perhaps the archetypal signing in Benítez's revolution: young, talented (but not in a merely showboating way) and sourced from a part of the world — South America — that was previously out of bounds. Two years ago Benítez promised to look harder for talent in countries like Brazil and Argentina, and while his first few signings from that part of the world struggled to adapt, in terms of value for money it could be a really significant policy if just 50% of the signings show their class.

On the debit side, Mauricio Pellegrino was an ageing free transfer worth a punt; given it allowed Sami Hyypia some rest ahead of the 2005 Champions League latter stages (where the Argentine's off-field assuredness and invaluable experience of such occasions also helped the squad as a whole in its preparations); he proved a wise short-term signing, even if he didn't adapt to English football. Mark González never translated his Chilean and *La Liga* form into the Premiership, but was sold at a small profit. Then there is the promising Argentine centre-back, Gabriel Paletta, who, at just 20 years of age, looked out of his depth in some of his few Liverpool displays; he was not the first young centre-back exposed at a tender age, as Jamie Carragher may have reminded him. Those three signings cost approximately £6m, and González's sale to Real Betis generated £3-4m, while Paletta's exit to Boca Juniors meant the club recouped their initial outlay.

But that brings us to the successes. In January 2007 Liverpool signed two Argentines on 18-month deals. The first was Emiliano Insúa, taken at the age of 17 on loan from Boca Juniors. A regular in the Argentina U20 set-up, he quickly impressed both the coaching staff at Melwood and in his displays for the reserves; word from behind the scenes was that he could feature before the end of the season, which proved the case. In the summer of 2007 he was in the Argentina side that won the Under-20 World Cup in Canada, to further cement his promise. While he's a long way from becoming a Liverpool regular, the potential is there for all to see. It was reported that the deal that took Paletta to Boca Juniors included Insúa's permanent transfer to Liverpool.

But of course the deal of the season was when Benítez took Javier Mascherano — a star of the *actual* World Cup — from barely a bit part role at bottom-of-the-table West Ham to Liverpool's first team, for a nominal fee, with no major cost applicable until the end of his 18-month deal. In some quarters reported as a loan, in reality it was the case that West Ham handed over his full registration to Liverpool.

## Monster Masch

Javier Mascherano had surely one of the most mixed seasons in football history: arriving out of the blue in London with his toothy compatriot, Carlos Tévez, on a wave of euphoria at Upton Park, only for the team to rapidly nosedive, with every league game in which Mascherano featured ending in defeat. Mascherano then moved to Liverpool and, after some excellent displays in the Premiership and Europe, was Man of the Match in the Champions League final. However, neither he nor Tévez could escape the scandal that shrouded their surprise parachuting into Upton Park.

Kia Joorabchian, the man who owns one of the third-party companies responsible for the two players, was influential in Tévez and Mascherano's arrival at West Ham at the end of the August transfer window in 2006. Iranian-born Joorabchian is head of Media Sports Investments, which owns a large stake in Brazilian side Corinthians, for whom both Argentines played. Joorabchian was preparing a £70m deal to buy West

Ham, and ahead of that he was moving two of his star players to London. Although the takeover never came to fruition, the thinking was that the two stars would help West Ham become successful under Joorabchian, while simultaneously placing the two very much in the European shop window, for the continent's best clubs to covet.

And, in a bizarre and roundabout way, their moves did just that. Both players struggled for several months, before ending 2006/07 as two of English football's star talents, albeit 200 miles apart. With Mascherano frozen out by new West Ham boss Alan Curbishley in the winter of '06/07, it made sense for all parties concerned — including that infamous *third*-party — to have Mascherano playing football again. West Ham got him off their wage bill, Liverpool got a top-class player who would fit their system, and MSI had their player back in the shop window, either for Liverpool to make the deal permanent in time, or for another club to be seduced.

Even now, in the summer of 2007, there is much confusion surrounding the deal that brought the players to England. It is not explicitly against Premier League rules for a club to sign a player whose economic rights are owned by a third party — as in the case of Tévez and Mascherano. However, rule U18 states: "No club shall enter into a contract which enables any other party to that contract to acquire the ability materially to influence its policies or the performance of its team."

When signing Tévez and Mascherano, West Ham did just that, entering into a private agreement with the companies that owned their economic rights. The contract stated that those companies had the right to terminate the players' contracts upon payment to West Ham the sum of £2m (in Tévez's case) or £150,000 (in Mascherano's case) in any transfer window. By entering into that agreement, West Ham undisputedly broke rule U18. When the two were registered as players, West Ham failed to disclose that they had entered into an agreement with third-party companies. The Premier League's independent commission said: "This was not only an obvious and deliberate breach of the rules, but a grave breach of trust as to the Premier League and its constituent members. In our finding the club has been responsible for dishonesty and deceit." West Ham pleaded guilty, and somehow managed to escape the points deduction that would have seen them relegated.

What is true, and what gets obscured, is that there was never a problem with Tévez's or Mascherano's *registrations*. The commission ordered West Ham's registration of Tévez to be terminated; instead the club ripped up the third-party agreement, and Tévez was able to see out the remainder of the season, and score the crucial goals that kept them up. Of course, one party ripping up a contract does not make it void, and it is this point that Sheffield United continued to contest after they, and not West Ham, were relegated. After all, it would be very easy in life to get out of contractual obligations by simply shredding the paperwork. Kia Joorabchian said that West Ham "unilaterally terminated the agreement and I have left it in the hands of my lawyer".

The reason Mascherano was free to play for Liverpool, and for the Reds to not face any of the furore surrounding Tévez's continued presence in the West Ham side, was because of the different contract the player signed at Anfield. Mel Goldberg, a lawyer for Max Bitel Greene who specialises in sport, told the BBC: "Mascherano subsequently signed for Liverpool pursuant to a contract entirely different in form to that agreed by West Ham and which has been approved by the Premier League." There were none of the third-party agreements within.

Amidst all the headlines it's easy to forget how good the two players in question are. And, more specifically, how crucial Mascherano could be to the long-term future of Liverpool FC. Diego Maradona described Mascherano as "a monster of a player and destined for great things". But it remains to be seen what will happen when the player's loan deal expires. By doing so well for Liverpool, the Argentine is effectively increasing his own fee in order for the Reds have to dig deeper into their pockets to make the deal permanent. The fear would be a richer club gazumping the Reds for him. It depends on whether the Reds had a first-choice clause in the contract, which you would assume to be the case. It also depends how much say Mascherano himself has in the matter; Liverpool is clearly a club that suits his talents, and has that crucial aforementioned Spanish-speaking core. But the same could be said of teams in Spain, while Italian football would hardly be a culture shock for him. Will MSI want the player to be happy, and enjoying his football at a club like Liverpool, where he will presumably settle further in his second season, or are they merely interested in treating him like a piece of meat to hawk to the highest bidder? The West Ham precedent, where both players looked distinctly shell-shocked and baffled at their presentation to the media, perhaps suggests the latter. But each is now at one of the two most important clubs in the country.

Another bargain came in the form of Lucas. In terms of the potential the Reds are getting for the fee, the signing of the blonde midfielder can hardly fail; even if he doesn't settle, his value will remain high (although of course the Reds need men who can deliver the goods, not those who, in failing, will present some financial redemption). The Reds beat off competition from Inter Milan, Juventus, Atlético Madrid and Barcelona, amongst others, so landing his signature was clearly a coup.

Lucas certainly has the attributes to succeed in English football: more skill than the average Englishman, and more drive than the average Brazilian. Although obviously not a clone of Steven Gerrard, he shares many of the captain's all-round abilities: a box-to-box midfielder who can tackle, pass and score goals.

In 2006 Lucas inspired Grêmio to *Copa Libertadores* qualification, following their return to the Brazilian top flight. Having won the Golden Ball, Lucas earned a first call-up to the senior Brazil squad — for whom he duly played in a friendly, but not one recognised by FIFA. He then skippered his country to triumph at the 2007 South American U-20 Championship, scoring four goals in the process, and helped Grêmio — where he remained until the *Copa Libertadores* campaign was complete — to begin the new Brazilian season in sparkling form. Grêmio won through their group, and beat fellow Brazilian sides São Paulo and top seeds Santos, as well as Uruguayan side Defensor Sporting Club on the way to the final, where they were beaten over two legs by Boca Juniors. Lucas barely featured against Boca due to injury. In August 2007 he won his first official Brazil cap when he came on as a sub in his country's 2-0 friendly win over Algeria in Montpellier.

The nephew of Leivinha, who travelled with Brazil to the 1974 World Cup,

Lucas, like Mascherano, holds an Italian passport, negating any work permit issues. Only time will tell how he adapts to English football, and life in the north-west, but he is clearly the calibre of young player the club should be scouting, particularly before his value soars excessively. Just ask Milan how much Kaká is now worth.

So does Tim Vickery feel the move is too soon for Lucas, as it was for Paletta? I put the question to him. "In an ideal world I think Lucas would stay another year. But in relation to Paletta he has some advantages. He's had more than two years now with a big club — admittedly the first one was helping them out of the second division — Paletta had one year with a tiny club, no experience in the *Libertadores* etc — it was a massive step up — and is paying the price."

And what of Sebastián Leto? "Leto has had a couple of seasons now with Lanus," Vickery explains. "Argentina coach Alfio Basile has recently been working with a 21-strong squad of home based players and Leto was not included, which I think tells you that he's seen as a promising player, not as a world beater."

Leto was highly impressive in his one pre-season run out, against Feyernoord in Rotterdam. But at just 20 he will surely have to bide his time for regular first-team opportunities. His only involvement in August came in the second-leg of the Champions League qualifier against Toulouse, in which he did well without ever excelling.

## Gillett, Hicks and the South American Connection

Benítez's desire to scour South America for players made the arrival of Gillett and Hicks all the more opportune. In February 2007, Gillett, already thinking about the territory, told Reuters in a telephone interview, "We've got a Spanish coach and a number of Spanish players, and I think we can grow our fan base in Central and South America and Mexico."

It's a continent that Liverpool FC now have an eye on beyond simple scouting. Tom Hicks has a number of long-held interests in South American cable television. And Liverpool FC is not his first foray into 'soccer' — in 2001 Hicks, Muse, Tate & Furst invested heavily in two big Brazilian clubs, Corinthians and Cruzeiro. The latter, based in Belo Horizonte, had a phenomenally successful season in 2003, becoming the first team to win the 'triple crown' of Brazilian football: landing the Brazilian Cup, State Championship and Brazilian League, racking up over 100 points and scoring over 100 goals in the process. Corinthians were national champions in 2005, and the following season boasted a certain Argentine duo: Carlos Tévez and Javier Mascherano.

Hicks, Muse, Tate & Furst's investment in Brazil followed what was known as 'Pelé's Law', which stipulated that clubs had to become 'businesses' by the year 2000. Several other big overseas investors pumped money into Brazilian teams: Swiss marketing company ISL did so with Flamengo, Grêmio and Palmeiras; Atlético Mineiro and Santos received investment from Octagon; and Bank of America bought an interest in Vasco da Gama. But the law became a farce when changes in 2001 meant it went from being mandatory to optional (therefore making it somewhat pointless), and the ownership of more than one club was outlawed. Hicks, Muse, Tate & Furst got out of Cruzeiro and Corinthians almost as quickly as they'd arrived, as did those who invested in the country's other major clubs; all escaped with fingers badly burnt. But despite the financial fallout, Cruzeiro and Corinthians had significant success on the field in the aftermath.

The economist Luiz Gonzaga Belluzzo, an ardent football fan, was scathing about Hicks and co.'s investment strategy. Belluzzo told Brazilian magazine, *Revista Pesquisa Fapesp*, "We have the notion that the investors have knowledge of the market better than the common man, but they don't. They place bets that could win out, such as was the case of Hicks with Corinthians and with Cruzeiro", he said. "In football, they made projections that were almost carbon copies of businesses in Europe and the USA. Our people don't have this acquisition power and our capitalism is very poor."

In 2001 Hicks, Muse, Tate & Furst Inc formed a strategic alliance with Spain's Telefonica S.A. in a deal worth about $4billion, allowing Hicks, Muse, Tate & Furst to further expand its cable TV assets in Latin America. At the time, Tom Hicks said the newly-formed company would focus "on cable and pay television, one with significant programming assets that fit perfectly within our overall Latin America media strategy of acquiring synergistic content, sports teams, and pay and cable television assets."

So clearly Latin America is a market where Hicks has built up significant knowledge. Even if all his forays into the area haven't been a success — not necessarily through any fault of his own, such as with the unexpected changes in legislation with Pelé's Law — lessons about the needs of South Americans will have been learnt in the process, and contacts made. It remains to be seen how this will help Liverpool in the long term, but it certainly represents a further opportunity. Increasing Liverpool's exposure on Latin American cable TV will help land new fans, especially as interest in the English game grows in that part of the world.

## The Word *Red*, Spread Around the World

### Half Scouse, Half Yank

Mel Abshier was born six years after the end of WWII at Warrington Air Force Base, the son of a US Air Force father stationed in northwest England and a Liverpudlian mother. America, and Texas specifically, quickly became home at the time of the Cold War. But Liverpool Football Club went with him across the Atlantic like a scent that couldn't be shaken off.

"The early '60s is the earliest I remember," he told me, in relation to when he first recalled being a Liverpool fan. "We used to get the *Echo* and articles sent to Mum from my Gran and friends in Liverpool. But we were raised middle-class at best, and never took a holiday to England because we had four kids in the family. Following the Reds' exploits meant reading those newspapers or watching ABC's *Wide World of Sport*, when it showed the FA Cup or European Cup Final. Those were the only two matches ever shown on US television until the mid 1990s."

Mel has been back to England eight times — twice on business, six times on holiday — and saw the Reds' play a friendly against Celtic in Hartford in one of Rafa Benítez's first games in charge of the Reds. His last three visits to England were with his Liverpool-supporting son in tow. But Liverpool Football Club has somehow managed to follow him to Texas, home of the Hicks clan.

The first game of the 2007/08 season provided the perfect excuse to organise a get-together. "The Official Liverpool Supporters' Club has a branch in Texas," Mel explains. "I am a member and have a fan card through them. Each season we pay dues ($25) to be a member. We have had Ronnie Whelan over previously as a guest of honour. For the first match of the season an invitation was sent out to all members to get together for the Aston Villa match. Bear in mind we have three main cities where Reds gather to watch games: Dallas, Austin, and Houston."

Trinity Hall at 5321 E. Mockingbird Lane, Dallas, is an Irish pub that broadcasts English football. Its website ran an (inadvertently?) amusing announcement ahead of the new season: "Liverpool FC kick off the new season of English Premier League soccer matches at 11am. This is a new fan club for Trinity Hall so don't be surprised by the Red sea up front watching the Big Screen! (For our two Everton Fans, we'll have the SDD feed at 1:15pm.)"

Mel, a regular at Trinity Hall, explains the routine. "This is where all premier league matches are shown. So there is usually a mixture of supporters. As our match was on last with an 11:15 am kick-off time locally, instead of the 6:30am for early Saturday kick-offs, there were a few supporters from Bolton vs Newcastle and around 25 for the West Ham vs Man City match already there. As those were winding down we had more Liverpool supporters in the pub than the other four teams combined."

But there was to be a surprise visitor at Trinity Hall.

"When our match kicked off we had close to 80 supporters. To my surprise Tom Hicks Jr came in near 11am, although I was not sure who he was at the time. He had on the exact same polo shirt as me. As my friends Scott and Simon, who run the supporters' club, were busily registering members, I went up to Tom, tapped him on his arm and said 'Nice shirt'. He turned and said 'Hey, I like yours, too!' And then he went to talk to some of his friends who had nicked a prime table in front of the big screen. It was Simon who said, 'That was Tom Hicks Jr.' So now I was aware of who he was. I also noticed a family resemblence in another lad. Turned out it was Alex Hicks, the younger brother. Alex had come to a Champions League match to watch last season before the takeover. I didn't personally meet him then.

"As the place was virtually packed with all the chairs and specs taken to watch the match, there was a pole up near the big screen at the front-right that was an area to stand near and watch the match. So that's where I headed. The match was just kicking off, I started up the "Liverpool, Liverpool, Liverpool" chant and a lot of supporters chimed in, so we had some songs going. Simon and Scott came over and stood with me and as we were down front, we were just a yard from where Tom Hicks Jr was sitting.

"So into the match we go. All of us ooohing and ahhing as the team controlled possession, or groaning when they lost it. I noticed Tom Jr getting antsy and into the match just like a regular supporter. As the match progressed he joined in all the songs except the new best midfielders in the world one — but I bet he learns it! When we scored he jumped right up out of his seat, jumping up and down like the rest of us crazies and high fiving those near him. During a lull in the action — player down I think — he reached over and tapped me and asked me 'Why do you support the Reds?' So I told him my Mum's from Kirkdale, Liverpool, and I was born just outside Liverpool in Warrington." He said great. And then the match got going again.

"So half-time rolls around, we're up 1-0, and he heads out the door into 90° degree heat to have a ciggie. He chats with his brother, checks his Blackberry, talks with some friends, and to some well-wishers from our Texas chapter, as word had spread as to who he was. I caught him alone and thanked him for the Victory Plaza party for the Champions League Final, and my Mum, who I'd just called, wanted me to tell him the new Stadium pictures were superb.

"So as the second half was about to get rolling again he found his spec and showed those of us near him his Blackberry, which had a screensaver of his cowboy boots — which had a Liverpool crest on them! Into the second half we go, more songs, Fields Of Anfield Road chorus, Scouser Tommy full version, Liverpool-Liverpool, Best Midfield, which really only Simon and I knew — we'll break the rest of them in.

"Tom Jr gets up to go get another lager and he stays on the opposite side this time. He starts singing 'Liverpool, Liverpool' and no one joins in. I lean over to Simon and say, 'you know the Director is shit when he can't get a song going', and we have a big laugh. Tom Jr must have had enough of that side of the pub and came back over and stood behind me and Simon. I say to Tom Jr, 'Decided to come back to where the singers are?' And then we get the 'Liverpool, Liverpool, Liverpool' song going, Tom Jr joining in with an arm draped on each of us and this time we get the crowd into it. He then takes his spec with his lager.

"Well the team wastes chances and sure enough a handball by Jamie and they get a pen, which is duly converted. We were down and needed a lift. So we get the Liverpool chant going again. Minutes later Stevie G steps up and top-corners a free-kick. Cue bedlam. We're all jumping up and down hugging each other and Tom Jr isn't missing a beat either. Another round of high fives and I kick off the Steve Gerrard song. Tom knows the words to that too. Seconds before the final whistle we break out into a rousing YNWA.

"As we gathered to talk about our great win in groups, some of the supporters came up to Tom Jr and had a brief chat. While they were doing that Alex Hicks and I were chatting. He tells the story of the two of them being out one evening and seeing a big lad — mind you, Tom Jr is about 6'3" himself — with a Chelsea top on. Tom Jr yells at him: "Fuck off Chelsea FC, you ain't got no history ..." and over the lad comes to find out who this idiot is. It turns out this lad had just finished a kickboxing workout. Alex tells me that Tom thinks that's what you say to someone with a Chelsea shirt, as that's what they heard last season at the semi-final versus Chelsea at Anfield! Anyway, Tom Jr tells him who he is and they share a laugh. Into a bar they go, Tom Jr gets the beers in. So things got smoothed over easily. But we shared a laugh about that."

So what was the abiding impression of the Hicks clan?

"Tom Hicks Jr. is a very personable person. Has time for people. As does his younger brother, but Alex is a bit more reserved and less physically imposing. Alex told me they were off to Toulouse for the Champions League match then on to Anfield for the Chelsea match the following Sunday. I told them both 'bring us home winners'."

While George Gillett's son, Foster, will take up a role with the club in Liverpool to help bridge the two continents regarding communications, Tom Hicks' sons will be enjoying life as regular Liverpool fans. Very rich ones, at that. But hopefully ones, for their own enduring well-being, who learn to be more selective in which opposition fans they taunt!

## The Final Frontier

Foxfield, situated in the north-west of England, and Foxfield, located at the north of Ireland, are two towns where you'd expect to find a fair few Liverpool fans. But Foxfield, Colorado — a small town about 20 miles southeast of Denver — is by contrast a rather unlikely place to discover a devoted native Red. Indicative of the global reach the game now wields, Whitney Louderback, a 21-year-old American in a town of less than a thousand inhabitants, is a devout born-again Liverpool supporter.

Fadó's Irish Pub, in downtown Denver, is where 'proper' football fans in the area go to watch games. A large establishment with a soulless red brick exterior, it has a surprisingly authentic charm inside. Unlike Trinity Hall, the Irish-ness is almost overbearing, with so many details thrown into the mix. Despite it being part of a chain of pubs, with obligatory themed rooms, there is a lot of incredible rustic accessorising and beautifully thought-out interior design; the charm is faked so well it feels convincing, if a little overdone. It is where Whitney travels to watch games; on 23rd May 2007 it was heaving to the rafters with Reds.

Pretty, in a bookish, trendy-spectacled way, Whitney is studying International Relations at university in Ohio. She tells me that her hopes centre around "going into international conflict resolution or post-conflict reconstruction." (With that in mind she sounds perfect for a leading role at Uefa.) She was not a fan of any club in any sport until 2000, when, aged 14, she fell for the Reds like a schoolgirl developing a crush on Justin Timberlake. (Depending on your generation feel free to alter the cultural reference to Simon Le Bon/David Cassidy/Paul McCartney/Abraham Lincoln).

"I'm a late bloomer, when it comes to footie," she says, instantly surprising, and winning kudos by avoiding the dreaded s-word her compatriots are so fond of. When she does use it, she inserts her own quotation marks to highlight an understanding of how little us Brits like the word. "I started playing "soccer" when I was two ... and absolutely hated it. I much preferred to watch. My older siblings played for years, so at first my only exposure to the Beautiful Game was white suburban kids with orange slices."

It's clear Whitney is about as far as you can get from the kind of fans attracted to the club in Victorian Liverpool, who were male, working class, and from the city. But her love of the game actually has its roots in similar unpretentious surrounds. She continues, "At the time I started going to Mexico a lot, and noticed that every town has a church and a pitch. If they can't afford both, they tend to just have the pitch.

"I started to become educated in the socio-political aspects of the game through my travels, and football became even more fascinating to me. When I was 13 I was staying in the same hotel in Mexico as one of the Mexican youth teams, and they were so amazingly nice and mature that I promised I'd watch a game of theirs when I got back to the States. About that same time, my dad bought a television package with every sport imaginable, so I tried to catch a soccer game. It was in Spanish, and though it seemed relatively enjoyable (and especially entertaining when there was a *goooooooaaaaaaaaaaaaaaaaaal!*), my Spanish wasn't good enough to understand much. I decided to try to find a game in English.

"In late 2000 I found an English game on TV. A team in red was playing a team in blue. Shortly into watching, this one player in red hit the ground quite hard and when he got up blood was pouring down his face, but he refused to leave the pitch for treatment until he was basically forced to. It totally shocked me, because I was used to watching American football where fully padded guys hit the ground and have medics run out immediately."

I point out that this isn't a million miles away from what happens in the Premiership — no extensive shoulder padding or helmets, but more than a few players act like they need airlifting to hospital if they get a crease in their shorts.

"Right after that, this really tiny player in red got possession of the ball and took off from one side of the pitch, passed what looked like 17 opposition players and scored. I had very little grasp of the game as a whole or who any of the players were, but I just knew that I had to start watching football on a regular basis. I also knew that, for me, there would be no other team besides Liverpool."

It can be that simple: the moment love strikes. "Liverpool chose me; I had no say in the matter. I'm lucky to have stumbled upon that game, because every single day I find another reason to love Liverpool FC. To my mind there is no other team like it in the world, in any sport. I may not have been a fan for very long, but that's the one thing I'm sure of."

When not at home in Foxfield, Whitney spends time away at campus, studying at The College of Wooster, Ohio. "To be honest, part of the reason I chose to attend Wooster was due to the high percentage of international students, most of whom are massive football fans. I've converted a number of my non-international friends from Wooster into Liverpool fans. On any given weekend, there are usually a couple of us sitting in my room on campus watching a Liverpool game on my computer — the only way to watch games in that part of Ohio. I try to watch as many games as possible with the other two massive long-term Liverpool fans on campus: one is from Ghana, the other from Jamaica."

Do people take her seriously as a Liverpool fan? How does she think she will fare during the forthcoming year in Ireland, which forms part of her course?

"Every Liverpool fan I've ever met has been amazing to me. I'll admit some are skeptical that I'm anything more than a glory hunter, or doubt that I am true fan, but it doesn't take very long to convince them that my intentions are pure. I do, however, try to put more effort into being a fan, knowing that I'm an out-of-towner. I've done my best — and still do everyday — to learn everything I can about the club's past, and I know that I will never be able to rival the passion of someone who's held a season ticket for three generations [I resist interjecting to point out that these are usually the ones who are fast asleep in the Main Stand], but at the end of the day, no matter where we may be, we're all fans of this great club, and I think that's all that really matters."

So how is the profile of football changing in America? Has the influx of U.S. businessmen — such as Malcolm Glazer, Randy Lerner and Liverpool's Hicks and Gillett — seen an increase in awareness?

"Since the American takeovers, news about football is starting the hit the papers a lot more than in the past. Stan Kroenke, who owns the Denver Nuggets — our basketball team — is trying to increase his share in Arsenal, so that's been in the Colorado papers a lot recently. I'd say that the news of David Beckham's transfer to LA made a bigger impact on increasing football's profile than the American takeovers have. In the direct aftermath of the Galaxy buying Beckham this past winter, I noticed a lot of people on the streets — way more than ever in the past — were making 'soccer' a topic of their everyday conversation, whereas the American takeovers haven't had the same impact.

"I have definitely noticed that from the time I first started following Liverpool up to today, football is increasing — I'd almost say exponentially — in popularity. In comparison to the rest of the world, America doesn't really care about the game, but in comparison to seven years ago, the atmosphere here has improved leaps and bounds. I'm only going on anecdotal evidence and personal experience, but I honestly think a lot of it is due to the influence of immigrants — especially those from Latin America, particularly Mexico. Footie used to be a sport for richer, white upper-middle class suburban kids on fancy purpose-built pitches, but more and more I'm seeing it played by people of all ages and backgrounds on the streets and in the parks. It seems to be penetrating American society from the bottom up, in a way that I think might greatly positively impact the future of football in America — as long as our immigration policies don't become too oppressive, in terms of kicking people out."

(At the time of our interview, George Bush is proposing new laws that get tougher on immigration — when immigration was, after all, what formed modern America.)

"That said, David Beckham still seems to be what most Americans think of when they hear about soccer, and at that, he's often seen more as a model — he's in a lot of print ads — or the husband of the Spice Girl. However, in the aftermath of the 2006 World Cup, Zinedine Zidane has become fairly well-known, albeit as something along the lines of "that crazy dude who head-butted the other dude". Things are getting better, but most Americans know very little about football, and I wouldn't say American knowledge is very nuanced. But then again, the sport faces a lot of competition for attention in the States. In Denver alone, we have eight professional sports teams, our football team has won the Super Bowl twice and our hockey team has won the Stanley Cup once."

Perhaps Whitney will remain in the vast minority: a genuine Liverpool fan from America, without the recent ancestry — such as English, Irish or Italian relations — to automatically draw her into the sport. How America continues to take to football remains to be seen. It doesn't seem that many British fans are desperate for the approval of the States when it comes to our national sport — seeing it as up to them if they take it or leave it, so long as they don't try to Americanise it. There's also that paradox between wanting to share something that is loved with all and sundry, and at the same time wanting to keep it all to yourself. Most impressive about Whitney is her genuine desire to learn about the club and its history, rather than just hop onto a ride already in progress without questioning previous stops along the way, and their significance. In that sense she is a credit to an ever-expanding fan-base.

## The Irish Red Sea

Westport, County Mayo. Its name gets straight to the point: a port on the west coast of Ireland, 30 miles north of Galway. A scenic town, Westport boasts the feel of a provincial French village, with winding avenues and shops arcing up hills. Old buildings with unusually colourful façades — yellow, lime, orange, deep red, bright blue — belie their age yet retain their charm. The town somehow manages to be both sleepy and vibrant; relaxed and busy. It has a quaint feel, but also modern amenities and trendy internet café bars. It's rustic without being an anachronism.

It is late August 2005, and the Westport Supporters' Club is meeting on the tenth anniversary of its formation. Over 100 members are present, here to sample the European Super Cup Final on a big screen with a pint of the black stuff, three months after gathering to witness the greatest night in their football-watching lives. For good measure, a re-run of the Istanbul final is also on the agenda; not that memories need refreshing. I am present as guest of honour, following the recent release of my first book.

There are a lot of Irish stereotypes around, but one which is deservedly true relates to an innate friendliness. It's also true that the country has a high proportion of Liverpool fans. As in the Far East and Australia, the following for English football seems to have arisen decades ago due to a lack of any meaningful kind of professional domestic league. Liverpool were high-profile during the '60s and '70s, and the city is a short ferry ride away from Ireland's east coast, so the attraction, as it is with Manchester United, is fairly logical. The Westport Supporters' Club was formed in 1995, after a gang of Reds met up in the local pub; a loose gathering quickly became an official collective.

At half-time, with the Reds trailing to CSKA Moscow in Monaco, I get talking to Peter Flynn, the club's treasurer and the man who has organised tonight's event. With genial face and gentle manner, he stands fractionally taller than Steven Gerrard in a picture I am shown of the two: Peter presenting the Liverpool captain with

Westport's 2004 Player of the Season award. Also in the picture is Christy Moran, a small man in his late 40s with a slightly lazy eye but a sharp mind regarding Liverpool. The chairman of the supporters' club and I had a brief chat earlier in the evening, when he spoke ten-to-the-dozen about the Reds, with an almost religious fervour. The man is an *intense* fan. I sense that if cut, he would bleed red with microscopic white Liverpool crests.

Peter tells me more about how their supporters' club came into existence. "The formation coincided with a time when the country as a whole was emerging from a long period of depression, when jobs and cash were very scarce. At present we have a hardcore group of about 60 people with about another 50–100 who tend to change over time. Many of our new supporters are parents who decide to take little Mary or Johnny to their first Liverpool game and we are more than happy to assist if at all possible. Ultimately, these kids are the next generation of Reds supporters and if we can help to keep the Liverpool legacy alive then we feel we are playing our part even it is only a minor contribution.

"The first official trip to Liverpool was organised at the start of the 1996/97 season after we got confirmation from LFC that we would receive an allocation of 30 tickets for the home game against Villa in January 1997."

There was another first that day: a full league debut in midfield for Jamie Carragher, who marked the occasion with a goal. Little did the Westport boys know they were witnessing something that would prove about as frequent as Halley's Comet.

"For nearly all of us that travelled over in January it was a first time ever to see the Reds live. It was also a time before low fare airlines so the only option for people was to travel by boat to England. Our travels started Friday morning at 7.25am when we got a train to Dublin, which took just under four hours. From the train station in Dublin we then had to make our way to Dun Laoghaire to catch the ferry at 2pm. We got into Holyhead just before 5pm and two trains later we finally arrived in Liverpool, roughly 12 hours after leaving Westport.

"It was my first time ever seeing Liverpool playing in the flesh, and my first experience of Anfield. Even after multiple visits since then, the memory of seeing what looked like a green carpet and hearing *You'll Never Walk Alone* at the beginning of the game will always remain with me. The journey back on the Sunday followed the same route as getting there, and although it took us over 24 hours coming and going it was worth every minute just to be there.

"Since then 30 to 40 of us travel over two or three times a year, with a few of us also trying to get to a European game whenever possible. Thankfully with Ryanair and Knock Airport we can now get to Liverpool in about three hours."

So why Liverpool?

"I have been supporting the Reds since the age of four when my friend and neighbour Paul O'Grady and I used think we were Kevin Keegan and Stevie Heighway! Back in the early '70s in Westport we had one TV Channel (RTE) which only showed events like the FA Cup Final and European Cup. To follow Liverpool it was the newspaper, *Shoot* magazine or BBC Radio, which had a brutal reception most of the time! That said I can especially remember tuning into games mid-week against Wolves, Derby, St. Etienne, Borussia Mönchengladbach, to name but a few. I hadn't a clue at the time where any of them were but it didn't matter once we got the result. We only hit the big time in the mid '80s when the west of Ireland finally got BBC and *Match of the Day*.

"I fully sympathise with locals not getting tickets, but knowing the gang from our fan club in Westport there is no-one lacking the knowledge, passion and voice required to be a true Red. I suppose not surprisingly since Liverpool won the Champions League in 2005, getting tickets via the Official Supporters' Club is getting harder and harder."

As in Istanbul, the game in Monaco goes to extra-time, with Djibril Cissé having got the Reds back in the game in the second half of normal time. This time penalties aren't required, as Cissé again, and then Luis García, wrap up a 3-1 victory, and the Super Cup is Liverpool's. Irish eyes are smiling.

## 'Rocket Ronny', So Much to Answer For

Haifa: the largest city in northern Israel and the third-largest city in the country, with a population of over a quarter of a million. A bustling and scenic seaport located on Israel's Mediterranean coastline in the Haifa Bay, about 60 miles north of Tel Aviv, it has the bizarre distinction of being twinned with Hackney and Newcastle. Clearly, with its palm trees, blue skies and shimmering turquoise waters, it is the glass-slippered Cinderella to those two ugly sisters. Haifa is home to a mixed population of Jews, Muslims and Christian Arabs, who are mostly secular. As such, Haifa stands apart from the rest of Israel because its public transport runs on Saturdays, the Jewish Sabbath. Hi-tech companies like Intel, IBM and Microsoft have opened Research and Development facilities in the city, while Haifa also hosts two world-class academic institutions: the University of Haifa, and the Technion — Israel Institute of Technology. It is a modern metropolis in every sense.

Ran Stotsky, native of Haifa, writes about Liverpool for the Israeli Liverpool FC Supporters' website, and translates news and opinion pieces from the English media into Hebrew.

So what attracted him to Liverpool in the first place? "Being a Maccabi Haifa fan practically from birth, and being a not-quite-over-developed kid during the late '80s/early '90s, I collected newspaper clippings of my heroes in green, and pasted them into notebooks. When any of the players left Maccabi and went to play for European clubs, I continued following them, until I came across a photo of Ronny Rosenthal signing for Liverpool FC wearing that Candy-sponsored Adidas shirt.

"The Israeli TV, which only had a single channel back then, used to broadcast one English football match every week, on Saturday evenings. Most weeks it featured Liverpool. So I had no problem watching Ronny on an almost weekly basis. And then I saw Grobbelaar, and Barnes, and Rush, and before I knew it — I was hooked. I was 12 at the time, re-born as a Liverpool fan.

"I know Ronny Rosenthal might not count as the best reason of all to become a

Liverpool supporter. If anything, he might serve as a good excuse to switch to rugby or something! But, nonetheless, that's how it happened. I know other supporters here in Israel have similar stories. Some followed Rosenthal like me, others — a bit older, obviously — followed Avi Cohen, who was at the club from 1979 to 1981. Some just watched Liverpool in black-and-white broadcasts every single week and just couldn't say no.

"So I became a Liverpool supporter around the age of 12, in 1990, which means my support for the club was shaped in a period during which the club didn't exactly rule European or English football. The drought years. I am aware, of course, of the history and heritage. Since then I've also tried watching as many past matches as I possibly could, but still — Liverpool, to me, is quite the underdog, really. And I actually think I like it better this way. This way I can experience the rebuilding of a new legacy, instead of living in the past. Plus it suggests I'm not a glory hunter — or at least not a very successful one. Until 2005, that was.

"So then over the years it slowly grew, until I found myself, six years later, making an extremely expensive phone call to the Liverpool official store hot-line from a payphone in the army base where I was stationed, spelling my name and address to the nice lady on the other side — 'S' for Steve, 'T' for Toshack ... to order my original shirt.

"And then came the internet. The internet, naturally, had a huge impact on the options a foreign Liverpool fan had, and on the depth of support one can delve into. Suddenly you had access to all that information — the history, the names, the folklore. What is that strange bird on the crest? What exactly *did* happen in Hillsborough? Suddenly the developing obsession had found all this food for its soul.

"And, of course, all of a sudden you had the option of communicating with fellow Liverpool fans. Not like those who were around you in Israel, who *liked* Liverpool but were real supporters of some godforsaken Israeli team or another, but rather actual Liverpudlians, who feel the atmosphere, who breath the air, who live the dream!

"However, then I discovered that being an Israeli Red comes with its very own inferiority complex. You know that the team you support, the club that means more to you than anything else actually 'belongs' to the people of a city you don't have any roots in, or any historic relations with. When you talk to fellow Reds on internet forums, you read a lot about OOTS and although you resent the hierarchy in supporter-classes, and although the energy, emotions, time and money the club costs you can be just as significant as any Scouser's, deep down you know they're right. After all, you do have your own hometown football club, what are you doing leeching on to theirs? But there isn't much we can do about it now, is there? I imagine this feeling is shared amongst all foreign Liverpool supporters, but probably has more impact on people who don't speak English as a native tongue.

"Despite what one might think, especially after watching one too many Eurovision song contests, Israel is not exactly all camels and barefoot people walking on non-paved streets wearing sheets. It's actually quite a developed, western and modern country, so today everything's much easier. With the internet and satellite/cable TV we can watch almost any official Liverpool match live in the comfort of our own homes — the Premiership is on pay-per-view — or in a sports bar. There's one pub around that I know of that even broadcasts reserves matches occasionally, and when we happen to come across a ridiculous amount of money, Anfield is just a five-hour-flight away. Istanbul was even closer. Quite a few of us were in Istanbul, on *that* night in May.

"So now we have our very own supporters' club, and our very own website with forums where we discuss everything related to LFC. Occasionally we dress up in our favourite LFC kits, and meet in a pub to watch the match together. Of course, there is one problem, though — our weekend doesn't include Sundays. Our work days are Sunday to Thursday, and Friday to Saturday is the weekend. Since missing Liverpool's Sunday action — or Sunday's big match in general, when Liverpool play on Saturday — isn't really an option, once I left the army and found a proper job, I cut down 20% of my salary together with 20% of my work hours, so I can conveniently work four days a week — Monday to Thursday, and have Sundays all to myself and the Reds. Without a doubt, the smartest decision I've made career-wise, bar none."

Ran clearly speaks in the universal language of football: the pain of a defeat. It's a good way to judge how much we care. I tell him that I've learned to recover from a terrible result more quickly than in the past, but when the final whistle sounds the sick feeling in the pit of the stomach is hard to shift.

"A loss, especially when coupled with a below par performance, can ruin my entire week. A great win can lift me for a few days. April 15th is a memorial day, even if I don't know anyone who's actually been there. Hey, if there's one thing us Jewish/Israelis are good at — it's memorial days. There is one major difference I can think of: I don't hate Everton quite as much as the average Liverpudlian does. I can empathise with the emotions a derby match arises, and I do get more excited when Luis García scores a goal against the bitters than when he does against — let's say — Sunderland. But when none of your next door neighbours, or your classmates, or your work colleagues, is an Evertonian — it's just not the same. It's not that I like them or anything, but let truth be told — I despise Manchester United and recently Chelsea much more."

This backs up the theory that, for overseas fans, rivals for trophies are more loathed than those contesting city bragging rights: the threat of inflicting pain is what drives inter-club conflicts, and that varies depending on where you live. For a Scouser, an Everton victory can have a major affect. That flawed football logic arises in the Toffees' taunts: beat your neighbours twice in a season and it confirms you are better than them, even if the league table or European success tells the opposite story. I'm sure Liverpool fans have felt the same thing in recent years, when doing the double over Manchester United.

So how complete is Ran's transformation from Maccabi Haifa to Liverpool?

"I no longer follow Maccabi Haifa that closely. It's true that they're my hometown club, and they are actually the reason I discovered LFC, and I do watch their matches whenever I get the chance — for nostalgic reasons, mostly — but being the monogamist that I am, I've found it possible to contain only one true love, albeit a long distance relationship."

After my first conversation with Ran, in the spring of 2006, Israel began to play a more prominent part in Liverpool's story. First, in August 2006 the Reds drew Maccabi Haifa in the Champions League qualifier, a game that would take place against the backdrop of continued Middle-Eastern troubles; as such, the tie was moved to the Ukraine, much to the chagrin of Israel. Then, almost a year later, came the signing of Yossi Benayoun, the country's most gifted player. It was a good excuse for Ran to update his story. Will it change the lives of Liverpool fans in Israel?

"For the past three years or so we've had two pay-per-view channels that have been broadcasting live football from the Premiership and from our own national football league. During the last couple of seasons, West Ham — with Benayoun, and briefly Yaniv Katan — and Bolton — with Ben-Haim, and briefly Idan Tal — were shown live considerably more often than any other Premiership team.

"In fact, when either team played at the same time as Liverpool, they always chose to show the 'Israeli' team, so chances of watching the Reds live on TV in the comfort of our homes were not as widespread as we'd hoped, especially after Istanbul, and we were forced to find a bar with a satellite dish, or get a satellite dish installed ourselves.

"As for Champions League matches, we have two channels that broadcast them live, which means four matches are broadcast live in each double match-day, two on Tuesday and two on Wednesday. [One game being truly live, the other broadcast as 'live' later in the evening.] For some mysterious reason they usually favour showing Barca/Chelsea/Milan matches over LFC ones, at least until they were left no options, e.g. we've reached the quarter-finals again. So we've been having the same problem there, too.

"So now that an Israeli player has signed for Liverpool, I imagine you'd expect all of us here to be thrilled — if not for Liverpool FC, at least for ourselves as Israeli supporters. Indeed, Liverpool is bound to be shown all over the place: Premier League, Champions League — even the pre-season friendlies against South China and Portsmouth were shown live on pay-per-view. Plus, news coverage of Liverpool will grow immensely, no doubt about it: it could be seen immediately, with minute-by-minute match reports of our friendly against Crewe Alexandra in Israeli sports and news sites, which never used to report anything Liverpool-related."

So what about the Maccabi Haifa game a year ago? How did the tensions surrounding the tie affect Israeli perceptions of the Reds?

"Rafa said it would be mad to make Liverpool go play in Israel, which instantly made him and Liverpool FC public enemy number one [— Palestinians aside, I hope —] for a brief while among some Israelis who probably weren't Liverpool supporters, and who obviously were colossally unaware of the greater scheme of things. Liverpool got plenty of media coverage back then, and extremely negative coverage at that. And now, Benayoun has signed, and Liverpool FC have instantly become the 'Israeli' premier league team. The nation's pride. The great red hope. What a difference one year can make, eh?"

Ran's last comment highlights the fickle nature of fans who are actually just following a favourite player, like Reds will have done when Kevin Keegan went to

Hamburg or Ian Rush to Juventus. It's not the club they support, but the player. Perhaps it's more pertinent for those who follow David Beckham rather than the teams he represents. But the example of Ran also shows that when that favourite player has moved on, as in the case of Ronny Rosenthal well over a decade ago, some genuine fans are left behind, caught in the thrall, to continue following the club they have since fallen head-over-heels in love with.

## Asia: The Rising Red Sun

Singapore: a small island nation at the southern tip of the Malay Peninsula, with a densely-packed population of almost five million. A former British colony, dating from the time Association Football was taking root back at the heart of the Victorian empire, English is still one of its official languages. English football is definitely a strong part of its lexicon. Having merged with Malaysia in 1963 upon breaking free of British rule, Singapore was expelled from the federation just two years later, and subsequently became an independent country.

Malaysia, situated to the north, consists of two geographical regions divided by the South China Sea. Peninsular Malaysia (or West Malaysia), which borders Thailand to the north, is a federation of thirteen Southeast Asian states. It consists of nine sultanates, two states headed by governors (Malacca and Penang), and two federal territories, including Kuala Lumpur, the capital. Malaysian Borneo (or East Malaysia) occupies the northern part of the island of Borneo, bordering Indonesia and surrounding the Sultanate of Brunei.

Asia remains the strongest outpost for Premiership passion. With no great tradition of indigenous football — although the sport continues to grow at local levels — fans looked overseas for its professional representations, and especially to England.

Asia is the continent where English clubs most keenly fight for supporters. The Reds' trip to Hong Kong in the summer of 2007, to participate in the Barclays' Asia Trophy — where they played South China FC and Portsmouth — was met with delirium in stands awash with red. The players of Portsmouth and Fulham (the other English team competing) dubbed the event the 'Barclays' Liverpool Trophy', such was the interest in the Reds and relative apathy towards the two smaller Premiership clubs. If it's unfair on Liverpudlians to suggest such fans can match their unique passion for the club on their doorstep, there does seem to be a greater *hysteria* in the Far East: more idolising, perhaps, given how the distance makes the players seem that much more *exotic*. The footballers are seen more like Hollywood actors.

"The one thing that many Englishmen fail to realise is just how big the premiership is in this part of the world," Dinesh Selvaratnam, a 37-year-old pilot for Malaysia Airlines, tells me. Dinesh has been a Liverpool fan since the age of ten, dating back to the club's European heyday. "Premiership clubs are now beginning to understand the scale of the fan base in Asia, hence the tours that have now become commonplace. Traditionally, clubs like Liverpool, Manchester United, Arsenal and Spurs have had the largest following in Malaysia for many years, and of course in recent times amongst the youngsters Chelsea has become popular due to obvious reasons. During our family reunions, there is constant argument amongst the cousins about whose team is better, etc.. As a matter of interest, four are Liverpool fans, three Man United, and one each supports Arsenal, Spurs and Newcastle. There are official fan clubs for most teams and most do congregate in certain venues on game day. The atmosphere is great. Everyone comes out in their jerseys and they follow they game intensely.

"The TV coverage we get over here is comprehensive to say the least. Thanks to ESPN Asia and STAR Sports, almost all the premiership games are telecast either live or delayed. Of course there are repeats of the choice games during the week. Most households subscribe to our local satellite provider which carries these channels, unless you don't opt for the sports packages.

"Personally, I prefer to stay at home and watch Liverpool games alone because I find that there are less distractions and I can take in more of the little details. I also get pretty annoyed at most of the stupid statements and remarks from some other viewers — including the less-knowledgeable Liverpool fans. I find that I take in more of the game this way and enjoy it better."

Upon this we are in agreement. There are two distinct ways of viewing football: the more concentrated focus of intently 'studying' the action in quiet isolation; or as part of a group, either in a pub or at the game itself; where thoughts can be influenced by reactions of the crowd, and where, at times, getting the best view isn't always possible — but where atmosphere, and the bond amongst fans, is paramount.

"These games are easily viewed at almost every pub and most local cafes in Kuala Lumpur," Dinesh says. "On my travels, I have found it so much more difficult to catch a game on TV in England than in Kuala Lumpur! During the entire season, I watch almost all of the Liverpool games live. That means waking up at 3am for midweek matches. This drives my wife up the wall but she has given up trying to change me. I have missed weddings and birthdays and other occasions simply because there is a Liverpool match on!

So how much money does he spend on following the Reds?

"I spend about RM 1080 a year on satellite TV. Don't convert the currency as it will give you a false idea — better to compare that to the average annual income in this country. I have bought three jerseys and three polo/T-shirts over the years. My four-year-old son has an LFC kit, and my daughter a cute top, albeit a fake. I also buy some of the club's DVDs. Last year I travelled to Istanbul to catch the Liverpool vs Galatasary match. I'm planning to make a trip to Anfield this season. If Anfield was in my country, I would watch any and every match I could get a ticket for."

Chua Wee-Kiat, known as Kit, a Singapore government worker, started supporting LFC in 1993 because of a certain Robbie Fowler, who broke onto the scene in spectacular fashion. "Before that," Kit tells me, "I was more of a general Premiership football fan with a slight preference for Spurs. After 1993, my support for Liverpool just deepened with every passing season.

"In Singapore, there are legions of LFC fans. Two years ago, in a local paper, a survey was done to find out which of the two most supported clubs in Singapore — Manchester United or Liverpool — has more fans. It was done via SMS — one mobile phone number per vote — and the result was hardly surprising. LFC fans outnumber Man United fans by a mile.

"Many of my friends who are die-hard supporters of LFC do go to bars to catch live games, but I prefer to stay at home to watch cable, being a family man. With regard to how much I spend following the Reds: basically, I pay for the cable TV subscription, buy the LFC magazine, occasional shirts online, and some training shirts/jerseys. We get almost every Liverpool game here live on cable. It's just that the hours for the European games are typically between 2am — 5am so that's quite tough due to work commitments the following day, but I never miss any games — and haven't for the past several years."

Kit and Dinesh are just two fairly representative examples of Far Eastern support. Both buy a reasonable amount of official club merchandise, and as such contribute to the club's finances; a contribution that will presumably be better tapped into across the whole region once the commercial activities of the club are better executed. Both men are committed to following the Reds, and not casual observers. Watching the games on TV at ungodly hours is a priority, and that's definitely a genuine kind of fanaticism.

## Tapas Time

A cramped tapas bar, tucked away on a narrow *Las Ramblas* side street, and near the famous Boquería Market in the heart of Barcelona. It is lunchtime on the day after the night before: Liverpool's unlikely comeback to beat the reigning European Champions on their home turf. And some occasion it had been. Official attendance figures suggested 88,000 were present, and after 20 minutes 87,999 of those felt Barcelona were going to win at a canter. The only person who didn't was Pablo 'El Loco' Cazorla: a man of such limited mental capacity, and so high on crystal meth, he thought the game would be won by either the Boston Red Sox or the mixed doubles pairing of Björn Borg and Martina Navratilova.

In the bar with me is Taskin Ismet, a man in his mid-30s who works co-ordinating Spanish and Portuguese medical assistance as part of the travel insurance of tourists from Britain and Ireland. Much of his summer is spent dealing with the patching up (or, at times, scraping up) of Brits who've had too much sangria and fallen — or leapt — from their lofty hotel balconies. Thankfully, February is a little quieter in his line of work, and he can indulge his passion for football with a couple of days out of the office.

Taskin somehow manages to combine in his heritage the major landmarks of Benítez-era Liverpool to date: he is part English, part Turkish (though not from Istanbul), and has been living and working for a number of years in Spain. (Okay — Catalonia, if we're being precise.) A Red since his younger years growing up in the UK, he spent the previous evening in the home section of the *Camp Nou*, where, from time to time, he watches *La Liga* games as a neutral with his Barcelona-supporting friends.

So how was his presence in a red shirt the night before received?

"I had some healthy banter along the lines of two European Cups as opposed to five," he tells me, "and about a certain group of supporters having no passion, no songs and no faith in their team — this was when the surrounding mute Barça fans complained about the Reds among them singing. There was also some collective white hanky waving as the not-so-faithful began to troop off with a full ten minutes to go. It was all in good humour, except for one woman who threatened to kill me. My joy was complete when her husband screamed 'shut up woman, he's speaking the truth!'"

As I try my luck with the menu — the Catalan/English translations are inept, and it's somewhat alarming to think what '*mussels nailed to a sailor's blouse*' could possibly be — Taskin runs me through the reaction of the local papers laid out before us.

"They're crying out with every excuse you can think of: the Barça fans were 'diluted' by the Liverpool fans dotted all around, and so lost their effect on the team as they were out-sung. They blame the officials and stewards — the fact that they don't generally sing seems to have been ignored. Ronaldinho is fat. Ronaldinho is mentally exhausted. Ronaldinho is fat, mentally exhausted and his heart isn't in it. The pressure has got to Frank Rijkaard and he has lost his marbles, hence his decision to drop Iniesta and also to play Saviola. The team has a superiority complex and thought they'd won in the first 20. And my personal favourite: the squad are still in a state of shock from their loss in the World Club Championship in Japan, some three months earlier."

## Dizzy Heights

Taking up a spec in the away end at the *Camp Nou* is akin to watching football from an airship overlooking the stadium. The very back row in the away end gives a distorted view of the city above the roof of the stand opposite. You are so high you feel you are looking directly down on play. It is hugely disorienting. You have to rely on the players' running styles to tell who's who.

The Reds seem to start without too many nerves, and are exerting some control on the game. But Barça look capable of working a bit of magic on the edge of the box at any moment. In a statement of intent, the Reds flood forward early on, getting into some half-decent positions in the first three minutes. Then, in the fourth minute, John Arne Riise is put in behind the Barcelona back four, but he fails to pick out Bellamy who has faced open goal in a central position.

Pepe Reina is facing his former club, and Xabi Alonso lines up against his father's club. Luis García, another ex-Barcelona player, watches from the stands. New Spanish right-back Alvaro Arbeloa is making his full debut, mirroring Rob Jones in both style of play and by being equally comfortable at left-back. (He will go on to snuff out the threat of teenage prodigy Lionel Messi, both home and away.) Peter Crouch, who has done so much to get the Reds to this stage of the competition and whose height worries Barcelona fans, has been left out, with Dirk Kuyt starting in a midfield-striking link role, behind Craig Bellamy. Benítez goes into the game on the back of two wins and a draw at the stadium during his time with Valencia. He knows how to get a result at the *Camp Nou*.

Bellamy's inclusion is notable, given that it comes just days after the infamous incident in Portugal. But it proved a masterstroke, with his headed goal cancelling out Barcelona's early lead, and the Welshman's incredibly astute pass setting up John Arne Riise — the very man he was accused of assaulting — for the winner. As if to prove that you just can't make up this kind of stuff, Riise used his *right* foot.

After those promising early moments, Liverpool were caught out by a quick Catalan counter, with Deco stealing in at the back post to head past Reina. For the next 15 minutes it looked like Liverpool could have had 30 players out there and not got close to the ball. But somehow the Reds held out; while possession was nine-tenths of Barça law, as they gave-and-went and wove intricate triangular passages of play, they couldn't get past a resolute back line that did enough to deny any clear goalscoring opportunities. With half-time approaching, Bellamy rose to head past Víctor Valdés, who had mocked Liverpool's chances of success in the build up to the game. Valdés fumbled Bellamy's header which, given the tight angle, he could only direct towards goal. Dirk Kuyt followed in with a poacher's instinct, but the ball had already crossed the line. With less than 17 minutes of a worry-free second-half remaining, Riise struck the killer blow. Rijkaard had been throwing on attacker after attacker, withdrawing more defensive-minded players, in an apparent obsession to win the game rather than take a draw to Anfield. That left his team unbalanced, and rather than pose problems for the Reds it undermined his own team's chances. (In a fortnight's time, the Catalans would scrape a victory courtesy of a late Eidur Gudjohnsen goal, but Barça lacked belief on a night when the Reds twice hit the woodwork at 0-0, and totally dominated. It really would have stretched credibility if Momo Sissoko's instinctive 40-yard first-time shot had dipped just under the bar rather than striking it full-on, following another Valdés howler.)

Back in the tapas bar the day after the first game, Taskin tells of the reaction to Reds invading the city: "Liverpool fans are being roundly praised overall and there have only been the odd quotes about anything remotely nearing trouble. Most complaints have been about getting covered in beer at each goal. The general feeling before and after the game seems to be of awe. We are regularly quoted as the loudest, most passionate and best behaved.

"It's a theme here that whenever I mention that I support Liverpool, I'm asked if I've experienced hearing *You'll Never Walk Alone* sung on the Kop. Anfield is described as a 'mythical stadium' and many Barça (and Espanyol) fans hold it as an ambition to go to Anfield and hear *You'll Never Walk Alone* sung 'live' at Anfield. I can't speak for the rest of Spain, but we definitely come out on top here. Celtic are also occasionally mentioned as being loud, and at the same time friendly, but we always seem to be the most revered. This comes from the radio, TV, papers and also your average fan in the street. If you'd taken a walk into *Plaça Real* where the majority of the Reds fans congregated, or to the top of the Rambla where I went when I left you guys yesterday, you would have seen groups of locals with cameras and videocams filming the travelling Kop with big beaming smiles.

"A friend of mine — a Barça fan — who went to the game with us summed it up when he said that the very description of 'supporting' a team in Spain is alien. According to him, they go to the stadium to 'suffer'. He also said that it was billed as a 'classic' game simply because it was Liverpool, and that was due to our supporters as well as our history. I met him just after I left you as he'd taken the day off work to see the fans. Chelsea on the other hand are just considered to be your classic English 'hooligans' and are not to be mixed with.

"They appreciate the fact that 'we' are loud, passionate, but always friendly. They are amazed at the repertoire of songs and the fact that we even sing when losing. There was a quote in the local Barça rag the following day that the Barça fans had been diluted by a swarm of Red whose first reaction after going a goal down was not to fight, but to sing. It mentioned that the Barça fans could learn a thing or two.

"There is still a feeling of trepidation here for the return leg and the noise and passion of the crowd that they will face seems to hold the biggest fear for them. I think its incredible when you consider that their stadium holds double the amount of people as ours that fear of passion and noise should even be considered as an issue for them at all."

With Barcelona beaten, anything is starting to appear possible. Perhaps even reaching a second Champions League Final in three years. Or would that be getting carried away?

## The Scouse Descendent

The Best Western Hotel on the picturesque coastal resort of Glyfada, Athens. Its foyer is awash with light, streaming in through open patio doors, with bright beams spinning across the room every time the revolving front door is used. Men and women in Liverpool tops come and go, while others hang around in the large sofas or on bar stools. More sit outside in the searing heat. There are less than ten hours until the kick off to the 2007 Champions League Final.

I sit chatting with Adrian Mervyn, with whom I have attended over 200 games over the past 14 years, but mostly between 1993 and 2002. I first met Adrian in the early '90s, when I joined the Sunday League team for which he played, whose pitch was on the outskirts of West London. At my first training session he wore a Liverpool kit, so we got to talking. He was a season ticket holder at Anfield, along with his dad; both had been so for many years. Almost a decade older than me, he'd been at the European Cup Finals at Wembley in 1978, in Rome in 1984, in Heysel in 1985 and at Hillsborough four years later. A friendship was struck up, and before too long I was making use of his dad's season ticket when he was unable to go, or, when I could get my own ticket, travelling up with the two of them. Up until then I'd managed to get to a few games, having first gone to Anfield under my own steam in 1990. A few years after I met Adie my own season ticket came through, and I had my seat moved alongside Adie's and his dad's in the Lower Centenary at the Kop end.

Adie is an incredibly honest, straightforward person who has always been able to take a joke. One summer, a year or two after I first met him, we turned up for the first pre-season training session of the forthcoming season. Adie, who was as bald as a coot, somehow turned up with a full head of lush dark brown hair. Someone instantly quipped, "Fucking 'ell, Adie, where you been on holiday — Chernobyl?" He took it in good humour, although the hair didn't take quite so well after the revolutionary new technique failed him, and was gone within a few months.

Both of Adie's parents hailed from Liverpool. His father, Len, met his mother, Beryl, in the '50s, and by 1957 they'd moved down to Middlesex due to Len's work commitments. Beryl had once graced the Anfield turf in a half-time exhibition of

Morris dancing, before the two had met; Len was in the crowd, unaware his future bride was out on the pitch. Adie was born four years after his parents relocated down south. So does that make him an OOTS? A southerner to all intents and purposes, but one with strong Liverpudlian connections, and one christened in Liverpool.

Part of our match-going routine on Saturdays was to stop at his nan's for lunch after the three hour drive, and pop in again afterwards for tea, before heading home. Sadie, known to the family as 'Nin', lived in Litherland. In her mid-eighties when I first met her, she insisted on cooking hearty meals, and dessert often ran to three courses. She was still doing this well into her nineties, although she passed away a couple of years ago.

As the '90s wore on, Len went to games less and less following his retirement, and after Beryl passed away following a battle with cancer. By 1997 I'd joined another team, and met Matt Clare, a Red originally from Cheshire, and he took Len's place in the collective. When Adie and I first started going to games together, the M1 and M6 motorways weren't too busy; as the new millennium approached, it seemed every journey was met with delays, road-works and accidents. One journey in particular springs to mind: Newcastle at home at the end of August 1997. It took four hours to get to Liverpool, and six hours to get home. All that, and the game didn't even take place — it was postponed due to Princess Diana's death. We'd been intermittently checking the radio for news, but all we heard was unbearably sombre music, so kept switching back to the CD player and therefore missed the announcement of the cancellation.

By 2002 both Adie and I had become fathers — Adie to twin boys, whereas I had one son. I had been diagnosed with M.E. (myalgic encephalomyelitis) in 1999, and had to stop work in 2000 as a result, so getting to games was increasingly becoming more of a physical challenge. (Even now, my illness is used by some supporters as a way to question my commitment and validity as a *true* fan. But then most fans are judged by others as to their worthiness, and in return, they form their own judgements on others. And anyway, I've never claimed to be a *superfan* — those ultra-dedicated souls who would let nothing stand in the way of getting to a game.) Matt also became a father soon after, and it was no longer a case of just jumping in the car early on a Saturday morning without a care in the world other than who would be in the starting XI. Both Matt and Adie were working hard during the week, so to disappear up north for the whole of the Saturday or Sunday and leave the kids with their wives was not really an option. Meanwhile, by the end of 2002 I was in the middle of a divorce, and due to my ex-wife's work commitments, Saturday was my day to look after our son. For me, getting to a game had got to the stage where it was still possible providing I left a few days clear either side, in order to rest before the match and recover afterwards. (An overseas game, or any kind of long trip, obviously involves even more rest and recuperation, but is possible providing it's a short break, and only once or twice a year.) On the whole, going to games is not practical, or physically possible on more than the odd occasion, and it was complicated by the fact that I had commitments with my son at the weekend as well as midweek; seeing him would always take priority over seeing the Reds; there needs to be a special reason for me to spend time away from him. These days I tend to go to games when Matt, who has built up a successful company from scratch since 1997, organises the entire event, which we all treat as a special occasion.

Back in the hotel bar in Glyfada, I ask Adie if he misses going to games regularly. "Absolutely. If we do win the league next season it will be something of a damp squib to me because I won't have been to many games. Football has always been about going, hence all those miles on the motorways. Watching it on the TV leaves me cold. That's why I had to make the effort to go to Athens without a ticket, for everything that went on leading up to the game and to be there to witness and be a part of it.

With plenty to choose from, what are your best moments as a Liverpool fan? "Applauding the opposition keeper at Anfield has always made me feel proud to support the Reds. Staying behind to applaud Arsenal in '89. Rome '77, although I wasn't there. Rome '84, when I was there. Dortmund in 2001, and Istanbul of course. Strangely, I haven't included winning the title because we did it so often when I was younger that you get blasé about it."

Does he expect his two young sons to be Liverpool fans? Or would he prefer them to support a more team local, given them he knows how much of a hassle it is getting to games?

"I'm still undecided on this one. If they actually want to go to games I will probably take them to Watford. If they are going to be armchair fans then I will definitely expect them to be Reds. I can't imagine trekking up to Anfield regularly."

Has the way he identifies with the club and its players changed?

"The biggest change has been not going to the games anymore. I've always had a love for the club and the city itself having spent so much time there when I was growing up. Stopping going to the match has also meant not going to the city so I definitely feel estranged from the club. As for identifying with the players, when I first started going it felt as though they were just like me but now, with the money and the status, I don't identify with them at all. I'm sure that getting older and having kids has a lot to with it too as your priorities change. However, if I was living in the city and going to all the home games as a minimum despite the kids, I'd be enjoying it as much as I used to."

Our lunch arrives, and soon it will be time to make a move with the rest of our group towards Syntagma Square, where tens of thousands of Reds are already gathered and in good spirits. Unlike two years earlier, the day won't end in riotous celebrations. But after a decade and a half of watching Liverpool together — with the comedy defending of the '90s and the eventual loss of direction under Houllier — it still feels slightly surreal to be in the European Cup Final at all.

# New World Order: From Kirkby to Kuala Lumpur

With all the fervour of colonial Victorians fired up on Bolivian marching powder, the name of Liverpool Football Club spread across the world — changing the colour of the map along the way — with the Reds' exploits in the European Cup in the 1970s.

In 2005, somewhat against the odds, the club sat proudly at the summit of Europe once more, and participation in the subsequent World Club Championship may have also helped entice a new generation of fans. Two years later the Reds were back at the top table in 2007, narrowly missing out on a sixth European Cup in Athens. In terms of being a world force, it was the second coming.

## Confessions of an Out of Town Supporter

My own love of LFC began when I was a young boy; in fact, from when I was too young to know any different. I recall staying up past bedtime to watch the Reds in Europe in the late '70s. At the age of seven I had no idea that you were supposed to support your local team. Besides, I didn't really have a local team. The town where I grew up had one non-league side, which many years later would make it all the way up to the Conference (before dropping back to obscurity). My father took me to a winter's evening game when I was 11 or 12, and I recall enjoying it, but it hardly had the same awe-inducing affect as would being taken to a packed Anfield. The surrounding areas had a few more lesser non-league sides, two of which I'd go on briefly to play for.

People from cities like Liverpool and Newcastle — real footballing hotbeds — often fail to understand or appreciate what it's like for football fans born in towns (or even countries) with no real footballing identity, and no obvious local team to support. Not everywhere has the sense of community that Liverpool possesses, let alone the passion for the sport. I don't think the denizens of such cities understand what it's like to grow up somewhere nondescript, the kind of place Ricky Gervais cleverly mocked by setting The Office in Slough; to have nothing with a magnetic pull on your doorstep — no local club to identify with. To be born into nothing special so far as football is concerned.

I grew up in a fairly humdrum town outside west London not far from the aforementioned Slough. There were probably 20 professional clubs in a 25-mile radius; but none was much closer than 20 miles away. My background was working-class — but as both parents worked, it was not one of financial hardship. My grandfather, originally from the Midlands, played for Aston Villa between the wars. (A fact I didn't know until I was too old to have any great affection or affinity for

Villa.) Both of my parents had grown up in football-mad families, with my other grandfather a keen player who ran a local football team in the 1950s; he also used to take my mother to football league matches when she was growing up. My dad was a dedicated player, although not so much a supporter. Football was in my blood, but supporting a specific football team wasn't. I was never indoctrinated into following a particular team, and as such was free to choose, or rather, wait for a team to choose me. When I was six an aunt bought me a Queens Park Rangers kit, and for a while it was the most exciting thing ever — even though, by today's standards, it was hardly a kit at all: plain cotton socks, white shorts and a blue and white hooped top that had neither a logo nor a sponsor's name. I loved that kit. But it didn't make me love QPR.

At my primary and secondary schools, in the late '70s and early '80s, diversity was the order of the day. Your choice did not boil down to either Red or Blue. It wasn't anywhere near that clear cut. There were fans of all manner of different clubs — Fulham, Chelsea, QPR, Luton, Watford, Spurs, Arsenal, West Ham, Millwall, Brentford, as well as a fair few following the glamour teams of Manchester United and Liverpool.

My peers would change their affinities like the popular kids' gameshow of the time, *Runaround*, where contestants would have to indicate answers to questions by aligning their allegiance by queueing behind one of three signs. Pre-Eastenders Mike Read would scream "*Runarroooounnndd*!" and everyone would switch positions. But my allegiance stayed with Liverpool, and never wavered. In fact, my passion only increased as Liverpool's fortunes faded in the 1990s. I may have been an inadvertent glory hunter aged eight, but I remained a fan long after the glory had disappeared.

I think I chose Liverpool; but maybe it chose me. Whatever the circumstances, I did not become a Liverpool fan to annoy anyone else; nor, indeed, to *please* anyone else, like a relative or friend. I did it for myself. And once you genuinely love something you shouldn't have to justify it to others.

## Anfield, and the 21st Century match-goer

So will Liverpool fill a 60,000 stadium — let alone one that might approach 80,000 — when the club doesn't always fill one with a capacity of 44,000? And if so, who will these fans be, and where will they come from? What has changed over the years?

For starters, the population of Liverpool has declined at a fairly alarming rate since the shipbuilding heyday of the Victorian age, when the city was one of the country's main ports. Liverpool 'lost' a quarter of a million inhabitants between 1901 and 2001. It sustains two major football clubs, both of which feel the need to move to modern grounds with increased capacities. Other two-club cities — cities close to Liverpool in size, such as Nottingham and Sheffield – are struggling to sustain one successful club, let alone two. Indeed, Leeds – a one-club city – has a current population even higher than Liverpool's in 1901. All other Premiership clubs are either from the three major cities (London, Birmingham and Manchester/Greater Manchester) or from single-club locations with a 100% captive market, such as Newcastle, Portsmouth, Blackburn, Wigan and Middlesbrough.

It's not totally unfeasible for a city the size of Liverpool to maintain two successful clubs: 2004/05 saw both in the top five almost throughout, and in 2006/07 both were in the top six. Of course, that's nowhere near as successful as the 1970s — when Liverpool were champions four times — and 1980s, when the city shared eight of the decade's ten titles, as well as numerous domestic and European trophies.

In 1901, Liverpool was home to 711,030 people. The latest figures, from the 2001 census, put the total inhabitants at 439,473. Of those, only 209,805 are male. While the numbers of women attending matches has increased, the majority of football fans remain men. One-fifth of those males are under 15. A further 20,000 are over 70, and therefore highly unlikely to still be regularly attending matches. Exclude also those too indisposed to attend games, those unable to afford ticket prices, and those who have no interest, and the remaining potential fan base in the immediate vicinity is substantially reduced. It's a totally different world from the one into which Liverpool Football Club was born, and a totally different city.

Anfield was constructed, in piecemeal fashion, at the back end of the 19th, and the early part of the 20th century, so that men — and it was almost exclusively men — could walk through the surrounding Victorian streets in order to stand shoulder-to-shoulder, gathering as a mass to watch a game of football. When the location was first used for organised football, in 1884, electricity was still in its infancy. No one had successfully flown, despite a series of attempts at aviation. The world's first practical internal combustion engine-powered automobile had only just been pioneered by Karl Benz. Cinema did not exist. John Logie Baird, credited with inventing television in the 1930s, was not yet even born. And although primitive computers would begin talking to one another in basic form in just 60 years' time, the internet would take another 40 years to reach global popularity. That was the world at the time of Anfield's creation. It's hard for us to imagine what it was like.

The only way to see football was to walk to the nearest game. A team called St. Domingos had been playing its games in Stanley Park. In time they changed their name to Everton, and moved to Anfield. The first ever game played on the now-hallowed pitch saw Everton beat Earlestown 5-0 in 1884. Everton moved to Goodison Park eight years later (possibly around the time it was last renovated). On 23rd September 1892 the newly-created Liverpool Football Club played its first competitive match at Anfield, and unbeknown to the 200 people in attendance that day, something very special was born. (No doubt some fans are still claiming to have been there that day.) The nearby Sandon public house and hotel — still a popular haunt for fans on match-days — provided the team's dressing room. From such small acorns ...

Back then there was no such thing as an 'out of town supporter' (OOTS), as there was barely even local support. The club grew over the following decades, as the game itself became more popular, drawing in more fans as a result. Terraced stands were added to various parts of the Anfield Road stadium, and then, in 1906, the Kop was constructed.

Football used to be all about the local community, as that was the only practical way to support a club. Anything else would have been illogical. There really was no alternative, especially as it was a working-class game, and as such, to those with incredibly limited finances, it could only exist in its local roots. The gentry could have travelled further afield in search of another team if they'd wanted, but they had no interest in the sport. It would have been sheer lunacy for any normal working-class man to walk, take a horse and cart, or ride trains and trams to another city, when he had a club right on his doorstep — especially when his network of friends and family were strolling to either Anfield or Goodison Park. But in time, the appeal of Liverpool stretched beyond Merseyside, out into Wales and Cheshire, then further down England and up to Scotland, before finally spreading all over the world like the virus from Terry Gilliam's *Twelve Monkeys*.

There is no rule book that states a person has to support his or her local team. There is of course a strong history and tradition of such activity, but nowhere is it written in stone. Does it have to be the football club closest, as the crow flies, to where you grew up? At what point does somewhere stop being 'local'? Who decides? What if you move to another part of town, or another town altogether? This is the 21st Century, not the 19th. Fans can now fly to Liverpool from various parts of England in the time it takes others to walk to the game; does that make Liverpool 'local'? Where once it would have taken months to speak directly to someone in Australia — via an arduous journey by sea — we can now speak to, and even see, someone on the other side of the world at the touch of a button. As Liverpool's success of the 1970s was transmitted, in glorious technicolour, to a global audience, many had no resistance to falling in love. Just as the world fell head-over-heels for the Beatles, Liverpool's footballers captivated those who, in years gone by, would not have had access to the team. A musical group from Liverpool could not have conquered the world before the advent of the phonograph; even then, it still required radio, and then television (and specifically in the Beatles' case, *The Ed Sullivan Show*) to reach a mass audience.

Distinctions in all walks of life continue to grow more blurred over time. It's a more diverse, racially mixed society, and technology has made the globe a much smaller place. This is the world into which the new Anfield will be born.

It would be fascinating to go back in time, to the 1890s, and try to explain to those men clomping through the cobbled streets in their hobnail boots just how the game would change towards the end of the next century; telling them that a good percentage of regulars at Anfield would not be their descendants, but men and women from all over the UK, and even from further afield.

Can you imagine explaining to the working-class Victorian shuffling down Walton Breck Road in his thick winter coat that, in years to come, people will be sitting in a fully-seated arena, watching multi-millionaires from almost everywhere but Britain kick (with what are apparently leather slippers) what to him would be considered a balloon, as up to a billion people around the world tune in to view the match on small boxes? Given that the Wright Brothers had yet to take to the air, can you picture his face as you outline the notion that hordes of people fly to matches from Norway and Asia, America and Australia? I imagine you'd receive a mouthful of Scouse wit peppered with with a plethora of choice profanities.

## Out of Town Supporters and Disharmony

There can be no doubting that OOTS irritate a fair amount of local supporters. Something the Liverpudlians hold dear, and which is part of their identity and culture — their club, their heritage — has become diluted by the influx of what they see as 'Johnny Come Latelys', some of whom do not seem to respect the traditions of the club.

Most of what we hold dear in life actually 'belongs' to us in some form or another: our families, our partners, our friends, our pets. A football club, however, is not a faithful mistress; she sees an unlimited amount of other men on the side. And, of course, women too, because these days she swings both ways. (If she's starting to sound like a bit of a slut, then that's not intentional.)

But what we love most can also drive us over the edge. The obvious suspect in any murder case is almost always the victim's partner, because the vast majority of killings are carried out by someone emotionally close, who is most likely to have felt significantly hurt or betrayed. We do not like being let down by those we cherish. Especially when it means we lose all sense of control. And when it comes to being a football fan, that sense of having no control is particularly strong. You can shout and scream, and sing songs, but your input and influence as an individual is minimal. So unconditional love from any fan to a club and its players is never a straightforward issue.

OOTS could perhaps be likened to the 'invading' West Indians of the 1950s, who came to England upon the promise of better times, only to be perceived on arrival as immigrants 'taking our women and jobs'. Except, in this case, it's 'our season tickets and seats'. There's a similar urge to protect what people see as *theirs*. And while the racism — or 'placism' in the case of OOTS — is never palatable, a desire to protect one's own world order is all the same a natural response. Sharing what you love with those you don't know is never easy.

But as with racism, generalising about any group of people is always dangerous. As the joint-most famous Liverpudlian once sang with Stevie Wonder, *'There is good and bad in everyone'*. (And no, that wasn't Robbie Fowler duetting with Steven Gerrard.) In the same way that everyone wants success for their favourite obscure band, only to then feel resentment when they get so massive that concert tickets are impossible to come by, so the locals cannot really do much about those who have joined the 'bandwagon', whether or not those joining are in for the long haul. Nowhere is the OOTS issue drawn into sharper focus than on the occasions the Reds meet their Blue neighbours.

The Merseyside derby, when it comes to supporters, no longer represents one big happy family: it's a tense affair, littered with ill-feeling and smatterings of violence. Not on a massive scale, but enough to matter. There are still touching fan-organised tributes between the clubs in time of sorrow: Everton playing *You'll Never Walk Alone* after Hillsborough, and on 28th August 2007, Liverpool playing the Z Cars theme tune — the Evertonian anthem — following the murder of 11-year-old Blue, Rhys Jones. But the tensions between the two sets of fans are far greater than in years gone by. It's no longer the 'friendly derby'.

Brothers with split allegiances might not suddenly find themselves fighting each other, but that doesn't stop Reds and Blues who don't know each other facing off. The Blue half of Merseyside takes great pride in teasing their Red counterparts about the cultural diversity of those who attend Anfield. 'Spot the Scouser on the Kop' is an all-too-familiar chant. As a result, Liverpool fans from the city are made to feel apologetic for the team's 'mongrel' following.

In many respects Evertonians are provisional, parochial, and there can appear a kind of xenophobia to their chants and taunts. Everton, in the eyes of their fans, remains a pure breed; Liverpool's authenticity, meanwhile, has been diluted by contamination of the bloodline. Everton doesn't have a particularly large appeal beyond Merseyside, and so, to their fans, it is the *true* club of Liverpool in the sense that its appeal lies solely within that area (and possibly parts of north Wales). That doesn't mean that there are more Blues than Reds in Liverpool; just that the Scouse Reds are supplemented by millions of fans from far and wide. If Everton is the club of Liverpool, then Liverpool Football Club is something altogether bigger — a club of the world, and the world, of course, *includes* Liverpool.

Everton cannot realistically hope to be the biggest or the best club on Merseyside in the near future. As a result, Evertonians can only cling to a belief that they are the *best* fans, according to criteria they themselves set.

## White Rappers

My first regular visits to Anfield were with my friend Adie and his Liverpudlian father. It became a regular routine for me for a number of years: doing the 400 mile round trip to every home game, and at least half of the away matches. As any Scouse fans who regularly travel to the far flung reaches of the country know, it's a long drive home after a bad result, and no fair-weathered fan would last long.

I was introduced to the workings of the club, and the behaviour expected, by those who knew the way fans were supposed to behave. I knew that *You'll Never Walk Alone* had a repeated chorus (although I only needed a pair of ears to deduce this), so did not applaud after the first. While I'd never feel it was my right to tell other people what to wear, a jester's hat was not something I'd ever be tempted to don. However, I can also understand the appeal to some fans of wearing something fun and red-coloured to the game. But just because you come from outside the city it doesn't automatically mean you don't understand how to behave.

Despite this, people such as myself are the white rappers of the football world. We have entered into a movement that is not part of our local history or tradition, but one which, for one reason or another, we have been drawn to and love nonetheless. Perhaps it's a different kind of love to that experienced by locals, but it's ours all the same — it's what *we* feel, after all. What anyone else feels is their business. You cannot dictate a person's emotions.

We struggle for credibility, constantly having to prove we are worthy, when, to the key members of that community — at least the ones who do not know us personally — we are misfits. Just as white rappers speak with an affected African-American accent, we too have been known to occasionally slip into Scouse vernacular, at the risk of being found out, or seen as a fake (and little in modern life is seen as worse than being a fake). We strive for the credibility of Eminem — who can rub shoulders with Dr Dre, 50 Cent and D12 — all the while fearing we instead come across like Vanilla Ice.

But just as there are clueless OOTS, who don't understand the history or traditions of the club, it doesn't automatically follow that, whatever their birthright, every Liverpudlian is a footballing genius who instinctively understands the game, or cares passionately about the club. These locals are the MC Hammers of Merseyside: they meet the correct criteria, but somehow are not in touch with the culture, or attuned to the passion. They could of course argue that, as they were born there, their indifference towards the club is their right. Perhaps it is. But their ambivalence won't exactly help the club flourish.

There can be no denying that Liverpool Football Club 'belongs' to the people of Merseyside by way of heritage — that it was passed down to them from their forefathers, like a helix of genetic coding transferred at the point of conception. The club was founded on the passion and pride of the locals, without which it would almost certainly have floundered many decades ago. Over the years it was they — the Liverpudlians — who made the club what it is today, with its famed Kop recognised worldwide for the unique wit and volume of the 24,000 who once stood on its terrace; even if it is now a different entity, and only half that size. Anyone from outside the city needs to respect the tradition they are entering into, and learn the correct protocol.

But it's also true to say that locals cannot stop other people from supporting the club, or buying tickets to games. As the club looks to expand, in the way its competitors have, it has to be happy to accept the money of anyone prepared to pay; not all will be die-hard Reds who could pass a 'knowledge test', but plenty will be, wherever they are from. It cannot discriminate.

One argument is that OOTS deny 'real' fans the chance to go to Anfield. Those who oppose this view tend to point to the empty seats at Anfield; attendances can fall a fraction short of capacity for league games, and well-short for most run-of-the-mill cup matches. Midweek games are the hardest hit — the games most suited to the locals, who don't have to take a day off work to get to Anfield, or face a drive, coach ride or flight home in the early hours of the morning. Clearly something is amiss with this theory. However, in midweek games when prices are reduced, there is more activity through the turnstiles. Perhaps it's a financial issue? Having said all this, the season ticket waiting list is reported to run into tens of thousands; while some names will be duplicates from those trying various guises to be successful, it suggests that massive demand exists, if people can be guaranteed of having a ticket each week.

Buying a ticket for a match is less straightforward these days: you no longer simply queue for one, or turn up on match day. There are season tickets (which are now just swipe cards), the Priority Ticket Scheme, tickets sold on the club's website, and all sorts of voucher retention schemes to reward those committed (or lucky) enough to attend earlier games. The ticket phone lines are often jammed as a result of heavy demand, and some locals may lose patience as a result. Having said that, the ticket office still opens windows at the back of the Kop, and many midweek games still take cash on the turnstiles. As with anything in life, it's no good Liverpudlians moaning about the situation if they opt to not go when the chance is there; making their own individual presence felt would mean they were redressing the balance, if they indeed feel a balance needs to be redressed. Keeping away because of the amount of OOTS only increases the chances of another out-of-towner snapping up that ticket.

Maybe the prices are more prohibitive for working-class Scousers, but Liverpool still set their prices fairly low when compared with the competition — especially clubs such as Chelsea and Arsenal, with whom the Reds still need to compete on the pitch to keep those very same fans happy. It's unrealistic to expect the Liverpool board to charge 1980s prices for tickets, and yet maintain its position as a major club, given that being a major club relies so much — if not exclusively — on money. (Funnily enough, Chelsea, given Abramovich's involvement, could probably afford to charge a fiver per game. Of course, they don't.) Manchester United charge a similar amount to Liverpool, but gain an extra £1m–£2m from ticket revenue every single game due to there being 33,000 more seats at Old Trafford. It's a difficult balance to strike: keeping up with the Joneses without upsetting the people who helped build up the club in the first place.

In August 2007 I spoke to Tony Barrett, *Liverpool Echo* feature writer on the Reds for a balanced view on the issues of the club's identity from a die-hard local who follows the team all over Europe.

"I'm 31 now," he told me, "and I've been going to the game since my dad first started taking me as a toddler. I first got a season ticket in 1987. I know I spend a small fortune following Liverpool each season. It probably comes in at around three or four grand a year when you take into account season ticket, travel and tickets for away games and European trips. In the last few years it has been more expensive than previously simply because we have been more successful in the Champions League. I would imagine the club benefits from around a third of my annual spend.

"We are lucky at Liverpool to still have players we can identify with. The likes of Jamie Carragher and Steven Gerrard come from a similar background to a lot of the fans and I think it is vitally important that Liverpool always has players who the supporters can identify with."

So would he rather Liverpool be a moderately successful club with a handful of local players, or a highly successful one without them?

"Good question. I suppose it comes down to whether or not you think success is more important than identity. I don't want success at any cost and I don't want Liverpool to become the kind of club where mercenaries can come and go as long as we pick up the odd trophy along the way.

"When I say it is vitally important that Liverpool have players the supporters can identify with I'm not necessarily talking about locals. It's more about shared values and experiences. Most local Reds I know identify with the likes of Alonso and Hyypia because they clearly love the club as much as we do. The same goes for Dalglish, McAllister, Hansen etc. Even Erik Meijer! Ideally, we would have more local players in the first team squad but if not enough quality players are being produced from the

Liverpool area then that's never going to happen. I'd much rather have Xabi Alonso in the Liverpool team than Kevin Nolan, and if someone told me Liverpool were replacing Daniel Agger with Alan Stubbs because he's from Kirkby I think I'd pack in!"

So if non-local players are welcome, providing they are of sufficient quality and actually care about the club, what about fans from outside the city?

"I have no problem with out of town fans or supporters from abroad. Anfield is a public place and they have as much right to buy a ticket to watch Liverpool play as anyone else does. My only concern is if the balance shifts too much and the local heart of our fan base becomes diluted. I won't use the word disaster, but that would be a terrible thing to happen to the club.

"Liverpool Football Club is a global brand, there is no getting away from that, but its heart must be kept local otherwise it will just become any other club. At times in Istanbul and in Athens it felt more like following Man United, such was the sheer volume of fans from other parts of the world who had attached themselves to us."

Of course, those overseas Reds in Istanbul and Athens were most likely there to watch the game in the Uefa section; that was certainly the case with those I spoke to in researching this book — many of whom found it easier to get to those two cities than to England. One such person was Eric Cordina, a pilot for Air Malta and administrator of Reds' fan-site www.bootroom.org. I first met Eric in 2001, when we sat together at Anfield to see the customary home victory over Spurs. We'd got chatting on a forum about a year earlier, and he was hoping to get over for his first game since the bizarre 6-3 Anfield victory against FC Sion in 1996. I had a spare ticket for the Spurs' match, which I offered him. I'll never forget the voicemail he left on the day in question, when on a train from London to Liverpool. In a deep European voice, sounding a bit like Arnold Schwarzenegger, he said: "I'm almost halfway to Liverpool. Approximate time of arrival one hour 43 minutes." All that was missing was "the cabin crew will shortly be passing through with a selection of drinks and duty free items". In 2005 he had been in Istanbul in the neutral stand, having made a trip similar to the Milanese, with Malta just south of Italy, albeit slightly closer to Turkey than Milan. In 2007 he wanted to make the trip to Athens, but the only ticket he could source was in the AC Milan end, and the price was prohibitive.

So rather that diluting the core of regular match-goers assembled behind the goal, they were mostly supplementing it with support in the side sections of the stadium; sections that could otherwise have been filled with neutral or opposition ranks — although locals could, and no doubt did, find themselves clambering for tickets in this part of the ground too, given official allocations were so low. It would have been highly unlikely that these overseas Reds could have come into tickets through official club channels, as to do so required attendance at previous matches. If they did, it was probably because someone who had qualified for a ticket sold it on the black market. That meant that the official away section was where the hardcore support congregated.

At a guess, the 40,000 in Rome in 1977 would have been 99% Merseysiders. The 40,000 in Istanbul and Athens may have been closer to 50%, with the rest made up of Reds from all over the world.

"We are at saturation point at the moment," says Tony Barrett, regarding the influx of new fans, "and it is incumbent on the club's new owners to get the balance right. Yes, out of town and foreign fans are welcome at Anfield but they must ensure that local supporters do not feel their club is being taken away from them."

## Worldwide Exposure

The advent of regular televised football led to people outside of their home towns getting to see rival clubs in matches other than the FA Cup Final or in competition against their local side.

Starting in England with *Match of the Day* — which, with a nod to things to come, debuted with Liverpool beating Arsenal 3-2 at Anfield on August 22nd 1964 — a process commenced whereby before long, anyone with a TV could watch the BBC broadcast to the nation on a Saturday night. As the show began on BBC2, which was only available in the London area at the time, it did not have an immediate effect on what were football's deeply-embedded traditions, but over a period of time, as the show became more widely watched, there was a shift towards casual followers of teams from other parts of the country, and what we now know as 'armchair fans'. Such an evolution was inevitable.

While Liverpool's enormous success of the 1970s and 1980s came before the astronomical rise in profits available to the best teams in Europe — money that came with the advent of the Premiership and Champions League — it did coincide with football, now in colour broadcasts, on national TV. While the club was unable to immediately cash in in the way Manchester United did in the mid 1990s, it did generate a massive fan-base across the UK. These games were also soon going out in numerous other countries; some saw Liverpool through their own country's broadcasting of the English Football League, although others will have been alerted to the quality of Liverpool's football through the European Cup. And so a global fan-base was gathering.

In August 2007, HitWise, a firm that monitors internet activity, announced that Liverpool's official site, www.liverpoolfc.tv, had a 17.3% share of the UK's Premiership market — almost 2% greater than that of Manchester United's official site. Only Arsenal, with 10.9%, could also boast a share above 7.5%. Everton were 8th, with 5.3%, while Chelsea were way back in 11th place, with just 4.39%. But the study also showed that seven out of ten Liverpool and Manchester United fans using their clubs' official site lived outside the north-west. It also put United's unique global user levels at 2.4 million, to Liverpool's 1.7m. However, Liverpoolfc.tv's own figures show that it served an audience of 2.8 million unique users during July 2007, fractionally short of the number who visited following the Champions League success two years earlier.

Include those Liverpool fans without access to the internet, and those who use only unofficial fan sites, and the numbers will be immeasurably higher. In October 2005 Rick Parry discussed some research undertaken by a company called Sports Market. Parry explained that at the time it indicated that Liverpool had "18 million fans in Europe's five major markets," which made the Reds the country's most supported club. "The research is updated every six months," Parry said, "and this was the first time for a few years that we have leapt ahead of Manchester United, obviously boosted by our Champions League triumph over AC Milan. The point is that in a European sense clubs like Chelsea and Arsenal are not on the same radar. It doesn't mean that all of those supporters actually see us as their first club, but we are more than happy to be topping this particular English table. The survey shows Real Madrid on top with Barcelona second and Liverpool third. Once again, it highlights our standing in the world game and it is something we can all be proud of." Of course, it's hard to know what kind of fans these 18 million were, and how much the club meant to them.

## Daytrippers

As well as the OOTS there is another distinctive category of fan: The Daytripper. (An apt title for LFC, given the Lennon and McCartney song of the same name.) Unlike the song, it doesn't take long for them to get found out. A daytripper is characterised by the look of a tourist: camera at the ready to photograph the match rather than actually watch it, and an inability to join in with any of the songs. A daytripper is the fan who doesn't necessarily understand everything about what's going on, but is having a great time all the same. They might be known by the phrase Roy Keane used to castigate sections of Manchester United's support — the prawn sandwich brigade — although his words were perhaps aimed at wealthier supporters.

On his or her own, there is no harm in the daytripper whatsoever: he or she is someone going to sample the atmosphere and experience something they will not be familiar with. Who is to say that they have no right to do so? It's much like how a Brit, if on holiday in Barcelona, might consider taking in a game at the Nou Camp. The difference here is that daytrippers are Liverpool fans going to watch their own team, but doing so in a way that can irritate the hardcore. If new to Anfield, there will be awe and wonder in their eyes. It is only once the percentage of daytrippers grows to a significant level that it starts to affect the event itself: no longer bystanders, they begin to affect the football.

For instance, if Anfield was 100% populated by daytrippers, all there to experience the singing and ebullient atmosphere, they would find themselves somewhere more akin to a public library; as a result *they* would be bitterly disappointed. The fewer hardcore fans well-versed in the tradition and song, the less there is to enjoy — or *experience* — for outsiders when it comes to the famous Kop. A big club like Liverpool needs its crowd to be a 12th man, in the manner to which Shankly alluded when he claimed the Kop could suck the ball into the net if it so chose, or blow it out if Liverpool's goal was under threat. At the very least it could scare the bejesus out of the opposition goalkeeper (after sportingly applauding him into the arena, like lions applauding a Christian at the Coliseum ... before devouring him).

Personally, I feel a sense of pride when I see a small group of wide-eyed Japanese tourists wandering around outside Anfield as if they're at the true Mecca of football. It makes me aware of the great pull of the club; in those moments it feels incredibly special, as if the whole world wants to be there. It also reminds me of the very first time I got to go to Anfield in 1990. But 40,000 'tourists' would be a different proposition.

## Stand still and shrink

In the early 1990s I played in the qualifying rounds of the world's oldest club competition, the FA Cup, for one of the world's oldest clubs: a team formed in Middlesex in 1868, 24 years before Liverpool Football Club came into existence. While the club I represented was never a shining light, it had fallen on hard times. Finances were so tight we had to train with only half the floodlights illuminated, and the club suffered successive relegations after mid-table finishes, on the grounds of the *ground*: it was deemed of an insufficient standard, despite having aforementioned floodlights, covered seating and standing areas. Payments to players were deferred. It was a local village team that, as the world became more connected, remained an isolated outpost, where a percentage of the 400 inhabitants walked to watch us play. (And often ran as fast as they could to get away at half-time.) Unlike a couple of the local rivals in the same league, who came from the larger surrounding towns, we couldn't expect crowds of 200 or more every week. As a result, the club slipped ever further into decline, to the shocking point where even I was too good to play for it.

In many ways that club represents time stood still. It shows how, even at the lower levels of the game, having too few local fans and not enough money can cripple a club. It had no way of moving with the times, because moving with the times takes money.

If success hadn't visited Liverpool Football Club, and fans from further afield hadn't been attracted to it, it would still be a big club given the size of the city. But the success of the 1970s was built upon the success of the 1960s, and the success of the 1980s on Paisley's all-conquering teams of the 1970s. By the time the '90s had arrived, and the real success had dried up, the club was set up on a bigger scale. Did the worldwide support help sustain the club during those recent fallow years, contributing in terms of merchandising and television deals, and more recently, internet-related arrangements? Certainly. The Premiership came into existence in 1992, just two years after the Reds' last title success. Football became big business when Liverpool's name was still of major importance, even though it was Manchester United who were cashing in most directly. The first nine Premiership years were largely trophy-free for Liverpool, but the new financial footing for the game gave the club the chance to continue to build in a number of ways: money spent on expensive players, Melwood revised, The Academy constructed. And plans began for a move to Stanley Park. The worldwide appeal of the club, and the money those fans spent, certainly helped contribute in all of these areas. In many ways, Everton, whose major success ended just a few years earlier than Liverpool's, in 1987, are an example of what happens to a club if it cannot exist near the top of the financial tree. Take away the revenue streams from those outside the city itself, and clearly Liverpool would have less money. And less money would almost certainly have made it harder for Roy Evans, Gérard Houllier and Rafa Benítez to keep the club in the top four, where more money could be earned, and more regeneration could take place. Everton have started to do well again in recent seasons, but they are still a long way behind Liverpool when it comes to winning trophies and qualifying for the Champions League.

Perhaps one major difference between local fans and those from further afield is this: Liverpudlians see the team as an inextricable part of the city, whereas OOTS just see a team. Of course, the average OOTS wouldn't want that team taken out of the city (no one's proposing moving to Milton Keynes, God forbid), and the city is in the thoughts of those fans. But it's not completely *central* to those thoughts.

## The New Age

A common refrain from a lot of fans, no matter where they are from or whatever their age, is 'I've lost that old feeling', highlighting a sense of disenchantment, perhaps even disenfranchisement. It's hard to know how much of this is due to the game going wrong, and how much to people simply growing up and experiencing shifts in priorities. We all want to support our team for life. Indeed, the option to change teams is never on the agenda for a true fan, just to those who follow success or, perhaps, move to a totally new part of the country and fall in love with a club from a different division. Only fly-by-nights fully change their allegiance.

But we cannot support our team in our 50s and 60s in the way we did in our teens. For a start, it grows increasingly difficult to relate to the players, because it becomes increasingly difficult to relate to people of a different generation. You can idolise a 19-year-old at 13, but at 53 it's just not the same; rather than getting the desire to copy groin-gyrating goal celebrations over the park, they merely baffle. Everything that is new an exciting about being a fan as a young boy or girl has worn off by the time you are well into your adult life. Responsibility brings new priorities. Along come marriage, kids, work, a mortgage. Some particularly dedicated fans will always put off such distractions, but for the majority they get in the way to some degree or other.

The most far-reaching changes to English football took place in the early 1990s, but since then everything has been fairly stable. Hillsborough led to the legislation on all-seater stadia, which saw the facilities at top-level clubs improved, but at the expense of the old working-class preserve of the terrace. So if you were still in love with the game in the late '90s, by which time English football had undergone its Incredible Hulk-on-steroids transition, it's most likely to be you — the disillusioned fan — who has grown away from the game rather than vice versa. That is not to say that everything about the modern game should be tolerated or embraced — progress always brings about change for the worse as well as the better — but many of the far-reaching changes have been in place for a number of years. And if anything, there's an increased awareness of the need to hold onto heritage: amongst Liverpool supporters, moves are afoot to safeguard the important aspects of the club's tradition, while the hierarchy want to take the best elements of the current Anfield to its replacement across Stanley Park. Rather than build stands that resemble multi-storey car-parks of corporate boxes, the needs of the average fan are being met in its design.

Although it took a few years to react to the changes seen in the '90s, the Reclaim The Kop (RTK) movement sprung up towards the end of 2006, aimed at protecting the Kop's heritage. At its best — and the reason for which it was created — RTK is an invaluable charter that educates new fans in how to behave at Anfield, to ensure valuable traditions are upheld, and in so doing, retain the uniqueness of the world-famous stand. At its worst, it is there for its name to be hijacked by militants with more extreme agendas, to *exclude* those who don't fit the correct profile. It wasn't long before stories arose of fans being abused, or beaten, in the name of Reclaim The Kop, for crimes that were hardly more than minor transgressions. (And even major transgressions of Kop etiquette would not merit such behaviour.) Of course, RTK can't easily legislate for those whose intelligence is too limited to understand its true aims, or for those who wilfully distort its doctrine.

As well as Reclaim The Kop, there's the Keep Flags Scouse campaign. It is rather bizarre to think of a Liverpool flag that has the name of another part of England as its focus. Such flags are arguably acceptable for the back of a coach travelling up the motorway to Anfield for a game. But once at the match, Liverpool should surely be the only focus. Are you supporting the team, or supporting your supporters' club?

But ultimately, no club can simultaneously please all sections of its support; no organisation — especially not one where pure unbridled emotion is at the forefront of the relationship with its customers — can keep everyone happy. As the saying goes, you can't please all of the people all of the time. (I have come to understand the truth of this through writing for the club's official website. On any given day I can get emails praising something about a piece I've written at the same time as emails vehemently criticising the very same thing. I also occasionally get complaints from deeply disgruntled fans wondering why I don't 'represent their views'; ultimately, I am providing my own views, and not representing any section of the support. And anyway, no one alive could represent the views of *all* fans, as those views span the entire broad spectrum; indeed, some are off the scale at either end!)

Dissatisfaction is also an intrinsic part of modern life. Ever since Edward Bernays — the nephew of Sigmund Freud, and the man seen as the father of public relations — first began to use psychology to influence the masses in the 1920s, a process was set in motion. Advertising changed from selling wares on the basis of the practical benefits they offered — it does *this, this, and that* — to making people feel inferior if they did not possess the item in question. It became about lifestyle, about appearances. It was about playing with people's emotions. If consumers and customers were content with what they had, the problem was that they wouldn't want more. And football fans almost always want more.

Fans are sold on the idea of ultimate success, and sometimes the shades of grey between success and failure get whitewashed. Whether or not a club's leaders make a promise to deliver that ultimate success, as fans we feel let down by the club we support if it doesn't appear to be doing everything in its power to appease us.

By the summer of 2007, expectations amongst many Liverpool fans had risen to the point where it seemed little joy could be derived from anything short of a 19th league title. The arrival of the new American owners further increased expectations. A pre-season draw against Portsmouth was greeted by many with an unusually strong sense of despair. This was due in part to a Premiership-or-bust psychology, which in itself thwarts satisfaction. While all Reds obviously want that 19th league title, the three most recent seasons were notable for an interest in silverware held deep into May. After years of nothing to play for after February, the recent relative success should perhaps have been valued a little more. Two European Cup finals, and one FA Cup Final, gave fans something to look forward to, even if Athens ended with unlucky defeat. Have some fans become so blasé after 2005 that they can forget all the years when reaching a European Cup Final was the most far-fetched pipedream possible?

These might not be the very best times for Liverpool FC, but they are good times all the same. In his book, *Affluenza*, the noted British psychologist Oliver James talks about how many people in wealthier western societies are depressed and frustrated by the immense range of possibilities presented to them: the more we can have, the less happy we become. We are made more and more aware, by advertising and the media (particularly through TV, films and lifestyle magazines), of what we should be aspiring to be, but ultimately just draws our attention to *what we are not*. The middle-classes are attaining things in life, and garnering possessions, but rather than be satisfied, the desire is always for more. And as promised, some are escaping the lower classes for a similarly privileged lifestyle, but not even that is good enough, because there's always something better out there.

Alain de Botton's book, *Status Anxiety*, tells a similar story to James': how the perceived ability to move up in life just leaves people discontented. He contrasts how the lower classes were happier in bygone eras because they 'knew their place': there was no room to move up in life and so they accepted things, and made the most of a bad hand. Life was more simple; it had its limits, but this stopped the mind and heart from incessantly wandering. The same people are now told they can be anything or have anything they want if they just put their minds to it — or apply for a lot of credit cards. Buy the lottery ticket for dreams to come true. Turn up for the *Pop Idol*-type shows irrespective of a crushing lack of talent. As a society we are made to constantly want more, even though only a select few can enjoy such success, and as a result we appreciate what we have less and less. Everything is devalued, particularly by the glow of what those around us possess.

Is this also the way it is for football fans? Keeping up with Joneses is the crux of *Status Anxiety*. For Liverpool fans, it's keeping up with the Mourinhos and, in particular, the Fergusons. Manchester United's title last season, and their subsequent spending, only heightened Kopites' need to win no.19, and win it soon. But does it have to be this season at all costs? Of course not. There's nothing wrong with ambition in life, and especially in sport. Indeed, can you be a sportsman (or sports fan) without it? But if you can't enjoy achievements and accomplishments along the way because you're already thinking about the next task, or looking at your neighbours and what they're doing, why bother?

These are exciting times to be a Liverpool fan: new owners, talented new players, and a state-of-the-art new stadium under construction. Success on the pitch should be forthcoming — but whatever form it takes, will total satisfaction be found?

Perhaps it's asking too much to expect all sections of Liverpool's support to exist as one very big happy family. But if an end to the long wait for another league title finally becomes a reality, many will be united in toasting the success — from Bootle to Bangkok, Old Swan to Oslo, Toxteth to Texas, and Woolton to Wagga Wagga.

# Chelsea Déjà Vu

*Shit on a stick.* No, not a new form of frozen summer delicacy aimed at culinarily-challenged kids, but the phrase coined by former Real Madrid coach and World Cup-winner Jorge Valdano in Spain's best-selling newspaper, *Marca*, following the Reds' Champions League semi-final victory against Chelsea. Valdano is clearly not a man to mince his words. "Football is made up of subjective feeling, of suggestion — and, in that, Anfield is unbeatable," the Argentine said, in a prelude to his stinging diatribe. "Put a shit hanging from a stick in the middle of this passionate, crazy stadium," he added, "and there are people who will tell you it's a work of art. It's not: it's a shit hanging from a stick."

While an extreme point of view that has little basis in reality — the semi-final was neither a work of art nor stick-mounted faecal matter — as well as being an insult to the intelligence of Liverpool fans, it's an interesting thesis all the same, given that it captures the age-old essence of results versus entertainment; an argument that seems to follow Benítez in particular.

While entertainment is an important part of football, it is never more important than the result to the people whose jobs depend on victory. And you don't get to the very top of the game with purely functional football; you can perhaps muster a one-off fluke, as did Greece in 2004, but they quickly found their level again. While the semi-final in question was not the best advert for the beautiful game, it still provided great drama, and pure theatre; unlike a lot of big games seen over the years. Both teams were trying to win, and that guarantees entertainment, even if the quality isn't reminiscent of Brazil circa '70.

Valdano was correct in a small part of what he said — the semi-final was not one for those pesky purists — but he ignored the pressure of the situation, in a win-at-all-costs grudge match, and the fact that it was an incredible *15th* meeting between the two teams in just two and a half years. It's hard for teams who have played so many high intensity, high-stakes matches against one another to find that spark and to avoid cancelling each other out. There can be little room left for surprises. Especially when the two teams are so evenly matched when they take to the pitch together, and when it is the fifth semi-final match between the two sides in that time.

Liverpool versus Chelsea was not a 'normal' semi-final; it was one played out in exceptional circumstances, after 30 months of jibes and barbs; of fiercely contested battles; of gripes based on accusations of cheating, as seen when Eidur Gudjohnsen got Xabi Alonso booked and Tiago punched a clearance on the goal-line in front of the Kop (which only referee Mike Riley failed to spot), and sickening tackles, as seen when Michael Essien 'did' Didi Hamann with an over-the-ball lunge; and of Luis García's 'ghost' goal in the 2005 semi-final, which Chelsea still believed hadn't crossed the line. Then there was the part the Kop played, particularly in the Champions

League semi-final, which everyone present described as a white-hot atmosphere up with the best ever known. Add a large dose of stirring by Jose Mourinho, for whom a dose of verbal diarrhoea would constitute quiet reflection, and you have a boiling pot. The two managers are almost identical in age, and arrived in England within two weeks of each other, from either side of the Spanish/Portuguese border, fresh from fresh from domestic/European doubles at their previous clubs. To add extra spice, it had also been mooted that Mourinho either wanted, or was offered, the Liverpool job before he ended up at Stamford Bridge.

Then there was Chelsea's desperation to finally reach a European Cup final, after investment of around half a billion pounds — only to twice fall at this very stage in the previous three years. It was also Liverpool's only chance of a trophy following a fairly turbulent season off the pitch at Anfield. If all of that doesn't put the occasion into context, nothing will.

The first leg in 2007 was more open than expected, with the Reds going at Chelsea early on, and the home team hitting back on the break, and in so doing, creating a couple of excellent chances. Frank Lampard forced a fantastic stop from Pepe Reina, but it wasn't long before Chelsea deservedly broke through. The game was won by Joe Cole's 29th-minute goal, with the midfielder losing Alvaro Arbeloa to find time and space in the centre of the box. At the same time, Didier Drogba (on the ball) turned Daniel Agger in the inside-right position, and ran with pace and power, finding a square pass just as the Danish centre-back, who'd managed to stay fairly close to the striker, was about to make a recovering tackle. Cole — scourge of Liverpool in recent seasons — turned the ball past Reina. It was the first Champions League goal the Blues had scored against Liverpool, at the fifth time of asking. Apart from a fairly bright opening, the Reds didn't really get going until the second half; the first 45 minutes were largely insipid and lacklustre, and infuriated Benítez on the bench. It took just eight minutes after the break — and its resultant team talk — for Gerrard to force Petr Cech into action, with a stinging volley from 20 yards that the Czech keeper tipped around the post. It was lovely technique from Gerrard, although it would probably have been saved by lesser keepers. But the key moment in the whole tie occurred with less than ten minutes to go, when Reina was again at full stretch to deny Frank Lampard. A goal then, and the second leg would have likely proved beyond Liverpool.

The first leg ended with one of the most surreal sights seen all season: Jose Mourinho launching a tirade on TV against the referee for not spotting what he felt to be a definite penalty, for Arbeloa's deliberate handball in the 50th minute. The only problem with his assertion was that the incident occurred *ten yards outside the box*. "I don't understand how we don't have penalties," he ranted on Sky television. "When the penalties are so clear, I don't understand. I go for the facts and it's a fact." Rarely has a manager looked so incredibly stupid, and referees everywhere will have been smiling to themselves. Mourinho continued: "The penalty is a big chance for us to be 2-0. Then it would be a completely different game and a different story. I feel it is not fair." He even found time to resurrect the Luis García goal gripes from 2005. "They had their mistake but it was not [according to the referee] a penalty. I hope after the second leg we are not crying and thinking again about a big decision. Two years ago we were. I hope we are not looking back on the penalty."

Rafael Benítez's response was short and sweet. "If he says it was a penalty, I am sure it was a penalty," he remarked, tongue firmly in cheek.

The second leg could not have been more perfectly poised. The game was evenly balanced, with Chelsea holding the lead but Liverpool able to harness the power of a baying Anfield. An away goal for Chelsea, however, would virtually guarantee them their first ever Champions League final. They huffed, they puffed, but on the night they couldn't even blow the fluffy white achenes from a dandelion clock, let alone blow down the Kop. In return, the Kop didn't just blow the ball out of the net, as Bill Shankly once suggested, but it seemed to force Chelsea, as a team, away from the goal. It was in stark contrast to the first leg, and the Blues simply never got up a head of steam. It was a mark of Liverpool's progress that, unlike two years earlier, there were no real worries — there was not a heart-in-mouth 'Gudjohnsen moment' — and there was little of the territorial pressure Chelsea exerted in 2005.

The most intrigued spectators were Tom Hicks and George Gillett, taking their places in the Directors' Box. Speaking after the game, Gillett said he believes nothing in world sport compares to what he experienced at Anfield on May 1st. Describing the night as "magical", he went on to say, "It was like attending the greatest sports event you ever go to — on steroids. Nothing can compare to it."

Plans for the demolition of Anfield were almost hastened after just 22 minutes: the roof, already shaking, was nearly taken off by the tumult as Daniel Agger stroked home the Reds' equalising goal. It was a goal that mixed inch-perfect technical execution with expert training ground planning. In that sense, Benítez must have been as pleased with it as any goal his teams have ever scored.

While everyone in the Chelsea ranks focused on Peter Crouch as Steven Gerrard lined up to take the expected inswinging left-wing free-kick, the captain instead played a perfectly-weighted square pass towards the edge of the area. With Dirk Kuyt, in a blocking move the Americans would have expected to see in their native brand of football, holding off a Chelsea defender (something Mourinho *could* have felt aggrieved about, although it's a tactic Chelsea also use), Daniel Agger strode forward and sweetly curled a first-time left-footed shot around Cech and just inside the post. Agger never had to break his stride, and Cech stood no chance. It's hard to imagine something transferring so well from the training ground to the high pressure arena. Even at Melwood it would never have come off so perfectly.

Back in Spain, Valdano wasn't sufficiently impressed to mention this in his article, instead continuing his invective on how the Reds and the Blues were killing football. "Chelsea and Liverpool are the clearest, most exaggerated example of the way football is going: very intense, very collective, very tactical, very physical, and very direct," Valdano continued. "But, a short pass? Noooo. A feint? Noooo. A change of pace? Noooo. A one-two? A nutmeg? A backheel? Don't be ridiculous. None of that. The extreme control and seriousness with which both teams played the semi-final neutralised any creative licence, any moments of exquisite skill."

Football history has been full of dire teams holding onvaliantly for penalties

– such as Steaua Bucharest and Red Star Belgrade in the late '80s and early '90s — too scared to leave their own half to make a game of it. That was not the case at Anfield in the semi-final, with Liverpool still pushing forward for the winner, which should have come through Dirk Kuyt's extra-time strike, which was incorrectly ruled out for offside. Kuyt also hit the bar with a thumping header, and Petr Cech pulled off smart saves from the Dutchman and also from Peter Crouch, whose point-blank header he somehow saved with his feet.

Both teams went direct at times, but Chelsea did so almost pathologically, with Ashley Cole opting to hit hopeful angled balls all game rather than use his pace and ability to overlap in the style that made Arsenal so effective a couple of years earlier. Liverpool had skill and trickery on the right, with Jermaine Pennant tormenting his former Arsenal team-mate, and it was only after Pennant limped off with a slight injury that the Reds lacked a skilful edge. Once Pennant joined Luis García, Fabio Aurelio and Harry Kewell — all injured — on the sidelines then of course Benítez had less skilled artistes at his disposal as the game wore on. Luis García epitomises everything Valdano thinks the game should be about, but it was not Benítez's fault that the little Spaniard was injured; whenever he was fit and eligible he was used in the big games, no matter what the stakes.

Previous dour encounters in world football did not mark the end of the game as we know it, nor did the Argentine team of 1966, who kicked England out of the game. (Perhaps poetic justice follow when Maradona was kicked out of the 1982 tournament, although he was so good four years later no one could get close enough to kick him.) Indeed, the 1990 World Cup final, between Valdano's countrymen Argentina and West Germany, was a nadir. Compare that with Benítez's team winning the Champions League in 2005 in a six-goal thriller! Liverpool may not be the most skilful team on the planet, but on big occasions the entertainment is rarely lacking. In the previous six years the Reds had contested and won what many felt to be the best FA Cup Final in recent memory, as well as almost certainly the best European and Uefa Cup Finals. These three finals alone produced a staggering 21 goals.

"If football is going the way Chelsea and Liverpool are taking it, we had better be ready to wave goodbye to any expression of the cleverness and talent we have enjoyed for a century," Valdano concluded, with an over-dramatic flourish. No team should be judged on one must-win game. Any team worth its salt will do what it takes. Even Barcelona punt in hope in the last minutes of matches.

Football cannot always be about art or beauty; sometimes it's a battle. But to judge Liverpool so conclusively — and to find them guilty of ruining football — on the basis of this one tie was to ignore a season's efforts that compiled a thick dossier of evidence to the contrary. It included Peter Crouch's two beautiful bicycle kicks, against Galatasary and Bolton, and his hat-trick clincher against Arsenal, when he showed the skill of a Maradona (admittedly a Maradona on stilts). There was Agger's stunning goal against West Ham, when the centre-back swerved a 30-yarder into the top corner, or his numerous runs from the back with the ball; Xabi Alonso with the vision and technique to score from his own half against Newcastle, for his second consecutive goal from such a distance; Jermaine Pennant's volley against Chelsea, or any of John Arne Riise's rasping drives. There was the backheeled one-two between Pennant and Arbeloa in setting up the first goal against Arsenal, and Luis García's array of flicks and turns (when they came off) that bamboozled the opposition. There was Robbie Fowler's audacious dinked finish against Reading in the Carling Cup with the outside of his left foot, and Dirk Kuyt's volley against West Ham. And while Steven Gerrard didn't have his best season, you could still compile a montage of his best moments — passes, shots and pieces of skill — and it not be a short collection. These are just a few of the examples that, far from showing how Liverpool are killing the game, show a healthy regard for skill, expression, and technical ability.

All this is not to say that Liverpool played with the élan of Barcelona at their best, because clearly that's not true, and probably never will be while Benítez is manager. But that doesn't mean Benítez instructs his teams to play unattractive, percentage football. While Liverpool in 2006/07 were not up there with the most entertaining sides in the world, the Spaniard had instilled a nice balance between the two cornerstones of style and substance. The main problem was finishing chances, not creating them. On the eve of the first semi-final, Glenn Hoddle, himself a purveyor of the finer aesthetic elements of the game (both as player and manager), named Liverpool alongside Arsenal and Manchester United as teams that he liked to watch. The former Chelsea manager notably excluded his erstwhile club from that list.

Valdano explained why Benítez and Mourinho were to blame for the demise of flair and creativity: "They have two things in common: a previously denied, hitherto unsatisfied hunger for glory, and a desire to have everything under control."

It's hard to know how any manager can succeed without those two attributes. Who wants a manager — or indeed a player — with a satisfied hunger for glory? For a purported football intellectual, Valdano sounded more like a Teletubby. Having everything under control is not necessarily a bad thing for a manager, either — although the natural accusation is that it leads to a lack of expression from the players themselves, as they must follow the manager's orders.

Valdano's main thrust, with which he ended his polemic, was that Benítez and Mourinho, as failed players, were "channelling their vanity into coaching". He made a point about those who do not have the talent to make it as players, but this ignores the fact that Benítez was on Real Madrid's books until 21, at which point injury, not a lack of talent, saw him leave for a lesser club. Of course, he wasn't on course to be a world star as a player, but he wasn't without ability.

Italian legend Arrigo Sacchi — who won European Cups with AC Milan and a World Cup with Italy — once deflected criticism of never having played the game by saying: "You don't need to be a horse to be a jockey". Of course, you need some kind of serious grounding in the game somewhere along the line, as you need to understand how it works in order to form your own theories and ideas, and to relate to the players, who can quickly suss someone who doesn't know his stuff; it just doesn't need to have been at a professional level. Holland is a place noted for its technical ability and its managerial acumen. Its most famous footballing son, Johan Cryuff, always claimed it was absolutely essential to have been a top player to be a top manager. But Louis Van Gaal, Dick Advocaat and the great Leo Beenhakker were never major players; Beenhakker was an amateur until, like Benítez, he took up coaching in his mid-20s. While other players were busy thinking only of themselves until their mid-30s, men like Beenhakker and Benítez spent a decade thinking about the game and developing their theories.

Managers who never made the grade at the top level need not have lacked talent as players; perhaps just luck. But it needn't be "vanity" that makes them strive for the top as leaders of men, but perhaps ambition and a will to win.

Valdano claimed that the type of manager Benítez and Mourinho represent does not believe in the improvisational abilities of a footballer. In fact, it could be argued that they provide a firm framework for they players to express themselves, but in the areas where expression is most useful, and not where it puts the team at risk. And all creative players flourish better ahead of a strong defensive unit, because the opposition aren't allowed to keep the ball for too long.

Not every manager can go out and buy the best players in the world in order to sit back and let them get on with it. And if, like Benítez, you're used to working on less than half the budget of some of your competitors, you need systems, ideas and tactics, to help close the gap in natural playing ability.

In the end, the 2007 semi-final was even closer than those seen in 2005 and 2006. This time it went to penalties, where the hero, as he had been at Cardiff less than a year earlier, was Pepe Reina. Liverpool scored all their penalties, with coolly taken spot-kicks from Zenden, Alonso, Gerrard and Kuyt, with Robbie Fowler waiting on hand, as he had been for England way back at Euro 1996, to take the crucial fifth. Geremi missed Chelsea's third penalty, but the tone was set when Arjen Robben, such a villain to the Kop when his theatrics got Reina sent off at Stamford Bridge 15 months earlier, discovered what Eidur Gudjohnsen had in the 2005 semi-final: that cheating to get an opponent booked or sent off is not always the end of the matter. It wasn't that it was necessarily karma — although some may believe that — but rather that he'd put himself under so much more pressure with his previous antics; the Kop hadn't forgotten the incident and nor had he, clearly. His penalty was put to Reina's left, where the keeper parried it clear. Robben put his hands to his face but, for once, didn't collapse in a heap from such gentle contact.

While all this was taking place, Rafa Benítez sat cross-legged in his suit near the touchline: a bizarre sight. He looked the picture of calm collectedness, but in such an unusual manner. He later said he did it to let the spectators in the Main Stand see the action, but in doing so he radiated a sense of control to his players. His posture said: *look how much I trust you*. It would have been no surprise to see him light up a cigar.

Of course, Jorge Valdano is entitled to his opinion on the nature of Liverpool's football, but in this instant it was one gleaned without knowledge of the context, and, it seems, at odds with the evidence of many of the successful managers in world football. 'Shit on a stick' may be the memorable phrase in the public domain following the semi-final, but it is the not the legacy of that game. That was the joyous scenes of celebration at the final whistle, and confirmation of yet another European final for Benítez, his third in four years.

# Athens Heartbreak

Football is heavy with perplexing paradoxes, grand ironies and the combined and somewhat sadistic Laws of Sod and Murphy. Or in other words, sometimes it just plain *sucks*.

In 2005, for all but 15 minutes, Milan gave Liverpool a footballing lesson, blowing the Reds out of the water to such a degree that, in terms of the metaphor, *there wasn't any water left*, just big black rain clouds forced up into the sky. They were three-nil up, and somewhere way beyond cruising. But the *Rossoneri*, against the longest of odds, ended up humiliated, in what became the toughest defeat they had ever had to take in an illustrious history. Two years later they were easily second best for the first 44 minutes, and barely able to create any chances all game, but clearly their luck had changed. In those few remaining seconds before half-time, as the ball ricocheted into the net off the upper arm of Pippo Inzaghi from what had been an average Andrea Pirlo free-kick heading into Pepe Reina's grasp, it became apparent that God had laid a tenner on the Italians and was very much in the mood to collect.

The first minute of the game presented a microcosm of how much better Liverpool played in Athens when compared with Istanbul. In 2005, the final was already slipping out of the Reds' reach after 52 seconds, when Paulo Maldini's scuffed shot, following a free-kick on the wing, looped off the turf and into the top corner. Liverpool's first meaningful touch that day was when Jerzy Dudek retrieved the ball from the back of the net.

It's hard to say whether or not that Liverpool side, who were largely inexperienced in games of a similar magnitude (including World Cup and European Championship finals), would have settled without that early setback. The Milan players had played in all manner of these types of games: those at the very pinnacle of football. But in Liverpool's case only two substitutes, World Cup runner-up Didi Hamann (2002) and European Championship runner-up Vladimir Smicer (1996), could boast such experience. By contrast, the Italians had innumerable Champions League Finals between them, not to mention appearances in the 2000 European Championship and 2006 World Cup Finals. Benítez's introduction of both Smicer and Hamann helped steady the ship in the second half, but once that first goal had gone in, a nervy 45 minutes followed, as the team's collective composure ebbed away and the Italians moved in for the kill.

In Athens there was no sign of the uncertainty that marred the Reds' efforts in that first meeting. The progress of the players was clear to see. In the opening minute they kept the ball with assurance right from the kick off, and bar one tackle on Xabi Alonso that gave possession straight to Steve Finnan, no Milan player touched the ball until Dida took a goalkick on 55 seconds. In those opening seconds Liverpool had worked the ball well, eventually moving into the Milan half, with Zenden finding Kuyt whose lay back fell to Gerrard in space. The captain's lofted cross was a fraction too long for Pennant arriving at the far post, and the ball sailed harmlessly behind, but it showed a determination to work the ball quickly and get men forward. Milan were the team put on the backfoot.

This was in total contrast to the team which, in 2005, suffered RIHS (Rabbits In Headlights Syndrome). The opening minute in Athens set the tone: this Liverpool team was wiser, and not about to be overawed.

The game continued in similar vein; Milan obviously went on to have a lot more possession than in the opening minute, but it was the Reds who showed the greater attacking intent. It was hard to reconcile the two teams with those who had contested the final in Istanbul. Were Liverpool that much improved, or was it a case of Milan having weakened, too? The Italians' semi-final mauling of Manchester United suggested they were far from on the wane.

Although seven players started both the 2005 and 2007 games, their shape had changed in the interim, with Pippo Inzaghi the only recognised forward in Athens. This was in contrast to the two out-and-out strikers of the first final: Andrei Shevchenko, who'd since moved to Chelsea, and Hernán Crespo, who had been on loan to Milan from Chelsea in 2005, but who had now become a *Serie A* Champion while on loan at AC's city rivals, Inter. While Inzaghi lacked the overall qualities of the two men from 2005, he was the ultimate poacher: always on hand to tuck away the loose ball.

Milan's deployment of Kaká in the hole, behind one striker rather than two, meant a more solid shape than two years earlier. It also meant the Brazilian playmaker could get forward that much more, without having to worry about filling in in midfield. His improvement as a player could be seen in the fact that he was the competition's top scorer going into the final, with ten goals to his name; four ahead of Liverpool's Peter Crouch in second place, although Crouch had started fewer games.

Elsewhere the Milan midfield was stronger than 2005: the same players were now two years older, and all firmly in the peak of their powers. And where Clarence Seedorf, as the oldest of that quartet, might have been expected to be edging over the hill, the Dutchman had gone through something of a renaissance.

The defensive set-up was not that different, with Dida still in goal, and the legendary defensive barriers of Alessandro Nesta and the indefatigable Paulo Maldini still in place. Gone was Jaap Stam, with Maldini switched to a central position. Cafu, just days from his 37th birthday, had once been known as *Il Pendolino* (the Express Train) due to his forceful and tireless raids down the wing; now he was more Thomas the Tank Engine, and fit for no more than the bench. Into the side came the attack-minded Czech, Marek Jankulovski — purchased after impressing at Udinese — and Lazio's Massimo Oddo: two accomplished full-backs. Oddo's career path had somewhat lived up to his name: he spent seven years on the books of Milan between 1993 and 2000, only to be loaned to six different clubs in that time, without ever representing the *Rossoneri,* until eventually they sold him. Then, after spells at Verona and Lazio, Milan bought him back in January 2007. Aged 30, he had more luck second time around. On Milan's bench were Kakha Kaladze and Serginho, as they had been two years earlier.

Liverpool retained five starters from 2005: Carragher, Finnan, Alonso, Gerrard and Riise. Luis García was still out with a long-term injury, and Harry Kewell, who limped out of the Istanbul game, trotted on in Athens. Jerzy Dudek was an unused substitute two years after his finest moment in football, along with Sami Hyypia, veteran of Liverpool's previous seven cup finals, six of which had been successful.

Jankulovski's evening was not made easy by Jermaine Pennant, who was was a real live-wire on the right wing, always looking to get in behind the offensive-minded Czech. Pennant's use of the ball was mixed, but as he won the possession on a number of occasions he could be forgiven intermittent aberrations. His energy and pace made him a constant menace in the first half, and he tested Dida with a low drive, albeit without ever looking totally convincing.

Indeed, it was interesting that three of the most assured performances came from Reina, Pennant and Mascherano, who were all new to this level of football. While those who had played in 2005 generally performed well, and didn't freeze second time around, it was encouraging to see three of the new boys rise to the occasion. While Reina had little to do, he exuded confidence in his handling and distribution. Standing absolutely no chance with the first goal, the second was one of those situations where a keeper gambles at the feet of the striker, but if the opponent gets the ball wide enough in the one-on-one he can evade even the best efforts of the man sprawling to stop him.

It was perhaps no surprise that Mascherano, with 20 caps for Argentina, including several at the World Cup, coped with the pressure. More surprising was how Pennant, uncapped, and largely untried in European football during his spell at Arsenal, showed no sign of nerves. And the same applied to Reina, whose biggest game to date was the FA Cup Final.

Dirk Kuyt was another who did well, scoring and having a goal-bound shot blocked by a superb piece of defending, as well as setting up Pennant's chance and generally working as hard as ever. In many ways it was a typical Kuyt performance: nothing showy, but a consistent, busy involvement in the game; the diametric opposite of someone like Djibril Cissé, who could quickly mix a showman's flourishes with a magician's vanishing act.

Peter Crouch, while only on the pitch for a few minutes, also came close to scoring; rather than show signs of being overawed, he entered the fray with a positive mindset. It was testament to how far he had come in his two years at the club. Perhaps the only new boy who looked nervous and played below his usual standards was the normally unflappable Daniel Agger. As the game wore on, and perhaps also due to the nervous energy of the occasion taking its toll (no doubt a reason why you see so much more cramp in cup finals than you ever see in normal league games, no matter how frenetic), he seemed to lose the power in his legs, and mistakes crept into his play as the encounter became stretched. As the Reds' youngest player on the night, and the least experienced, there was always a chance the Dane was going to feel the pressure. He didn't have a bad game, just a poor one by the high standards he'd been setting.

Another player new to the club since 2005 — Bolo Zenden — didn't necessarily look nervous, but he did revert to his disappointing form after a fine semi-final against Chelsea. Despite over 50 caps for Holland and his career at a number of big clubs — including the Reds' three previous opponents: PSV Eindhoven, Barcelona and Chelsea — this was a man who'd played in few meaningful finals during his career. While he put in the effort in what he surely expected to be his last hurrah at a major club (although a move to Marseilles followed), and did the donkey work that was part of his role, he may have found himself too desperate to succeed before his career moved into its winding-down stage. He had also injured his ankle in the build-up to the final, and needed to pass a late fitness test. It's fair to say that had Harry Kewell been match-fit or Luis García recovered from a serious knee injury, Zenden would probably have sat out the game. Then again, with an out-and-out winger on the other flank, Benítez might always have wanted Zenden's steadier approach and tactical awareness to stop the Reds becoming too open. Unfortunately, while Zenden's experience would always help the team keep its shape, he didn't do enough with the ball when the chances came his way and the crowd began singing the name of Harry Kewell: in stark contrast to two years earlier.

It probably helped the new players that the established core of the side was not overawed; with the platform provided by the five who also started in 2005, there was a strength to the team that enabled the others to feel confident. It's also the case that Benítez seeks out mentally strong men when making his signings, and players like Kuyt and Mascherano were unlikely to wilt in the way a more nervous character like Djimi Traoré had.

Every time Kaká received the ball, the terrier-like Mascherano was snapping at his heels. The battle between the contrasting South Americans had been seen as the key clash, and it lived up to its billing. Or rather, the Argentine lived up to his, while the Brazilian — such a maestro all season, and responsible for tearing Liverpool open like a psychotic surgeon on speed two years earlier — was hounded out of the game. Some pre-match pontifications had Benítez pegged as a killer of football for his obvious intention to set out to thwart Kaká. But never has it been a manager's remit to sit back and admire an opposition player tear his team to pieces, in the way a sour-faced Alex Ferguson had witnessed Kaká do in the semi-final.

Disappointingly, Steven Gerrard didn't hit the heights he was capable of reaching. It wasn't that he was poor, and he certainly had more influence than in the first half in Istanbul, but in key moments he just couldn't make decisive contributions. He is someone who burns a lot of nervous energy before big games, and while he was less overawed than he had been for the early stages in 2005, he still wasn't as effective as he could have been. Perhaps, as captain and the team's undoubted go-to man, he carries that much more pressure on his shoulders in the tensest situations, and he can only rid himself of that tension as the game wears on.

Never the happiest with his back to goal — his game is mostly about striding forward — his control unexpectedly let him down on a number of occasions, and he couldn't exert the influence he eventually had in Istanbul and Cardiff: two finals that were virtually renamed in his honour. From a tactical point of view, however, he performed the role asked of him — namely helping Dirk Kuyt unsettle the ageing Milan backline by pressing them high up the pitch, and by dragging Andrea Pirlo back from his playmaking duties into defensive areas.

But in playing Gerrard further forward Benítez had banked on his captain's ability to get in behind teams with his pace and finish chances. In the 63rd minute, Gerrard should have obliged and made the tactic look inspired, by breaking free after a mistake by Gennaro Gattuso, and speeding past Alessandro Nesta into the left side of the box: typical Gerrard. The ball never sat quite right, but rather than shoot with his right foot, as he opted to, the chance demanded a left-foot finish. In opening up his body to such a degree in order to strike with his right instep, not only could he not generate enough power to place it past Dida, but he also clearly signalled his intent to the keeper. Had it been a league game then Gerrard would almost certainly have swung his left foot at it, but it takes a brave man to use his weaker foot in the defining moment of a monumental match, especially when he's had a number of seconds to ponder the consequences; an instinctive first-time chance might have seen him use his 'swinger', in the way John Arne Riise, who uses his right foot less than Paris Hilton shuns publicity, had seen off Barcelona in the Nou Camp.

In Fernando Torres, Benítez went on to buy a player whose physique, skill and pace are in keeping with Gerrard's, but who could perform that same role far more naturally. Torres was arguably the only player the Reds lacked in Athens to really tip the match in their favour; had Gerrard been dropped into midfield at the expense of Zenden, and the Spaniard played up front, the Reds' chances of winning would surely have improved greatly.

The main criticism that Benítez faced over the final was in choosing not to start with Peter Crouch and then, once the game was slipping away from the Reds, not introducing him sooner. The plan to start without Crouch was vindicated from a tactical point of view — the performance bore that out, even if the dominance wasn't turned into goals. But the effectiveness of the big striker, once he belatedly entered the fray after what seemed an eternity warming up, suggested Milan may have struggled to handle him. It's always easy to conclude that it would have been that way from the first minute, but that's something that can never be put to the test. It's always possible that starting with Crouch could have backfired; maybe his presence would have tempted the more nervous members of the team on the night to look long for him at the first opportunity. What's fair to say is that introducing Crouch earlier — even if only ten or fifteen minutes — looked a gamble worth taking. Benítez appeared slightly indecisive as the second half wore on with his team running out of ideas — or, perhaps more pertinently, the belief that they were ever going to score. The chances began to dry up.

But the difficulty for Benítez was that his team was still very much in the game, which remained delicately in the balance. That was until the 74th minute — just ten minutes after Gerrard's defining miss — when Inzaghi, again against the run of play, broke free of the Liverpool defence, took the ball round Reina and stroked it into the empty net. It was only then that Mascherano could be sacrificed and Crouch sent on to attempt another remarkable rescue mission against Milan.

The introduction of Crouch clearly panicked the Milan defence. Of course, that doesn't mean they'd have been so unnerved early in the match, but it would be nice to see how that alternative might have played out (in some parallel universe). The no.15 showed how good he is on the deck as he skipped past a challenge and fired in a rasping drive that tested Dida, who had to tip it over for a corner. Crouch's presence for another corner a few minutes later might also have distracted the Italian defence, as Agger found freedom at the near post, flicking on Pennant's delivery towards Kuyt, who calmly headed back across the keeper to score from close range.

A lot was made at the end of the season about how Crouch scored all of his 18 goals in 2006/07 as a starter. In some quarters it was used as a kind of proof that he does not make a good substitute, but the final in Athens showed just how much he can change a game, even if he doesn't get on the scoresheet himself. Too good to be a perennial sub, and a certainty to get a good few starts as Benítez continues to rotate his strikers, he is someone who unsettles defences. Ideally a substitute will have something so different — searing pace, or clever skill — he will shake a resolute defence from its comfort zone. With his combination of height and technical ability, Crouch does just that.

Harry Kewell, the earlier sub sent on in the hope of changing the game, tried to take on the Milan back line, but it was clear that the necessary extra yard of pace was lacking after almost the entire season out injured. He'd looked extremely sharp in the final league game, against Charlton, in a 30 minute cameo, but it now looked somewhat of an illusion. However, he still used the ball intelligently, and it was another case of 'what might have been'. A fully fit Kewell would certainly have been a welcome option, especially in the absence of Luis García.

After Kuyt's 89th-minute goal it looked as if another miracle was possible, but Milan's time-wasting antics were allowed to profit them. The referee — Fandel Herbert — had been overly fussy all night, not to mention allowing Gattuso to escape a second yellow card for what looked a bookable offence. Herbert also somehow failed to add on the necessary stoppage time as Inzaghi intermittently and inexplicably lost the use of his legs; somewhat akin to Little Britain's wheelchair-faker Andy, he seemed perfectly fine when the referee was not looking. Meanwhile, the physio was looking for any chance to run on with Maldini's zimmer frame. The game petered out, and the Reds failed to pull a third successive lost final out of the fire at the death. But it was close.

If it was impossible to argue that Milan deserved their victory on the night, it was equally true that one win each from the 2005 and 2007 finals was undeniably fair.

## Aftermath

As the fireworks faded and the smell of sulphur dissipated into the Athens air, anyone would have thought Liverpool had won their sixth European crown, such was the continued noise, even as much as 30 minutes after the game had ended. Despite some faults that were highlighted on the night, as turnstiles were forced by a minority of irresponsible gatecrashers, it's hard to think of any other club whose fans could be this gracious in defeat or — as had proved the case two years earlier — inspiring in adversity. After the final whistle the masses of Reds stayed to applaud Milan and show their appreciation to Benítez and his boys. Milan's players were shocked much later in the night when, having milked the applause of their fans like suckle-hungry calves, they finally prepared to head in, only to realise that the remaining few thousand Liverpool fans were still applauding them. They came over to the English end for more appreciation, and appeared genuinely humbled. It was a great moment.

The next night, fans of both clubs would party in Monastiraki Square; while most news reports involving any two sets of fans will inevitably centre around conflict, when it exists, it was a reminder of how fans can also unite. Reds' fan and poet, Nigel Shaw, described the scene: "Coming out of the tube station at midnight 24 hours after our defeat I assumed it must be *Rossoneri* fans singing this unfamiliar tune, and sure enough the first fans I saw in the square were Milanese. But I soon realised that they were dancing and clapping along in admiration and amusement while hundreds of Reds sang the new 'Best Midfield in the World' song non-stop. They were awestruck, as a conga line of merry Reds gave high-fives and handshakes to every Milan fan around. I heard them say in Italian 'Imagine what they're like when they win'."

So the latest European odyssey was at an end. While losing is never easy to accept, this defeat didn't come close to the sickening emptiness felt by many at half time in Istanbul. And while that night saw the most remarkable recovery imaginable, it also left another enduring memory burned into people's minds after a truly awful first 45 minutes — the recollection of just how badly a final can go. In contrast, losing 2-1 in Athens was relatively easy to shrug off. In 2005 there was also the feeling that reaching the final was a one-off, after 20 years in the European Cup wilderness; two years later there was proof that it could be repeated, so thoughts quickly turned to Moscow in 2008. No one in Europe had outplayed Liverpool beyond a few minutes here and there, and the consistency across all '06/07 Champions League games was excellent. The message was clear: apply that to the Premiership.

## Final Fallout

Upon exiting the tube station at the Olympic Stadium in Athens, three hours before the kick off to club football's biggest game, fans are instantly ushered into this other-worldly experience; perhaps this is the norm for Champions League finals. With Istanbul it was the stadium in the middle of nowhere: lights beaming up ahead from what appeared like a crashed spaceship deserted on a remote Martian landscape. In Athens, it was the sea of Reds at the cordons on the tube station concourse, beyond which lay the expansive outer limits of the stadium, with its endless rows of elaborately decorative white arches like a half-mile ribbed sculpture, with beyond it in turn the surreal mixture of gushing fountains, riot police and scantily-clad dancing girls.

It was a final sandwiched with ill-feeling. Before the game there was the frustration of Liverpool fans who could not get tickets due to the limited allocation, which led to protests. Then, after the match came days of brickbats in the press, with Liverpool fans complaining about the organisation and Uefa launching scattergun potshots at the travelling Reds like over-eager police spraying all and sundry with tear gas.

Uefa appeared to be gunning for Liverpool. First of all, there was the negligence, perhaps borne of self-serving interests, in allocating a pitiful proportion of the tickets to a club with a history of getting 40,000 fans into far-flung finals. Allocating less than 17,000 tickets to each set of fans in a stadium that holds 63,000 left a lot of genuine fans in the cold. Every year the clubs that contest these games seem less and less relevant to the organisers. Once Liverpool had supplied its usual amount of tickets to those to whom they have a long-standing obligation — sponsors, shareholders, employees, players and ex-players — then only 11,000 remained for those who'd accrued the expected amount of credits through attending previous rounds. Rick Parry came under fire for only belatedly revealing this breakdown of allocations.

More than this, there was the thorny issue of the G14, the group of clubs (which now stands at 18) who have united to form a representative body, and who many feel will eventually usurp Uefa; at the very least, its existence puts pressure on Uefa, given the profile of the clubs involved. Michel Platini, the new President of Uefa, stated soon after the final that he wanted to see the G14 disbanded. The timing was interesting, given Liverpool were one of the founding members, along with AC Milan.

Then there was Uefa's policy of defending their own shortcomings over the Athens debacle by going on the attack. The reputation of football fans is easy to tar, and in the case of Liverpool fans, there's no forgetting Heysel in 1985 and the six-year expulsion that followed. Perhaps it's significant that Platini was a Juventus player that fateful day?

Liverpool will never escape that particular stigma, and while there was some shameful behaviour at the crumbling Belgian stadium, both sets of fans were engaged in ugly exchanges. The collapse of that mouldering wall, which resulted in the loss of 39 lives, was extremely tragic, but it was not a wilful act of murder. While Liverpool fans needed to take responsibility, so too did the Italians. The loss of life shouldn't have obscured the fact that their fans were partly to blame for the hostile situation that arose by launching missiles at Liverpool fans. Athens, while free of such tragedy, and with few reported serious injuries, was easy to lump with Heysel as rowdy Reds misbehaving. With Heysel always in the back of people's minds, it was possible for Uefa spokesman William Gaillard to stick the boot in in the wake of disturbances around the Olympic Stadium in the Greek capital.

On June 3rd 2007, Gaillard claimed Liverpool's were the "worst behaved fans in Europe" — manna from heaven to the headline writers. Instantly there followed a whole host of articles quoting him verbatim, with little to redress the balance of the story in those initial reports. Like a lawyer who makes a damning statement in court which he knows will be struck from the record, Gaillard knew that his comments would not be so easily struck from people's memories. In that sense, he was highly manipulative. Gaillard said: "We know what happened in Athens, and Liverpool fans were the cause of most of the trouble there. There have been 25 incidents involving Liverpool fans away from home since 2003 and these are in the report — most teams' supporters do not cause any trouble at all."

A Liverpool spokesman countered with: "The shortcomings in the management of the situation in Athens were apparent to anyone who was there. This latest statement from Uefa should not deflect attention from that reality." Sports minister Richard Caborn rallied to the club's aid, helping it take the fight back to Uefa over shoddy organisation. Meanwhile, former Conservative leader and Liverpool fan Michael Howard was at the game and said ticket checks at the stadium were "a joke". While not the most credible of celebrity fans, he was at least someone unlikely to go to Athens with the intention of picking fights with Greek riot police.

Problems broke out over an hour before the kick off when fans with genuine tickets were denied entry into the ground. Police told fans going through the penultimate checkpoint to halt, then riot police formed a line to prohibit other fans joining queues to move through the checkpoint. Earlier in the day thousands of fans had passed the checkpoints by waving their tickets in the air in front of disinterested guards; some merely waved pieces of paper. Having queued for hours and patiently passed a number of cordons, the unfortunate final groups of fans were told that the stadium was full. There was some unrest, as tempers understandably flared, and fans were tear-gassed.

Andy Knott from the fanzine *Red All Over The Land*, and organiser of a number of the Kop's stunning mosaics, told BBC *Radio Five Live* that both the fans and the authorities were to blame for what happened: "It's a culmination of everything. The Liverpool fans weren't innocent and a lot of them have got to have a look at themselves and take that into account. But at the same time Uefa have got to look at it and instead of trying to give token games to people with big stadiums, they've got to do it in a proper way. I mean how you can have a football ground without a turnstile — where it's just a metal gate that opens and you walk through — its just not football is it?"

Gaillard spoke of his organisation's damning 25-incident dossier, but did so without making the document public. It was a bolt out of the blue. According to Gaillard the charges included the ludicrous charge of stealing Uefa flags from the Olympic Stadium; taking home a memento from such an occasion is hardly a major crime — if that's one of the examples Gaillard felt compelled to disclose to illustrate his disgust, you can only wonder at the nature of the charges he felt were less significant. Sticking chewing gum to the base of seats? And perhaps some fans felt they deserved a little more for the exorbitant €100+ tickets — priced by Uefa, not touts — than a stadium with limited amenities and no drinking water, unless you happened to be a Uefa delegate. Uefa were hardly in any place to accuse others of purloining.

Gaillard's invective just didn't tally with what the world — and his own organisation — has seen in recent years. Indeed, even his own memory seemed skewed. In 2001 Uefa gave Liverpool fans the Supporters of the Year award at a Monte Carlo gala for their behaviour at the Uefa cup final, where up to 50,000 were believed to have been present for the game against Alaves in Dortmund, Germany, which was a remarkable game played in a remarkable atmosphere. This preceded the 2003 start of Gaillard's dossier, but even so, it's strange that, within two years, Liverpool fans were suddenly a different proposition. Again, it still makes no sense when you consider that in Istanbul a further two years *after* the start date of the dossier, Liverpool fans were widely lauded for their behaviour by many (including Uefa), which produced not one single arrest. This is remarkable, given the heat and the alcohol consumption, and that 50,000 Reds were believed to have travelled to the edge of Asia for the game. After that final, Gaillard said: "Liverpool fans are wonderful people." What had happened in the meantime to make him perform such a dramatic u-turn, beyond having to somehow defend Uefa's woeful organisation of the 2007 final?

Uefa themselves praised Liverpool in 2005 following their match with Juventus, which was incredibly tense given that it was the first game between the two teams since the Heysel tragedy in 1985. Deputy chief executive Markus Studer said then: "Liverpool must be applauded for the way they handled the arrangements and the fans of both clubs understood the message. There was not a hint of trouble in the stadium, there was a fantastic atmosphere and both clubs must be praised. It was a very successful night for European football."

Rick Parry, countering Gaillard's accusations, mentioned the semi-final against Chelsea on May 1st 2007 as another example of when Uefa praised the Liverpool fans. "Let's not forget," said Parry, "that these same supporters who Mr Gaillard is claiming are now the worst in Europe were praised by Uefa President Michel Platini after our semi-final victory against Chelsea only last month."

The *Liverpool Echo* felt driven to respond to Gaillard's defamatory comments by writing a strongly-worded editorial, which included the following passage detailing a litany of serious events elsewhere: "When you consider some of the outrageous and downright evil incidents committed by hooligans throughout Europe in recent years, you realise quite how ridiculous Gaillard's position really is. On February 2 a police officer was killed in Sicily when fans rioted during a derby match between Catania and Palermo. On November 24, 2006, a French police officer shot dead a Paris-Saint Germain football fan after being turned on by a mob during racist violence that followed the team's defeat by Israeli side Hapoel Tel-Aviv. On Saturday night a referee was attacked on the pitch during an international match between Sweden and Denmark. The game had to be abandoned. On September 15, 2004, Anders Frisk was forced to abandon the Champions League match between AS Roma and Dinamo Kiev after he was felled by a lighter thrown from the stands. On April 4 this year twelve Manchester United fans ended up in hospital after Italian Ultra hooligans ran riot around the Roma vs United Champions League quarter final. Do incidents like these not pose a far greater threat to the very fabric of the game than those fans who

Gaillard claims stole banners from the Olympic Stadium in Athens?"

There were seven Liverpool fans arrested in Athens, out of an estimated 40,000 or more; none for serious incidents. There was none of the kind behaviour seen by Inter Milan ultras in 2001: stealing a motor scooter, setting it on fire and hurling it from the second level of the Stadium.

On a personal note, I have travelled to the continent for a handful of European games this decade, starting in Rome in February 2001. On that occasion, a number of Liverpool fans were stabbed, in the same manner as Manchester United fans suffered in 2007, and as a dozen-or-so Reds in the 1984 final: mostly with a blade to the buttocks. In 2001, Liverpool fans in the stadium were pelted with objects throughout. Some retaliated by returning said objects, but beyond that there was no trouble, just the joy of beating Roma 2-0. Perhaps with Heysel in mind, a great deal of Liverpool fans are extra careful to protect the image of themselves and the club, although of course that doesn't mean troublemakers are never present in the ranks. The club's followers remain a fairly broad cross-section of society, not a collection of Trappist monks.

As was the case two years earlier, I received a ticket for the 2007 final in the neutral Uefa stand. Although Uefa's bloated sections have ultimately allowed me to attend the two finals, the ticket system is still something I'd happily see radically changed. (Encouragingly, on August 31st Michel Platini said from now on he wants to see clubs share 75% of the tickets.) Of course, it's hard to refuse the chance to attend if the ticket is not being taken directly from the more deserving hands of fans who narrowly failed to acquire a ticket through the club's ballot. In a more just world, these tickets would have been part of a much bigger allocation to Liverpool in the first place. But once these Uefa tickets are on the 'open market' (or in other words, tied up to hospitality packages or floating around on the black market) it leaves them open to anyone who gets lucky. Those around me in the stadium were mainly Liverpool fans who had presumably paid massively over the odds for their seats. Boycotting tickets from touts or corporate event organisers would only work if everyone stuck to it; but football fans know that others will always be too tempted to resist, and prepared to find the necessary money at the expense of common sense. Until Uefa, whose responsibility it is, get their act together and make the entire system fair in the way Platini is proposing, this situation will not change.

The previous good behaviour of Liverpool fans at finals in 2001 and 2005 does not excuse the minority who went to Athens without tickets, and made sure they were going to get into the stadium at all costs. Most fair-minded Liverpool fans who were in Athens agree that there was an element of the support that let the club down. It's hard to say for sure why this occasion drew them out in more significant numbers than in the past, but the build-up to the game was filled with a lot of anger over ticket allocations, so perhaps some spotted an opportunity. A number of tickets were snatched at the ground; as my party stood outside the first cordon, a boy could be seen running frantically from a group of chasing men, one of whose ticket he had in his hand.

Then there were the forgeries. Touts were trying to pass off colour photocopies for in excess of €1,000, while others, accepting that their wares were clearly as real as Pamela Anderson's breasts, were selling them for €20, and suggesting the buyer tried his or her luck at the cordons. I got to closely examine one forgery when a young Danish lad, shady Greek shyster in tow, came up to my group. The tout was offering him a ticket for €1,200, and he asked if he could he check it against our tickets for validity. When comparing it with the real McCoy it's flaws were instantly clear: logos that should have been yellow were orange, fine details in the design were totally absent, and the hologram was more like silver baking foil stuck on with PVA glue by a short-sighted five-year old.

It's hard to judge the intelligence of those who bunked in, or passed the cordons with obvious forgeries. In some ways, they could justify it to themselves by saying that they, and perhaps their mates, represented only a handful of extra people inside a stadium with plenty of room in the aisles. And after all, it's part of Scouse football culture. Of course, if a few thousand people are thinking the same thing, then you have a potential for massive overcrowding. With Hillsborough fresh in the minds of every Liverpool fan, even 18 years later, it's remarkable that some would even countenance such an act, let alone do so while wearing Hillsborough Justice Campaign stickers. The lack of perimeter fencing meant another Hillsborough was unlikely, but that didn't mean it was safe. And any overcrowding in an upper tier is instantly dangerous, while a moat-like ditch that lay directly beyond the barriers to the pitch-side would not make for a safe escape route. The whole event was shambolic.

Steve Walsh, a Liverpool fan now living in Holland, had this story to tell me via email the day after the final: "I was in Athens last night and met up with friends I was in Istanbul and Dortmund with. These guys were from Leeds, Morecambe and Oxford. As a former Captain in the British Army, I can assure you that it's written as objectively and as factually as possible.

"I arrived at the Fan Zone 2.30pm. I saw no trouble at all there, nor on the train to the stadium which we left for at approximately 4.30pm. The queues to enter the Olympic Park were quite simply horrendous. There were plenty of riot police who were quite visible although not confrontational. At one point they were actually told by their superior to withdraw slightly to become less visible.

"After queuing for two hours we were finally admitted to the Park at approximately 9.15pm. After a walk through the park to the stadium we were blocked by a police cordon of officers and riot vehicles about 400m from the ground. I estimate there were 150-200 fans there. There was no attempt in this area to charge the police line and there was no reaction from the Greek police. They simply stood their line but refused to communicate with anyone.

"It was obvious that the situation may deteriorate. I asked several times to speak to the senior police officer myself and finally he arrived. He first said that people should stop pushing. In a raised voice I'll admit, I asked/told the group of fans to show some common sense, stop pushing and back off. Without one word of disagreement, the whole group of fans complied instantly. I then spoke with the officer and explained to him that we were all fans with genuine tickets and many of the group produced their tickets to prove this. He agreed and relented and allowed the group to proceed to the stadium. It occurred with no fuss at all.

"I would point out that most of the police in that line seemed to be very young constables who actually looked terrified and I felt sorry for them. This was caused by their lack of communication. You don't simply put up a cordon and then not communicate with your audience about what it is you want them to do. All that simply happens is police and fans end up standing face-to-face and eventually tempers are likely to flare. Acting dumb simply invites confrontation. Thankfully, on this occasion, that did not occur.

"On arriving at the stadium there was no scan to check the ticket [which had a barcode], the steward simply ripped off a corner. It was obvious when I took my seat that many sections of the stadium were overcrowded, including my own, never mind the hundreds of Greek stewards and police sitting in the main aisles — watching the match!

"If there had been less police in riot gear and more doing the security checks and ticket scans at the entrances to the Olympic Park then none of this would have happened. In the official Uefa guide to Athens, they introduced a coloured wristband system to avoid congestion in the early hours of the morning at the airport. For the several thousands who flew back in those early hours this was a system that worked well. If Uefa could work out that 10-15,000 people might cause congestion at the airport over a couple of hours, why did they not think that 63,000 people might cause worse congestion at the stadium over a couple of hours. If Pythagoras were alive today ...

"The match ended and I witnessed no further incidents on the way to or at the airport where my flight to Amsterdam departed at 5.30am."

Walsh offered an interesting insight into how tickets exchanged hands: "I paid over £1,000 for my ticket from a ticket agency in Rotterdam. I collected the ticket in Athens on the day of the final. The ticket is clearly marked as originally belonging to the "Uefa Local Organising Committee — Ticket No. 00100". The gentlemen in the seat next to me from this committee said some of his colleagues had sold them on, and he just laughed at this. I'm not so naive to think that this doesn't happen but Uefa needs to take a big look in the mirror.

"My overall feeling is that Uefa have little understanding of what the real fans go through. I get the impression they would much rather fill the stadium with guests and sponsors and use sound recordings and library pictures of the real fans. Uefa really needs to become a 'professional' organisation in the true sense of the word."

Architect Paul Gregory threatened to sue Uefa over the debacle. "As a former shareholder in Liverpool FC I am the recipient of three €140 tickets for the Champions League final," he told Henry Winter of *The Daily Telegraph*. "All are still unused as we were refused entry into the stadium. I was herded, tear-gassed, kicked and baton-charged by riot police outside the stadium for the hour leading up to kick-off and way beyond." He went on to tell of mass crushes that sounded reminiscent of Hillsborough, and of crying children caught up in the panicking, herded crowd.

In the end, Uefa promised to review their organisational procedures, and backtracked over Gaillard's outburst. Michel Platini said: "It's official, Liverpool fans are not the worst behaved." Of course, by then the damage had been done, both to the reputation of Liverpool fans, and to the hopes of many who'd travelled halfway across Europe to watch a game they'd paid a small fortune to attend, only to spend it being abused by riot police.

# Epilogue

The new season couldn't have started much better: the first two Premiership away games were won in style, whereas last season it took until December to register one, let alone two victories on the road; the Champions League qualifier against potentially troublesome French opposition was navigated as comfortably as could ever have been hoped for; and but for an outrageous refereeing decision against Chelsea at Anfield which helped peg the Reds back, the league campaign could have opened with a 100% record. As it was, it was Liverpool's best start to a Premiership season in years. All of the major new players had settled quickly, and each had shown why he was purchased. All four strikers had got off the mark, with Torres and Voronin both quickly reaching three goals. Ryan Babel also opened his account, with a stunning strike at home to Derby County. Meanwhile the defence was as stingy as ever, if not more so, with just two goals conceded in the first six games, and both of those penalties (one of which should never have been awarded). Even Steven Gerrard's broken toe, Sami Hyypia's broken nose and Jamie Carragher's broken rib and punctured lung could not halt progress in the opening weeks.

But then, at the end of August, a bombshell: Pako Ayestaran, Benítez's assistant for the previous 11 years at a number of clubs, announced that he was leaving Liverpool. Ayestaran had been linked to several managerial roles in Spain, but nothing had transpired and he was still an integral part of Liverpool's back-room staff. But it seemed that he and Benítez had fallen out in the summer, and a number of disagreements rumbled on until a breaking point was reached. It was clear that Liverpool needed a better start to the season than in recent years, and the manager's lessening of the intensity of pre-season training was believed to be one of the causes of the friction with the man who had previously planned the physical work. In that sense, with the Reds top of the league after the first month and with a game in hand on Chelsea and Manchester United, Benítez was vindicated. But with Ayestaran's help, Benítez's teams had always ended the season strongly, and it remains to be seen if this will be compromised by the new fitness regime. It's no good starting well only to fade badly; but after three years of slow starting, it was equally clear that the Reds could not leave a mountain to climb for a fourth successive season.

Another Spaniard, Angel Vales, had already arrived in the summer, as reserve team coach/head of technical and video analysis. His area of expertise was similar to Ayestaran's: Vales is a doctor of sports science who'd been teaching football to degree level at the University of La Coruña, and to Masters level in three other Spanish Universities. Perhaps it was also a cause of tension, with some overlap in the roles. Fitness coach Paco De Miguel was another new arrival from Valencia, and took Ayestaran's place alongside Benítez for the first game following the bust-up. But Ayestaran was much more than a fitness coach: he was Benítez's right-hand man, his confidant, his tactical co-conspirator, and his friend.

The timing of the split, on the eve of the home game with Derby, was potentially disastrous. Such a positive start to the campaign stood in danger of being undermined by the unrest. But the impressive results achieved in the month while the dispute was rumbling on, and immediately after, suggested the manager was right to facilitate a change of direction in the summer. Perhaps Benítez's goatee beard was more than a merely cosmetic addition, and a symbol of the newer, even meaner manager who would stop at nothing to bring success to Liverpool. After three years on Merseyside it had no doubt occurred to him just how massive an achievement it would be to land the Reds' 19th league title.

By the start of September 2007 it was clear that the first team was as strong as it had been in years, as was the squad as a whole. For the first time since November 2002 the Reds led the league table following the 6-0 demolition of Derby County. If issues with the coaching staff could be satisfactorily resolved then the chances of landing the title would at their highest since 1990. But even if 2007/08 doesn't prove to be the year the Reds have been waiting so patiently for, with such a young team, and with no key players nearing retirement age, not to mention two ambitious Americans in charge and keen to back the manager in the transfer market, the wait must surely be due to end sooner rather than later.

Time will tell ...

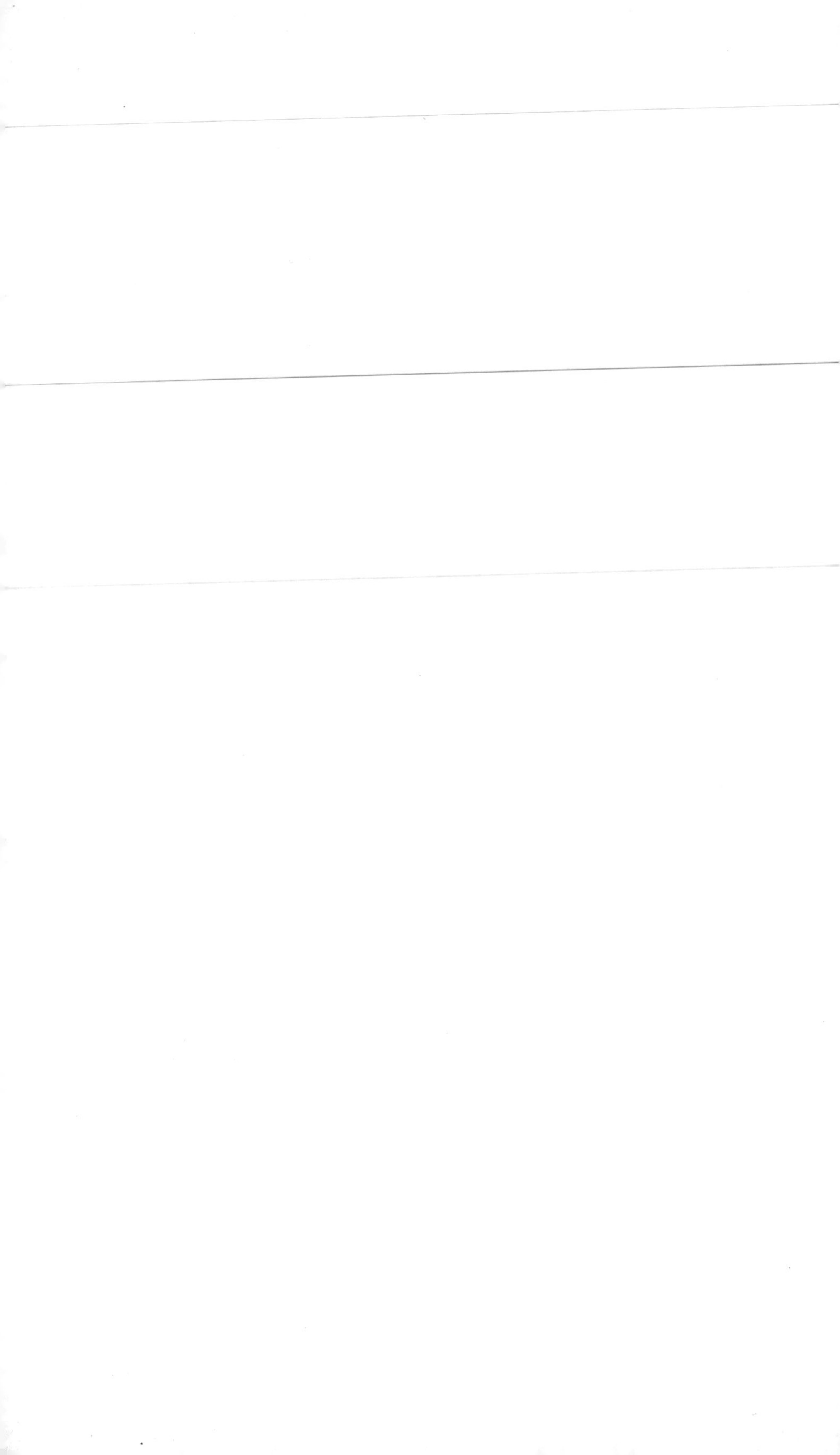